Country Homes

Edición Edited
Fernando de Haro • Omar Fuentes

Casas en el Campo

LIFESTYLES

Nature & Architecture

autores / authors **Fernando de Haro & Omar Fuentes** diseño y

producción editorial / editorial design & production **AM Editores**

S.A. de C.V. dirección del proyecto / project managers

Valeria Degregorio Vega y Tzacil Cervantes Ortega coordinación

/ coordination **Edali P. Nuñez Daniel** texto original / original

text **Luis Mariano Acévez** traductor / translator **Louis Loizides**

Casas en el Campo / Country Homes

© 2007, Fernando de Haro & Omar Fuentes

ISBN español 978-970-9726-75-6
ISBN inglés 978-970-9726-76-3

AM Editores S.A. de C.V., Paseo de Tamarindos #400-B suite 102, Col. Bosques de las Lomas C.P. 05120, México D.F., Tel. 52(55) 5258-0279. Fax. 52(55) 5258-0556. E-mail: ame@ameditores.com **www.ameditores.com**

Impreso en China / Printed in China.

Contenido Contents

Introducción Introduction

El campo es un reino intermedio entre la ciudad y la naturaleza virgen, la selva, la montaña, el desierto o el mar. Es en ese reino intermedio donde los seres humanos hemos desarrollado, a lo largo de la historia, las culturas más ricas y complejas, basadas en la agricultura. La agricultura es un invento de la humanidad para entenderse con la naturaleza, para domesticarla y convertirla en aliada y el campo es el lugar donde se expresa, todos los días, ese encuentro de la tenaz mano del hombre con los animales y con la tierra, las semillas, el agua y el sol. Un encuentro del que nacen los frutos más variados, el maíz y el trigo; mangos, plátanos, bellotas, queso y vino, miel y lechugas. Y con esos frutos, vienen también los diversos modos de vivir, los modos de comer y de beber, de conversar, de soñar y hasta de morir.

The countryside stands as the middle kingdom between city and virgin beauty, the jungle, the mountain, the desert or the sea. It is here in this middle kingdom that we human beings have, throughout history, conjured up the richest and most complex cultures based on agriculture. Agriculture is man's invention devised to live in harmony with nature, to harness it and turn it into our ally. The countryside is also where this encounter between the resilient hand of man and the animals, the earth, the seeds, water and sun is expressed each day. This encounter gives rise to a vast array of fruits, corn and wheat, mangos, bananas, acorns, cheese and wine, honey and lettuces. And these fruits, in turn, give rise to numerous ways of living, eating and drinking, conversing, dreaming and even dying.

Cada uno de nosotros es quien es porque hemos nacido en un tiempo y en un lugar que tiene rostro y nombre. El pertenecer a una familia, a una comunidad y a un lugar determinado, nos hace compartir una manera de entender el mundo: una manera de ser, una manera de andar, una manera de hablar y de callar. Esa manera de ser tiene en el campo una de sus raíces más viejas y más fuertes, nutriéndose permanentemente de la historia de los abuelos y los bisabuelos hasta el más lejano origen, en el barro blando del que todos fuimos hechos. En el campo abreva con avidez una nostalgia que duerme en el fondo de la memoria, esperando despertar para inundarnos con sus imágenes. En el campo surgen recuerdos sorprendentes por su frescura, con su recién nacido aroma de hierbabuena y de pino; con el eco de los arroyos de agua clara y de los leños crepitando en la chimenea; con el nervio vibrante del colibrí o el trazo fugaz del halcón; con el timbre de las herraduras chispeando sobre la cantera o el suave desliz del viento entre los árboles, al atardecer.

Así como el campo es esa frontera donde la compleja civilización urbana se encuentra con la indiferente naturaleza "un territorio domesticado pero no totalmente sometido", las casas de campo son el lugar donde los hijos de la ciudad celebramos el ritual del encuentro con un pasado que se hace visible, con enorme fuerza, para enriquecer el presente. El lugar para recargar el cuerpo de oxígeno y energía, y el alma de recuerdos y emociones. El lugar para descubrir en el interior de uno mismo los espejos donde se contempla la naturaleza cuando le damos permiso.

We are each who we are because we were born in a time and place that has both a face and a name. By belonging to a family, a community and a given place, we are forced to share a way of understanding the world: a way of being, a way of walking, a way of talking and being quiet. One of the oldest and strongest roots of this way of being is to be found in the countryside, where it constantly feeds on the history of our grandparents and our great grandparents all the way back to our most distant origins and the soft mud we once came from. The country exudes a nostalgia that sleeps in the deepest recesses of our memories, waiting to awake and flood us with its images. It is in the countryside that memories emerge with surprising freshness, with their newly born aroma of spearmint and pine; with the echo of clear springs and crackling of firewood in the hearth; with the vibrant pulsating of the hummingbird or the boundless soaring of the falcon; with the sparkling ring of horseshoes on stone or the soft surge of the breeze through the trees at sunset.

This is how the countryside stands as the frontier between the complex urban civilization and the indifference of nature, a terrain that has been domesticated but not fully conquered. Country houses are where the children of the city perform the ritual of encounter with a past that becomes visible with tremendous power to enrich the present. It is here where the body is revitalized with oxygen and energy, and the soul with memories and emotions. It is here where one finds mirrors inside oneself to contemplate nature when we allow this.

NATURAL IMPRESSIONS

accesos y exteriores
accesses & exteriors

Cuando en el campo convivimos con las luciérnagas y la granizada, los caballos y las palomas, con los mapaches y las orquídeas, volvemos al origen. Tocamos nuestra naturaleza elemental. Recordamos palabras del idioma antiguo: valle, cerro, peña, sendero, potrero, pirul, milpa, rancho, roble, lago, matorral, guajolote, apancle... Recordamos que fuera de la ciudad hay otra vida, de la que se alimenta la misma ciudad, aparentemente tan poderosa y definitiva . Otra vida tal vez más viva, más quieta y más sana, pero reservada a breves tiempos: a los fines de semana o a los fugaces días del ocio y el descanso. Y por eso más deseable. A la orilla del lago o frente a la montaña, en el bosque o en el llano, el campo trae consigo una llovizna de recuerdos de la que nace un flotante sentimiento de nostalgia. De esa nostalgia se alimenta la poesía de los espacios con que la arquitectura nos envuelve en estas casas. Casas en el campo, casas para el campo.

When we spend time in the countryside amid the fireflies and hail, with horses and doves, and with raccoons and orchids, we find our origin again. We get in touch with our elementary nature. We recall the words of ancient tongues: valley, hill, rock, path, field, shrub, cornfield, ranch, oak, lake, thicket, turkey, stream... We remember the existence of another life beyond the city, one that feeds the city itself and commands the same power and definition. This other life is perhaps more alive, more tranquil and healthy, but it is reserved for brief intervals only: for the weekend or those scarce days of leisure and relaxation, which makes it all the more alluring. On the shore of a lake or in front of a mountain, in the forest or on a plain, the country stores a whole arsenal of memories that give rise to a fleeting sense of nostalgia. And it is precisely this nostalgia that feeds the poetry of the spaces encapsulated in these houses through architecture. Houses in the countryside, houses for the countryside.

La ilusión es una constante de la arquitectura. Nadie puede ver el espacio, que es su materia prima. Pero se percibe su leve temblor al atardecer, su quiebre en reflejos y en sombras; los muros conduciendo la mirada desde los modernos acabados, hacia la cortina del cerro. La fiebre del campo penetrando en el espacio refinado y preciso de una arquitectura que sabe dialogar serenamente con su entorno.

Illusion is a constant in architecture. Nobody can see space, which is its raw material. But its faint quivering at sunset can be perceived, as can its dissolving into reflections and shadows; the walls turn the viewer's gaze from the modern finishes towards the face of the hill. The countryside's fever enters the refined and precise space framed by architecture that is perfectly capable of conversing serenely with its surroundings.

Otro recurso propio de la arquitectura es el contraste,
que en este caso adquiere un valor notable: las líneas
horizontales se desplazan decididamente creando un
movimiento fugado, como una prolongada nota musical
invitada para enaltecer la verticalidad titubeante de los
árboles. La terraza es una partitura viva, una especie de
teclado de madera, con notas agrupadas para enriquecer
con su contraste los rumores naturales del campo.

Another resource drawn upon by architecture is contrast,
which acquires a noteworthy value in this case: the
horizontal lines advance with determination to create
a fleeting motion, like a drawn out musical note, to
highlight the staggering verticality of the trees. The
terrace is a live musical score, like a wooden keyboard
with notes grouped together to enrich the natural
murmuring of the countryside with its contrast.

Cuando entre los árboles van levantándose los muros refinados, las ventanas de cristal y las puertas, las escaleras, las vigas de las techumbres y los pisos, la luz aprende a hablar en un lenguaje nuevo. Es otra su intensidad y son otros sus ritmos y sus intenciones. El paisaje, antes desparramado y suelto, se perfila y se convierte en cuadro para contemplar con admiración silenciosa. La casa es entonces un hallazgo, un objeto precioso, cuyo mayor mérito está en saber dar un sentido propio al lugar donde se edifica.

When refined walls, glass windows and doors, stairs, roof beams and floors stand proudly among the trees, the light learns to speak a whole new language. Its intensity changes, as do its rhythms and intentions. The same scenery that was one scattered and loose now becomes a painting to be contemplated in silent admiration. The house is a finding, a precious article, whose greatest virtue consists of affording a unique meaning to the place where it was built.

El caballo impone su propia escala, dándole a la casa un carácter especial. Con el caballo llega la música de sus cascos (tambor o campana) y el abanico vivo de su cola; el relincho y la nobleza, la fuerza y la docilidad; el aroma de su piel y la negra profundidad de su mirada.
La casa ha de saber enmarcar dignamente la imagen de ese ancestral compañero.

The horse sets its own scale, bestowing a special character to the house. It is accompanied by the music of its shoes (drum or bell) and the lively fanning of its tail; whinnying and nobility; the aroma of its skin and the unfathomable depths of its gaze. The task of the house is to frame the image of this age-old companion in a dignified manner.

La pequeña hondonada, con su ojo de agua, es un lugar que tiene carácter propio. La casa lo reconoce así, integrándose al paisaje con un inteligente respeto y haciendo que cada vista, cada ángulo del paisaje, adquiera valor. La selección de la madera para las columnas, tanto como la piedra y la teja, expresan ese respeto. La casa está precisamente en su sitio. No podría estar en otro.

The small ravine with its pool of water is a place with its very own personality. The house is aware of this and blends into its setting with a wise respect, enriching each view and each angle of the scenery. The choice of wood for the columns, along with the stone and tiles, expresses this respect. The house stands precisely where it should. It could not stand anywhere else.

Nacido hace siglos en las casas prehispánicas y también en el Mediterráneo, el patio es la forma en que la arquitectura rinde homenaje al buen tiempo, a la luz del sol y a la brisa tibia en las noches de luna llena. Los patios se han multiplicado en una extraordinaria variedad. Son la perfecta conjunción entre el espacio exterior y el interior: invitan a estar en ellos tanto como a cruzarlos, a pasar de largo o a contemplarlos. Le dan marco al cielo, encuadran las estrellas. En el campo, ofrecen el agua como un tesoro vivo. El patio es el corazón y la sonrisa de la casa.

Born centuries ago in the pre-Hispanic houses of the Americas and in the Mediterranean, the patio is the means used by architecture to pay tribute to good weather, sunlight and the cool breeze of night under a full moon. There is now a vast range of patios. They are the perfect conjunction between indoor space and outdoor space, inviting people to stay in them, cross them, go around them or contemplate them. They provide a frame for sky and stars alike. In the countryside, they offer water like a living treasure. The patio is the heart and smile of the house.

La generosa austeridad de algunos espacios, como este que sirve de circulación y vestíbulo para las habitaciones que enfrentan sus puertas, recuerda el ambiente de los conventos del siglo XVI. No hay pasos perdidos, aunque se trate de espacios secundarios o destinados solamente para circular. La atmósfera íntima provocada por el color y el piso de madera, se acentúa con la ventana, velada por una reja casi conventual.

The generous austerity of spaces like this one, which serves as a hall and allows for movement between the bedrooms whose doors stand face to face, is reminiscent of the atmosphere of Sixteenth Century convents. There are no wasted steps, even though they may well be secondary or for the purposes of movement only. The intimate mood created by the color and the wooden floor is enhanced by the window and its convent-style lattice.

Cuando el lenguaje contemporáneo de la arquitectura se hace presente en el campo, agrega una enorme fuerza a la naturaleza: cristales flotantes, metal, planos, volúmenes puros y transparencias, conspiran para establecer un poderoso contrapunto frente a las formas naturales. Como resultado, el confort y los servicios propios de una casa en la ciudad dialogan con el entramado del bosque.

When the contemporary language of architecture is spoken in the country, it provides a tremendous force for nature: floating windows, metal, planes, pure volumes and transparency all conspire to create a powerful counterbalance to the natural forms present. The result is a dialog between the comfort and services you find in a city house and the untamed lattice of the forest.

La casa echa raíces ajustándose en quiebres y desniveles. Hacia el cielo, levanta chimeneas que se suman a la danza de los troncos. El color y las texturas de los muros, las tejas y la madera, mantienen la doble referencia a la ciudad y al campo.

The house lays down its roots by adapting itself to slopes and split levels. Chimneys join the dance of the tree trunks surging towards the sky. The colors and textures of the walls, tiles and wood sustain a double reference to both city and country.

La fuerza de la estructura metálica, con sus líneas exactas, su posición geométrica y su color, teje una red para atrapar la vista teniendo al fondo el contraste de la naturaleza. La puerta roja anticipa una inminente sorpresa. Por la noche la casa recorta al cielo y se funde con el paisaje. Las sombras y las luces producen la ilusión del hallazgo de un refugio deseado por mucho tiempo.

The power of the metal structure, with its precise lines, its geometric position and its color, weaves a web to catch the eye, aided by the contrast of nature in the background. The red door awaits an imminent surprise. At night, the house cuts out an area of sky and merges with the scenery. Lights and shadows create the illusion of coming across a long sought-after refuge.

La piedra, la madera, las tejas y el tabique de barro parecen surgidos del mismo paisaje que envuelve a la casa y a él se sujetan. El cubo que le da forma y la audacia de su techumbre, por su parte, parecen salidos de la geometría pura de las ideas. La arquitectura concilia los opuestos: el espacio rompe las aristas, penetra al cubo, se derrama hacia fuera y hacia dentro en un juego sin fin, que rebota hasta el horizonte del lago.

Stone, wood, tiles and earth partition walls all seem to emerge from the same landscape that engulfs the house and to which they cling. The cube that gives it shape and the audacity of the roofing seem to be borne of the very geometry of ideas. The architecture reconciles opposites; the space breaks up the edges, penetrates the cube, and spills outwards and inwards in an endless game that goes on to the lake on the horizon.

El cobijo desciende del cerro del Tepozteco a la casa y se desliza, a través de una serie de muros, a la vida doméstica. Hechos de barro, estos muros multiplican el eco de la enorme cortina de rocas, refugio de leyendas y de mitos. La casa, asentada con seguridad sobre piedra maciza, dispone un centro para celebrar rituales de encuentro y conversación o momentos de silencio contemplativo.

Refuge swoops down from the Tepozteco hill to the house and slides through a series of walls into home life. These earth walls amplify the echo of the huge rock face, the home of myth and legend. The house sits sturdily on solid stone and boasts a center for rituals of gathering and conversation or for moments of contemplative silence.

Lentamente, conforme va sucediendo
el anochecer, el espacio del pórtico
gana la preferencia de los habitantes de
la casa, entre quienes están los cocuyos
y los grillos, encargados de acercar las
luces y el canto del campo. La quieta
presencia del agua, que duplica la
ligereza de la casa, hace del verano una
fiesta silenciosa. Todo reposa. Reposa
el cuerpo, reposa el alma, reposa el
mundo alrededor.

Slowly, as the sun sets, the space in
the portico gains popularity among the
house's inhabitants, including the beetles
and crickets, responsible for attracting
the lights and music of the countryside.
The gentle presence of water accentuates
the lightness of the house, turning
summer into a silent celebration. All is
rest. The body rests, the soul rests, the
surrounding world rests.

El recorrido entre un espacio y otro, a través de una galería o un pasillo, puede ser una rica experiencia más allá del mero traslado físico. Gracias al clima que permite disfrutar los exteriores, el paso se detiene por unos momentos para gozar con el canto del agua, con el leve susurro del viento y con el brillo de las diminutas estrellas caídas al piso.

The route between one space and another, through a gallery or corridor, may provide a rich experience beyond the confines of mere displacement. The weather that outdoor spaces make available for our pleasure encourages passers-by to stop for a moment and enjoy the splashing of water, the discrete whispering of the wind and the gleam of tiny stars fallen to the floor.

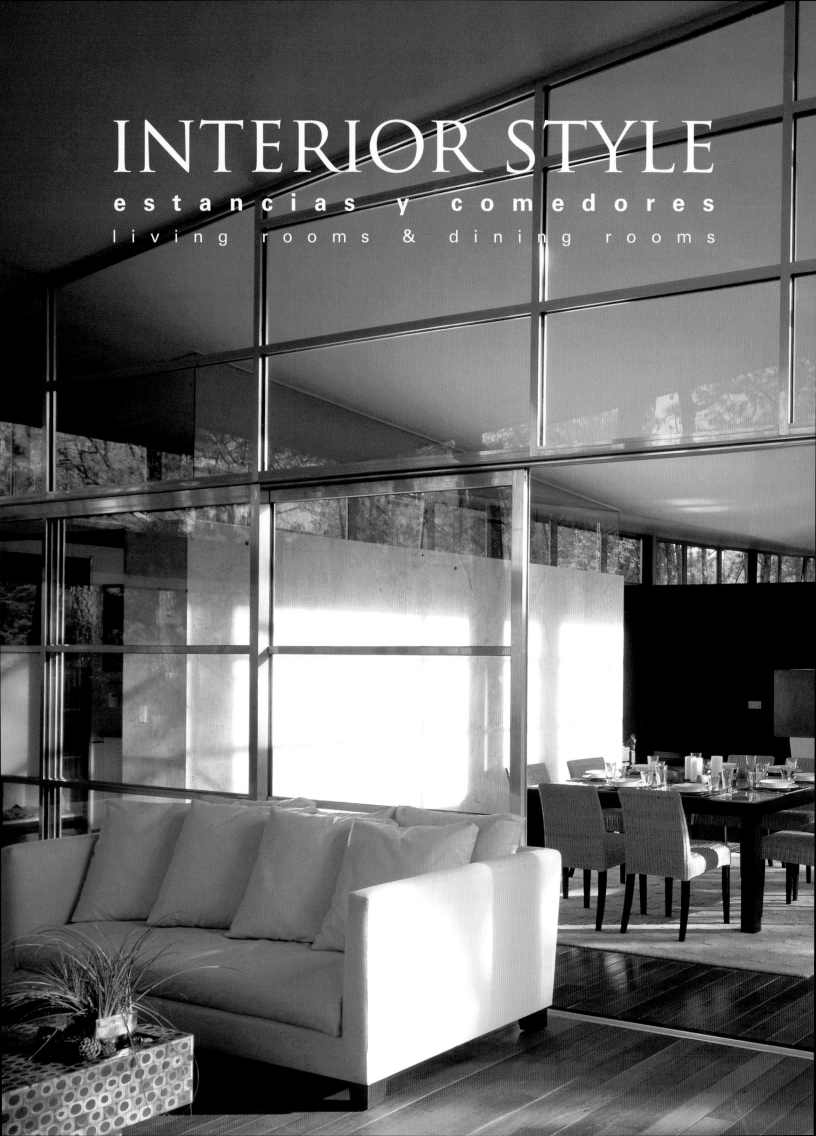

INTERIOR STYLE
estancias y comedores
living rooms & dining rooms

Comer y estar, en una casa de campo, son actividades que no tienen la formalidad que se vive en las ciudades. Sin embargo, tienen su propia cadencia y están matizadas por un ritmo especial: el de las costumbres y tradiciones de cada lugar. A la hora de comer y beber, el bolillo o las campechanas recién horneadas, las tortillas "echadas" a mano; la leche fresca, los tamarindos y la jamaica, el conejo o la codorniz; el dulce de leche, la miel y los tamales imponen su aroma, sus horarios y su modo de compartir. La cocina tiene secretos y trucos ancestrales, que exigen de sabias traductoras. En el campo, estar significa conversar sobre cuentos y leyendas, leer paladeando cada frase o contemplar mariposas o tejones; escuchar el llamado lejano de la campana o el retozo del agua, tan ligera como el trote de un caballo. Las estancias y comedores de estas casas son escenarios para que las mujeres y los hombres, felices con estos quehaceres, nos convirtamos en mejores personas.

Eating and spending time in a country house are activities that can be enjoyed without the formality required by the city. At the same time, they do have their cadence and are characterized by a particular rhythm borne of the customs and traditions of each place. When it comes to eating and drinking, freshly baked bread, hand made "tortillas", fresh milk, tamarinds and hibiscus, rabbit or quail, the sweetness of milk, honey or "tamales" all lay down their own aromas, times and form of sharing. The kitchen harbors age old secrets and tricks that require wise interpretation. Being in the country means that talk is about tales and legends, that reading a sentence is to savor it, or contemplating badgers and butterflies, listening to the distant ring of bells or the playfulness of water, as light as the trotting of a horse. Living rooms and dining rooms are the stage on which we, men and women -joyful with these tasks-, can become better people.

Al entrar en contacto con la
arquitectura contemporánea el
campo se "civiliza", invitando a
una nueva relación, indirecta y
sofisticada. Sobre la alta pared de
adobe o de tepetate (al fin tierra
domesticada al servicio de la casa),
el cuadro suelta su música quemada.
A través de la luz y los reflejos en
los cristales, las piedras proponen
una textura que hace más terso el
ambiente de la estancia.

The countryside becomes "civilized"
when we come into contact with
contemporary architecture to create a
new relationship that is both indirect
and sophisticated. On the high adobe
or rock wall (finally, earth tamed to
be put to the use of the house), the
picture releases its scorched music.
The light and reflections from crystals
afford the stones a texture that
highlights the flow of the living room's
ambience.

El espacio de la estancia se enriquece con el entramado de las vigas de madera, poderosas y sólidas, que llevan aún las huellas y el aroma de su nacimiento. Más atrás la escalera, como una secuencia de notas musicales, invita a nuevos descubrimientos. El sol tempranero y tibio cruza el espacio, de lado a lado, recortando presencias inesperadas y venidas de lejos para atestiguar su salida puntual.

The space of the living room is enriched by the intercrossing of solid and imposing wooden beams that still bear the traces of the fragrance of their birth. Further back, the staircase is a scale of musical notes that suggests new discoveries. The mild morning sun crosses the room from one side to the other, highlighting unexpected presences that have come from afar to witness its timely arrival.

El vino es del campo como la lluvia es
del cielo y como el calor del fuego.
Casi como un templo y muy pegada a la
tierra, la cava atesora en silencio deleites
adivinados: conversaciones cercanas,
saludos, convites y brindis por la vida
breve. En la fresca penumbra el buen
vino, que lleva la felicidad al corazón
de los hombres, duerme su víspera.
Despertará para traer nuevamente la risa.

Wine is from the country just like rain
comes from the sky and heat from
fire. The cellar, like a temple rooted
firmly to the earth, silently boasts
divine treasures: close conversations,
greetings, invitations and toasts to a life
all too brief. In the fresh penumbra, the
wine sleeps ready to awake and bring joy
and laughter to men's hearts.

En el campo la leña sabe cómo cantar. Por eso, nada convoca con tanta fuerza y con tanto afecto como el aroma del ocote ardiendo en el hogar de una chimenea. El fuego vivo o el fuego lento, las brasas, los rescoldos y las chispas, con su efecto hipnótico, abren las puertas del ensueño. En silencio, la reja responde cediendo el paso. Sobre el muro, arde también el cuadro.

Firewood sings tunefully in the countryside. This is why there is no more powerful convocation than the fragrance of wood burning in the fireplace. A lively fire, a slow-burning fire, embers and sparks, with their hypnotic effect, open up the doors to the realms of dreams. The gate silently responds by opening and showing the way. The painting on the wall is also in flames.

El campo rinde tributo: convierte al árbol en robusta columna. Así fue, acaso, la primera vez que levantó el hombre un techo para protegerse. Algo de ese gesto primitivo queda aquí, en la simple y clara manera como se arma la cubierta y en los grandes cuarterones de barro que cubren el piso. Por eso puede asomarse el campo con tanta naturalidad. La casa es su hija predilecta.

The countryside pays tribute: it turns the trees into a solid pillar. This is how it was the first time man raised a roof to protect himself; and some of this primitive gesture remains here, in the plain and simple way the ceiling is put in place and in the large earthen tiles that cover the floor. This is why the countryside can reveal itself in such a natural way. The house is its favorite daughter.

Por su luz y sus proporciones, por su altura y amplitud, puede ser majestuoso el espacio también en una casa de campo. El adjetivo parece inadecuado, más conveniente para un palacio o para un templo. Sin embargo la maciza madera y la combinación de tonos del color de la tierra generan una atmósfera, de tan grande serenidad, que recuerda los pabellones de caza propios de la nobleza.

The light and proportions of the space, its height and abundance, can lend a country house a truly majestic air. Yet, this adjective hardly seems appropriate, perhaps more fitting for a palace or a church. But the solid wood and combination of earth tones create a very serene atmosphere reminiscent of the hunting lodges of noblemen.

Otra virtud de las casas de campo
es que trastocan formalidades
opuestas a una vida libre y ligera.
La distinción entre comedor y cocina
no es tan clara como en la ciudad.
El fogón, el comal, la leña, cazos
y cazuelas se llevan bien con los
manteles y con la mesa para comer.
Asombra la poderosa trabazón de la
madera, que comunica la más sólida
sensación de seguridad.

Another virtue of country houses is
that they rearrange the formalities
that stand in the way of a free and
easy life. The distinction between
the kitchen and the dining room is
not as clearly defined as in the city.
The hearth, the *tortilla* pan, firewood,
saucepans and casseroles combine
well with the tablecloths. The
consistency of the wood, portraying
a very powerful feeling of safety, is
awesome.

Las haciendas mexicanas fueron
centros económicos de primer orden.
Pero su arquitectura mantuvo siempre
un lenguaje contenido y severo:
espacios amplios con muros lisos,
vigas disciplinadas, puertas anchas y
ventanas claras. Algunos sonidos, casi
musicales, brillaban fugazmente: una
espuela rozando el piso, el canto de un
pavorreal en el patio o el ladrido lejano.
Todavía quedan, en la arquitectura
contemporánea, resonancias de esos
años pasados.

Mexico's haciendas were top level
economic centers, but their architecture
was always created with a contained and
austere feel: large spaces with smooth
walls, disciplined beams, broad doors and
clear windows. Some sounds, almost
musical, would stand out for a fleeting
moment, like a spur scraping the floor,
the singing of a peacock in the patio
or barking in the distance. To this day,
architecture contains some echoes of
those years gone by.

La audacia se pinta toda de blanco y consigue un sorprendente efecto: los espacios se iluminan y las líneas de la estructura (las columnas, las vigas), capturan la mirada compitiendo con lo que se adivina está sucediendo afuera. En un espacio relativamente pequeño, un acontecimiento singular. La luz vibra de otra manera en los textiles, en el piso y en los muebles. Es el reino del color.

Audacity is painted in white and achieves a surprising effect: the spaces are illuminated and the structural lines (the pillars and beams) attract the observer's gaze competing with the suggested activities outdoors. A singular moment is taking place in a relatively small space. The light vibrates on the textiles, the floor and the furniture in a different way. Welcome to the kingdom of color.

Se trata de un privilegio. Habría
que inventar la palabra que designe
ese estar entre, que la arquitectura
ofrece, tan seguido, en los lugares
de buen clima. Ese es un espacio
que goza del bienestar controlado
del interior (el fuego, la suavidad
de los muebles y los tapetes), con
el exterior soleado hasta el final del
lago. Estar ahí, entre el exterior y el
interior, es un privilegio.

This is a privilege. The word to
describe being in a place of fine
architecture and good weather does
not exist. This space is blessed
with the controlled wellbeing of
indoors (the fire, the softness of
the furniture and rugs) with the
great outdoors illuminated by the
sun up to the far edge of the lake.
To be here, between the inside and
outside, is a privilege.

El arte contemporáneo puede encontrarse a gusto
en la estancia de una casa de campo, tanto como la
casa beneficiarse del contraste que trae consigo esa
presencia. El resultado es un ambiente muy acogedor,
gracias a la cuidadosa selección de la pintura abstracta
y de su marco, que conviven en armonía con las
vasijas de corte casi bíblico, los textiles artesanales y
las flores en su jarrón de vidrio.

Modern art can sit comfortably in the living room of a
country house, as much as the house itself can benefit
from the presence of modern art. The outcome is a very
welcoming atmosphere, thanks to the careful choice
of the abstract painting and its frame, which blend
harmoniously with the almost biblical amphorae, the
handcrafted textiles and the flowers in a glass vase.

La vasta cortina de árboles con su aroma siempre recién nacido; su color, la vibración de su luz con el lago al fondo y el rumor del viento, encuentran una respuesta equilibrada por la generosa amplitud de la terraza que permite experimentar —desde la comodidad— una sorprendente cercanía con el bosque.

The huge curtain of trees with its freshly born fragrance; its color, the vibrancy of its light with the lake in the background and the rustling of the wind, are balanced by the generous size of the terrace that affords an incredible –yet comfortable– closeness with the forest.

Con un lenguaje contemporáneo: la estructura metálica y los ventanales, los lienzos-parasol, los plafones y hasta los muebles, la lámpara y los cuadros, la casa se asienta claramente en el paisaje campestre. Un jardín, campo civilizado bien atendido y bien cuidado por la mano del hombre, se convierte en extensión de la misma casa. Es evidente que la comodidad no tiene porqué estar reñida con el campo.

The contemporary language of the house with its metal structures, the large windows, the parasols, the soffit and even the furniture, the lamp and the paintings clearly place it in the countryside. The garden, a piece of countryside that is civilized and well-kept by the hand of man, becomes an extension of the house itself. It is evident that comfort does not have to be in conflict with the countryside.

Las grandes cristaleras, logro de la
tecnología moderna, acercan de tal manera
al bosque que la casa parece flotar entre las
copas de los árboles. El espacio fluye entre
el exterior y el interior, en un movimiento
facilitado por las columnas y por los tiros
de la chimenea, que son un eco de los
troncos. Las duelas, tendidas en el piso,
mantienen vivo el aroma de la madera.

The large glass panes, a feat of
contemporary technology, bring the forest
so close that the house seems to be floating
among the treetops. Space flows smoothly
between inside and outside with the
assistance of the columns and the chimney,
which seems to reflect the tree trunks.
The staves on the floor keep the fragrance
of the wood alive.

INTIMATE SPACES

habitaciones y baños
bedrooms & bathrooms

La manera en que los humanos habitamos un lugar, cualquiera que sea, expresa siempre los anhelos del grupo o la sociedad a que pertenecemos, sus logros y los valores en que cree. La manera de ocupar y modificar un lugar para habitarlo dice todo acerca de las personas que lo habitan. Por eso la arquitectura es una llave maestra que da entrada al conocimiento de los seres humanos que la producen: con ella podemos saber cuáles son sus sueños, sus recursos, sus luchas y sus aspiraciones. En estas casas de campo, es notable la actitud de profundo respeto y la búsqueda de armonía en que se han empeñado los arquitectos al satisfacer las necesidades de sus clientes. De esta manera, la civilización se acerca al campo sin dejar de lado las ventajas de nuestro tiempo, pero con la actitud respetuosa de quien —al asomarse a la mañana por una ventana— reconoce el valor enorme de la naturaleza y el hecho de que los seres humanos formamos parte indisoluble de ella.

The way humans inhabit any type of place will always reflect

the aspirations of the group or society we belong to, along with

its achievements and the values it believes in. The way a place

is occupied and changed in order for people to live in it says

everything about these people. This is why architecture is a

master key that unlocks the door to the knowledge of the human

beings who make it; it allows us to know what their dreams are,

as well as their resources, their struggles and their goals. These

country houses stand out for the profound sense of respect and

the quest for harmony with which the architects have set about

the task of satisfying the requirements of their clients. In this

way, civilization approaches the countryside without overlooking

the benefits offered by our times, but with the respectful attitude

of someone who –on leaning out through the window in the

morning– recognizes the huge value of nature and the fact that

we human beings are an inseparable part of it.

Los espacios más íntimos, reservados para dormir y para amar, para el aseo y para el reposo, dicen más que ninguno otro sobre la calidad personal de sus habitantes. Al asomarnos a estos espacios, nos asomamos a lo más íntimo y nos damos cuenta de la nobleza con que podemos relacionarnos, desde esos espacios, con el bosque y el lago, con la montaña, el llano y el arroyo.

The most intimate spaces reserved for sleeping and loving, for washing and resting, say more about the people who inhabit them than any other space. On entering these spaces, we are entering the most intimate part of ourselves and we become aware that, from these spaces, we can nobly relate to forests, lakes, mountains, fields and streams.

La ligereza de las persianas de madera
y la puerta corrediza consiguen matizar
en el baño un ambiente ricamente
iluminado por el sol. Al mismo tiempo,
puede graduarse la vista para obtener la
privacidad necesaria. Así el espacio se
disfruta aunque no esté en uso, desde la
recámara, a la que agrega mayor interés
por los efectos de la sombra. Lejos de ser
solo un servicio adosado, el baño forma
parte sutil de la recámara.

The lightness of the wooden Venetian
blinds and the sliding door provide the
bathroom with an ambience exquisitely
lit up by the sun. At the same time,
exposure may be graduated until the
necessary degree of privacy is achieved.
This means that the space can be
enjoyed, even if it is not being used, from
the bedroom which is blessed by the play
of shadows. Far from merely fulfilling a
specific function, the bathroom becomes
a subtle extension of the bedroom.

Podría pensarse que en la vastedad del campo no existen limitantes graves para definir el tamaño de los espacios. Pero otras consideraciones, llevan a limitar las dimensiones para conseguir mayor cercanía, mayor convivencia o mayor intimidad. A pesar de eso, la precisa organización de los muebles y de los objetos da la sensación de amplia funcionalidad.

It is only too easy to think that the vastness of the countryside means there are no limitations for defining the size of spaces. But other factors impose restrictions on sizes for the purposes of achieving greater closeness, greater sharing or greater intimacy. Nonetheless, the precise arrangement of furniture and items creates a feeling of extensive functionality.

La soltura y la informalidad de la vida en las vacaciones o en los fines de semana dan permiso para que la fantasía juegue un papel destacado en la arquitectura. La escalera es una escultura de teclas musicales para trepar; la base de la cama de arriba es delgada como papel y la tarja del lavabo duplica su diseño como lo hace el cristal jugando con las velas.

The freedom and informality of life during vacations or at the weekend enable fantasy to play a leading role in the architecture. The staircase is a scale of musical keys to climb; the base of the top bed is wafer-thin and the curvature of the washbasin duplicates its design in the same way as the mirror does with the candles.

De la fantasía que sabe cómo jugar con el ojo y
burlarlo a veces (mediante reflejos, duplicaciones o
destellos inesperados), la arquitectura pasa al diseño
de espacios que destacan por su ambiente discreto,
pero muy sugerente: los pabellones hechos con gasa o
las cortinas-mosquitero forman un espacio dentro del
espacio, haciendo referencia a los juegos infantiles
y a los ambientes exóticos. Cada espacio adquiere así
su propio ambiente.

From fantasy, which tricks and sometimes mocks the eye
(through reflections, duplication or unexpected sparkles),
architecture moves on to the design of spaces that stand
out for their discrete but highly suggestive mood: drapings
made from gauze or mosquito nets create a space within
a space, in reference to children's games and exotic
settings. Each space acquires its very own ambience.

En el campo es indispensable abrir bien los ojos, conocer la hora por el recorrido del sol, y las estaciones del año por el aroma del viento. Las ventanas abiertas al frente, a los lados o en el techo, altas o bajas, enmarcan a la naturaleza siempre presente. Quiebran la luz del sol en astillas luminosas y convierten cada paisaje en un momento único para alimentar al alma.

In the countryside you cannot but open your eyes, see what time it is by the sun's position and identify the season of the year by the fragrance in the breeze. Open windows at the front, to the sides or in the ceiling, up or down, frame the constant presence of nature. They scatter sunlight into shards of light and turn each landscape into a unique moment that feeds the soul.

El espacio se contiene a sí mismo con sencillez y sobriedad. Se organiza con las vigas de la techumbre, precisa y sin pretensiones; con el piso de grandes cuarterones de barro y los muros lisos, simplemente aplanados y pintados. Todo el color del campo, todo su canto y su tibieza; todo su lujo, se mete y se queda afuera al mismo tiempo, gracias al prodigio de la ventana.

The space is contained within itself with simplicity and sobriety. It is arranged with the rafters of the ceiling, in a precise and unpretentious manner: with the large earthen tiles on the floor and the smooth walls, simply flattened and painted. All the color of the countryside, all its music and coolness, all its luxury enter and stay outside at the same time, thanks to the wonder of the window.

Los herrajes de las camas, las
cortinas y el pergamino en la
pantalla de la lámpara, son huellas
lejanas de la sobria grandeza
de las haciendas coloniales. El
adobe de los muros recuerda las
mejores obras de la arquitectura
vernácula, viva todavía en México.
La agreste vegetación, que puede
contemplarse plácidamente desde
la terraza, baila un jarabe en la
sombra junto con el color inocente
de los bordados.

The ironworks of the bed, the
curtains and the parchment on the
lampshade are fading fingerprints of
the sober grandeur of the colonial
haciendas. The adobe walls are
reminiscent of the finest local
architecture, still very much alive in
Mexico. The wild vegetation that can
be contemplated serenely from the
terrace dances in the shade with the
innocent color of the embroidery.

Frecuentemente, en la buena arquitectura, lo interesante de un espacio radica en lo que se adivina alrededor o fuera de él: en las luces y en las sombras, los sonidos, los silencios y los movimientos invisibles. De este modo, cuando un espacio nos deja intuir algo más allá, se prolonga el misterio y la aventura del descubrimiento. La misión de una puerta o de una ventana en ese caso, va más allá de ceder el paso al movimiento o a la luz, pues se trata de articular a la arquitectura como se arma un poema.

A common feature of good architecture is that the interest generated by a space lies in what is suggested around or outside it; in the lights, the sounds, the silence and the invisible movements. So when a space allows us to perceive something beyond the immediate, the mystery and adventure of discovery lasts just that much longer. The role of a door or a window in this case, goes beyond merely granting access to people or to light, as the aim is to create architecture in the same way a poem is created.

Por su capacidad para crear
ilusiones y fantasías, los espejos
son uno de los instrumentos con
que la arquitectura logra sus
propósitos. Amplifican la forma y
el tamaño de un espacio a veces
hasta el infinito; modulan la luz
y multiplican los reflejos. En los
baños, particularmente, los espejos
y los cristales crean ambientes
propicios para el relajamiento y el
bienestar, trayendo al interior la
atmósfera del campo.

The ability of mirrors to create
illusions and fantasy makes them
a vital instrument for architecture
to achieve its objectives. They
amplify the shape and size of a
space, sometimes infinitely so;
they modulate light and multiply
reflections. In bathrooms in
particular, mirrors and glass generate
an ambience that is conducive to
relaxation and wellbeing, bringing
the feel of the countryside indoors.

La luminosa claridad de la cal, aplicada sobre muros aplanados con textura espesa, es uno de los signos característicos de muchos pueblos y construcciones populares en el campo. Su fuerza expresiva se debe a su origen discreto y humilde, a su calidad artesanal. El deleite de la vacación en estas casas de campo recuerda ese origen, con una austeridad casi conventual, que sabe combinarse plenamente con el confort.

The bright clarity of lime spread thickly on flattened walls is a common sight in many villages and more humble buildings in the countryside.
Its expressive prowess is the result of its discrete and unassuming origins, as well as its crafted quality. The joy afforded by spending vacations in these country houses recalls these origins, with an austerity reminiscent of the convents, which is capable of combining perfectly with comfort.

Las grandes hojas de plátano, atrapadas en el cuadro, aseguran la identificación de la casa con el campo y establecen junto con el hogar de la chimenea, un eje que esparce vida alrededor. Hay aquí varios modos de estar, todos ellos colmados de bienestar. Como un resplandeciente testigo de luz y color, con ecos y cantos lejanos, el movimiento horizontal del lago es enmarcado cuidadosamente por el ventanal.

The large banana leaves trapped in the framed photograph guarantee the identification of the house with the countryside and create along with the fireplace, an axis that scatters life all around it. Here there are several ways of being, all of which are oriented towards wellbeing. Like a shining witness of light and color with distant echoes and song, the horizontal alignment of the lake is carefully framed by the large window.

156

Desde el siglo XVI y antes, el cerro del Tepozteco ha sido reconocido como uno de los más bellos paisajes de México, señor de mitos y tradiciones.

El gran convento construido por los frailes dominicos en aquél siglo tiene un bellísimo espacio destinado solamente a contemplarlo. Esta terraza, entregada sin reservas a la muralla viva del cerro, es una respetuosa caravana a la naturaleza y a la historia.

Since the Sixteenth Century and before, the Tepozteco hill has been acknowledged as one of the most beautiful spots in Mexico, as well as a place of myth and tradition. The large convent built by Dominican monks in that century includes a beautiful space set aside just for contemplating it. This terrace, dedicated without quarter to the sheer face of the hill, is a respectful monument to both nature and history.

La soltura y la informalidad se convierten en un gozo durante la vacación o el fin de semana en una casa de campo. Las literas son una forma de aprovechar el espacio pero también, a todas las edades, una manera de jugar. Una manera de trepar y de soñar en otro nivel, de cambiar los modos de convivir y de conversar; los modos de acercarse y de reconocerse.

Freedom and informality are a joy during vacations or at the weekend in a country house. Bunk beds are a good way of making the most of space, but they are also fun at any age. They offer a means of climbing and dreaming at a different level, of changing how people live together and converse, as well as how people approach and recognize each other.

OUTDOOR LIFE

piscinas y terrazas
pools & terraces

La cara amable del campo depende, en mucho, del clima. Así como las temporadas para sembrar y para cosechar están sujetas al comportamiento del sol y de las lluvias, así la vela en el lago, la cabalgata o la exploración de la montaña, dependen del buen tiempo. Las casas de campo tienen el privilegio de un clima que permite gozar largamente el exterior. Asolearse, contemplar las nubes de la mañana y las estrellas por la noche; escuchar el canto del ruiseñor o de los tecolotes, recoger los hongos de la tierra húmeda o aspirar el aroma de los eucaliptos, son placeres reservados por el campo. Las casas responden con patios, amplias terrazas, pórticos y albercas, estanques o piscinas. Al contrario de los interiores, que cambian poco porque están sujetos a los colores y a la disposición de las paredes, las ventanas, puertas y muebles, en el exterior la experiencia siempre es nueva. Como el cielo nunca repite su espectáculo, cada mañana, cada tarde y cada noche son únicas.

The friendly face of the countryside depends to a large degree on the weather. In addition, the seasons for sowing and harvesting are subject to the behavior of the sun and rain, in the same way that sailing on the lake, horse riding and exploring the mountains depend on good weather conditions. Country houses are blessed by a climate that allows people to enjoy the great outdoors at their leisure. Soaking up the sun, contemplating the morning clouds and the stars at night; listening to the singing of nightingales or owls, picking mushrooms from the damp earth or breathing in the fragrance of eucalyptus are the exclusive pleasures of the countryside. The houses respond with patios, spacious terraces, porches, pools and ponds. Unlike the inside of the houses, which change little because they depend on colors and the positioning of the walls, windows, doors and furniture, the outdoor experience is new. Just like the sky, its shows are never repeated and every evening and night is unique.

La claridad y la lógica con que está armada
la estructura hacen cantar a esta casa frente
al lago. Cada tirante, cada columna y cada
viga ocupan su lugar con una sencillez tal,
que recuerda los juegos infantiles con cubos
y volúmenes de madera. Parece fácil, pero
el recuerdo es engañoso: este resultado solo
pueden lograrlo aquellos arquitectos que,
con maestría, han hecho de su oficio un arte.

The clarity and logic with which the structure
has been put together allow this house to
stand vibrantly in front of the lake. Each tie
beam, column and rafter occupies a space
with such simplicity that it is reminiscent
of children's games comprising wooden
cubes and volumes. It looks easy but the
comparison is deceptive: this result can only
be achieved by architects who have truly
mastered their trade and turned it into an art.

El predominio de las líneas horizontales en el piso, en los cristales del pretil y en el agua dormida, serena las mentes y pone paz en los corazones. La piscina es un segundo lago, domesticado, que dialoga con el otro bajo la efímera luz del atardecer. La soledad del paisaje traslada el silencio al interior de quien lo contempla. Ante la belleza exterior, el callado reposo del alma.

The prevalence of horizontal lines on the floor, on the glass of the parapet and on the sleeping water soothes the mind and brings peace to the heart. The pool is a second lake, a tamed one that converses with the other lake under the fleeting light of sunset. The solitude of the landscape filters the stillness through to the inside of anyone contemplating it. The soul rests in silence before the beauty that surrounds it.

El doble pórtico forma una rica secuencia de espacios que van escalonándose de adentro hacia fuera, hasta llegar a la piscina. Las columnas juegan a la Alhambra. Así se van diluyendo las vistas, se entrelazan los colores, se matiza la luz y se consigue también una escala de temperaturas intermedias. Gracias a eso, la terraza se constituye como el espacio más pleno y más importante de la casa.

The double porch creates a rich sequence of spaces scaled from indoors towards the outside until it reaches the pool. The columns are reminiscent of the Alhambra. The views become diluted, the colors intertwined, the light takes on different tones and a scale of intermediate temperatures is also achieved. All of this makes the terrace the most complete and important area of the house.

174

Por un efecto sorprendente de la arquitectura, la "Peña"
—esa marca que da carácter al paisaje del lago—, se
convierte en un manso remate que casi puede tocarse
en la jardinera, en parte privada de la casa. Los muros
bajos contienen el espacio, pero el telescopio invita a
lanzar lejos la mirada en busca de detalles. La chimenea,
en el exterior, presagia una noche platicadora y quieta.

A surprising effect of the architecture turns the "Peña"
—that landmark that gives the lake's landscape character—
into a gentle crown that can almost be touched from the
flowerbox, into a private part of the house. The low walls
contain the space, but the telescope invites the viewer
to gaze afar in search of details. The chimney outside
predicts a quiet night ideal for conversing.

La poderosa columna sirve como gozne para que el espacio gire alrededor. De un lado, la privacidad de la terraza recluida y los macetones con las buganvilias poniendo límite a la verde explosión de los árboles. Del otro lado el espacio es para compartir. Lo atestigua el aroma del jugo de naranja en los vasos. La alberca, el sol y el piso mojado reflejan la proximidad del encuentro.

The powerful column is like a hinge around which space revolves. On the one hand, there is the privacy of the secluded terrace and the pots with bougainvillea defining a limit for the green explosion of the trees. The other side of the space is for sharing. This is complemented by the aroma of orange juice emanating from the glasses. The pool, the sun and the wet floor reflect the proximity of the encounter.

Frente a la áspera cortina del cerro,
la sofisticada calidad de la terraza
con el piso diluido en cristal. Ese es
el diálogo de las casas de campo
contemporáneas. La capacidad de
entender y apreciar los extremos
para colocarse en el medio y desde
ahí contemplar el cielo, acariciar la
tersura de los materiales, admirar
la vitalidad de los árboles y el juego
vibrante de sol y sombra.

In front of the rugged face of the
hill stands the sophisticated quality
of the floor diluted by glass. This is
the dialog of modern day country
houses: the ability to understand and
appreciate the extremes in order to
find the middle ground and, from
here, contemplate the sky, caress
the smoothness of the materials, and
admire the vitality of the trees and
the vibrant play of light and shade.

En medio de la solidez de la base y de la cubierta de la casa, aligerada por el color claro, el espacio se desenvuelve vigorosamente a lo largo y a lo ancho. En el interior, reina la chimenea. Afuera canta el agua quieta en la piscina, encendida en los surtidores. Los cristales se ilusionan con una separación inexistente. La noche de los grillos envuelve suavemente a la vida.

In between the solid base and the roof of the house, lightened by pale colors, the space vigorously stretches out lengthwise and breadthwise. The chimney is in charge indoors. Outside, the still water fed by spouts whispers. The glass creates the illusion of an inexistent separation. The night of crickets gently swallows up all life.

Como una acequia o un amplio bebedero
para caballos (podría ser un homenaje
a Luis Barragán), el estanque responde
con un acto de magia a la firmeza del
gran muro de piedra que respalda a la
casa. Las columnas apareadas juegan
con la mirada, queriendo retenerla
en su fuga hacia los árboles, hacia el
cielo. Lo consiguen por un momento, la
entretienen un poco y luego la sueltan.

Like an irrigation channel or a horses'
trough (this could be a tribute to Luis
Barragán), the pond responds to
the firmness of the large stone wall
supporting the house with its own magic
trick. Pairs of columns play optical games
on the eye, preventing it from moving
on to the trees or the sky. They achieve
this for a moment, entertaining the eye
briefly before setting it free again.

El culto al agua, en el campo,
forma parte de lo cotidiano. Sin
agua suficiente no hay cosecha.
Con demasiada agua, tampoco.
Atesorarla es una manera de ser,
de responderle a la vida. Que el
agua sea parte inseparable de la
arquitectura, expresa el respeto
y la gratitud a la naturaleza. El
agua salta y canta, escurre y grita,
se duerme y platica, cuando los
arquitectos saben amarla.

The worshipping of water in the
countryside is a part of daily life.
Without water, there is no harvest.
With too much water, there is also
no harvest. Treasuring it is a way of
life and a response to its demands.
The fact that water is an inseparable
component of architecture is a
testimony to the respect and
gratitude we owe nature. Water
jumps and sings, it pours forth and
shouts; it sleeps and talks when
architects know how to love it.

El agua es al campo lo que el árbol
es al bosque. El agua extendida en el
lago. El agua fría domesticada en los
estanques profundos o tibia en las
plataformas de las piscinas, ligera
en el arroyo, precipitándose en
la tormenta, en el granizo y en
la lluvia. El agua es protagonista
principal. Estas casas lo reconocen
y lo manifiestan con orgullo.

Water is to the countryside what the
tree is to the forest. Water stretching
out in the lake; the tamed cold water
of deep ponds or the lukewarm water
on the platforms of the pools; water
running light-footed along the stream;
water pouring down in storm, in the
hail and rain. Water plays the leading
role. These houses are aware of this
and express it proudly.

Así como el juego de los muros y los pavimentos, las jardineras y los macetones hacen que la casa se meta en el campo, los estanques y las piscinas llaman al lago, trayéndolo hasta casi inundar la terraza. Por su parte los distintos planos de la casa se van alejando hasta flotar sobre la serena superficie del lago. Como mariposas, las sombrillas conducen la mirada hacia el fondo.

In the same way that the walls, walkways, flowerboxes and pots place the house firmly in the countryside, the pools and ponds invoke the lake, pulling it in so much it almost floods the terrace. The house's different planes stretch out until they float on the calm surface of the lake. Like butterflies, the sunshades guide the eye towards the background.

El contraste sorprende, enriquecido por la geometría pura de los círculos, rectángulos y cuadrados, que se oponen armoniosamente a las formas orgánicas del campo. También el color y los reflejos cristalinos participan en la fiesta. Gracias a la arquitectura el paisaje adquiere un nuevo significado. Igualmente, la casa se honra con la visita puntual de los árboles, con su aroma y el suspiro del viento entre sus ramas.

The surprising contrast is enhanced by the pure geometry of the circles, rectangles and squares, creating a harmonious contrast with the organic shapes of the countryside. The colors and crystalline reflections are also present. The architecture gives the landscape new meaning. Furthermore, the house is blessed with a clear view of the trees, with their fragrance and the breeze whispering between their branches.

En el campo, el crepúsculo es uno de
los más bellos momentos. La mitad del
mundo se dispone a dormir: las ardillas
y los cenzontles; los halcones, los
escarabajos, las golondrinas, las vacas
y los caballos. Despiertan los grillos, los
tejones y las luciérnagas, los mapaches,
las lechuzas y otros mil personajes.
Arde la chimenea y se encienden luces,
como silenciosos testigos del milagro
de la noche joven.

Sunset is one of the countryside's most
beautiful moments. Half the world is
getting ready to go to sleep: the squirrels
and mocking birds, the falcons and
beetles, the swallows, the cows and
horses. The crickets wake up, along
with the badgers and fireflies, raccoons,
owls and a thousand other beings. The
chimney smokes and lights are switched
on, like silent witnesses of the miracle of
the new night.

La arquitectura acerca y aleja, contiene y desparrama, une y separa. Así es la vida hecha de encuentros y desencuentros, de sometimiento y soberanía. Siendo como es un invento humano, la arquitectura establece territorios y lugares con nombre propio, donde antes sólo había terrenos. Tiene sus propios límites y en reconocerlos está su grandeza. Una terraza abierta así al campo no domesticado es, en su pequeñez, contundente testimonio.

Architecture holds you close and hurls you away, it contains and scatters, it joins and separates. Such is the life of encounters and distancing, of submission and sovereignty. Being the human invention it is, architecture establishes territories and places with their own name, where once there was only land. It sets its own limits, and its greatness lies in recognizing them. A terrace open to the untamed countryside is, in all its smallness, an outstanding witness.

Esta es la arquitectura: el escenario para vivir todos los días, en todas partes. La articulación de espacios para pasar el tiempo, para crecer y para contemplar, para amar, para descansar, para callar y para compartir. Estas casas muestran la sensibilidad con que los arquitectos responden al paisaje del campo y enmarcan el modo de ser de quienes las habitan. Esta es la arquitectura hecha para la vida.

This is architecture: the stage on which each day is lived, everywhere. The definition of spaces to spend time in, to grow and to contemplate, to love, rest, be silent and share in. These houses show the sensitivity with which architects respond to the landscapes of the countryside and highlight the personality of the people who live in them. This is architecture made for life.

INDICE / INDEX

FOTÓGRAFOS / PHOTOGRAPHERS

Se terminó de imprimir en el mes de Junio del 2007 en China. El cuidado de la edición estuvo a cargo de AM Editores S.A. de C.V. **Printed in June 2007 in China. Published by AM Editores S.A. de C.V.**

First Published in 2021 by Motorbooks, an imprint of The Quarto Group,
100 Cummings Center, Suite 265-D, Beverly, MA 01915, USA.
T (978) 282-9590 F (978) 283-2742 QuartoKnows.com

Motorbooks titles are also available at discount for retail, wholesale, promotional, and bulk purchase. For details, contact the Special Sales Manager by email at specialsales@quarto.com or by mail at The Quarto Group, Attn: Special Sales Manager, 100 Cummings Center, Suite 265-D, Beverly, MA 01915, USA.

25 24 23 22 21   1 2 3 4 5

ISBN: 978-0-7603-6777-3

Digital edition published in 2020
eISBN: 978-0-7603-6778-0

Library of Congress Cataloging-in-Publication Data

Names: Codling, Stuart, 1972- author.
Title: Ferrari Formula 1 car by car : every race car since 1950 / Stuart
   Codling.
Description: Beverly, MA : Motorbooks, an imprint of The Quarto Group,
   2020. | Includes index. | Summary: "Ferrari Formula 1 Car by Car is the
   complete guide to every Ferrari Formula 1 car that has competed since
   1950"-- Provided by publisher.
Identifiers: LCCN 2020017086 | ISBN 9780760367773 (hardcover) | ISBN
   9780760367780 (ebook)
Subjects: LCSH: Ferrari automobile--Catalogs. | Ferrari
   automobile--History. | Formula One automobiles--Catalogs. | Formula One
   automobiles--History.
Classification: LCC TL215.F47 C635 2020 | DDC 629.228/5--dc23
LC record available at https://lccn.loc.gov/2020017086

Acquiring Editor: Zack Miller
Cover Image: James Mann
Page Layout: Landers Miller Design
Photography: Motorsport Images and James Mann
All photos used with permission Motorsports Images except where noted

Printed in China

Acknowledgments

I'd like to pay tribute to the diligence of my colleagues at *Autosport* magazine, past and present, for documenting the ongoing developments within Formula 1 in great and accurate detail, and to Kevin Wood for superintending its archive. My thanks also to John Barnard, for agreeing to an interview at the launch of his excellent book *The Perfect Car*, and to my esteemed colleague Giorgio Piola for his patience and generosity. Last but indubitably not least, thanks to my wife, Julie.

FERRARI FORMULA 1

CAR BY CAR

EVERY RACE CAR SINCE 1950

STUART CODLING

Contents

1

2

3

4

5

6

7

08 – 35	1950s
36 – 57	1960s
58 – 71	1970s
72 – 93	1980s
94 – 129	1990s
130 – 167	2000s
168 – 205	2010s

INTRODUCTION

Enzo Anselmo Ferrari—and the cars carrying his name—were embedded in the rich tapestry of motor racing history long before 1950, when the postwar Grand Prix racing scene coalesced around what we now call the Formula 1 World Championship. Born in 1898, the second son of a foundry owner, Enzo nursed dreams of becoming a racing driver . . . or a sports journalist, or an opera singer. The death of his father and brother during an outbreak of influenza in 1916 brought the family business to its knees and forced Enzo to set his dreams aside—for a while. Those who like to associate a person's psychology with their formative experiences point to this phase of Ferrari's life as the wellspring of his tendency to be harsh, cynical, intolerant, controlling, and, above all (in his own words), "an agitator of men."

Discharged from the army during the Spanish flu pandemic of 1918, Ferrari scratched around for a job before finding a position with CMN, a small Milan-based manufacturer that was converting war surplus vehicles into cars. Initially his job entailed driving the bare chassis to the coachbuilder. Later he would enter hillclimb events, and by the end of 1919 the Targa Florio, the famous road race around the island of Sicily.

Through a friend he gained an introduction at Alfa Romeo, then Italy's preeminent force in motor racing, and at the wheel of a 6-liter Tipo 40/60 he finished second in the Targa Florio in 1920. Though he continued to race with enough success to be honoured by the Italian state, first as a *Cavaliere* and then as a *Commendatore*, during that decade he gravitated toward team management, allying himself with Alfa Romeo and establishing Scuderia Ferrari in 1929. Alfa had undergone one of its periodic withdrawals from racing as a works force and Ferrari's organization serviced the demands of the many wealthy Alfa Romeo owners who wished to compete. It would later become the company's de facto racing division.

By then Ferrari had already adopted the symbol of the *Cavallino Rampante*—the prancing horse—and, as is fitting for a man who spent much of the second half of his life concealing his eyes and intentions behind dark glasses, the origin of this is enigmatic. It's widely believed he was gifted it by the parents of the late fighter pilot Francesco Baracca, whose squadron carried that as an emblem.

It's also claimed that Ferrari ceased to attend motor races in the late 1950s after the premature death of his son, Dino, but in truth he had long since withdrawn to his workshops, from where he could pull the strings with impunity. It added to the sense of mystique and, for those

John Gabrial Collection

charged with ensuring Scuderia Ferrari's Alfa Romeos performed on track, the perils associated with failure.

The Grand Prix racing scene of the 1930s became an arms race between the fascist government–backed German manufacturers Auto Union and Mercedes, as Alfa Romeo pitched in from the fringes. There was never quite the money, the political will, or the technological resources to tackle the Germans meaningfully or consistently. In 1937, under pressure from Italian dictator Benito Mussolini to be more on par with his Axis partners, Alfa Romeo became a majority shareholder in Scuderia Ferrari and folded it into the larger corporate organization as the official competitions department. Enzo's plan to build a new car for the voiturette subclass—in effect not really racing against Mercedes and Auto Union—didn't align with the new objectives and he was duly edged out. Not only that, but his severance agreement also included a four-year non-compete clause.

World War II rendered that largely irrelevant, as Ferrari's new company, Auto Avio Costruzioni, was pressed into munitions and machine tools manufacture. Postwar privations made motorsport an unaffordable luxury for a time. But soon Ferrari summoned his old engineer, Gioacchino Colombo, to his Modena works, where he said, with admirable understatement, "I've had enough of utilities. I want to go back to racing."

The Ferrari company as we now know it was founded in March 1947. Two months later, Franco Cortese won the grandly titled Rome Grand Prix—40 laps around the historic Terme di Caracalla site—in a Ferrari 125 S roadster. In supercharged form, that car's engine would power Ferrari's return to Grand Prix racing—and take it into Formula 1 as we know it today.

CHAPTER 1

Although it's easy to look back at 1950 as the genesis of the Formula 1 (F1) World Championship we recognize today as the pinnacle of international motor racing, in the context of the time it was rather less exciting. Motorsport for the most part was about making do: postwar material shortages and economic privation militated against the development of sophisticated new racing cars. Sports car events were often more popular and offered better prize money.

By the middle of the decade, though, F1 was beginning to establish itself as a leader in technology and was attracting greater interest from major manufacturers. Ferrari's journey to becoming one of the preeminent automotive marques began here, as Enzo Ferrari fought to survive against wealthier opposition. Well before the phrase "Win on Sunday, sell on Monday" was coined, Ferrari was building and selling cars on the back of his racing success.

As the architect of prewar victories with Alfa Romeo, he knew his value. The notion of receiving prize money for participating in a racing season would remain an alien concept until the 1980s. During this period, entrants would negotiate fees individually with race promoters—hence, famously, Ferrari did not participate in the first World Championship Grand Prix at Silverstone in 1950. They just weren't offering enough—world championship or not.

←

Juan Manuel Fangio didn't mind swapping teams if it meant accessing the best car. After Mercedes withdrew from racing in 1955, he moved to Ferrari, who had obtained the mold-breaking D50s from bankrupt Lancia.

Ferrari's first Grand Prix car was living on borrowed time, even as the world championship began in 1950. Though the 125 F1 was nimble on account of its relatively short wheelbase, this same characteristic made it twitchy and unstable in a straight line, as the varying surface quality of certain tracks overwhelmed the 125's crude suspension.

Work on the 125 F1 began shortly after Enzo Ferrari founded Ferrari S.p.A in Modena in 1947, though the 125 S sports car was the initial focus of development, perhaps because Ferrari was reluctant to compete against Alfa Romeo, his old employers. But since they were widely expected to step back from racing their aging prewar 158s—developed by Gioacchino Colombo at Ferrari's behest when Enzo ran Alfa Romeo's competitions department—there was no reason not to proceed with a single-seater racer.

Both the sports car and the monoposto were built around iterations of a 1.5-liter supercharged 60-degree V-12, also designed by Colombo. It was notably compact, with a single chain-driven camshaft actuating two valves per cylinder, a single carburetor mounted in the vee, and a single Roots-type supercharger mounted at the front. The five-speed gearbox was a bespoke Ferrari design driving an open propshaft to the final drive at the rear.

Colombo's chassis followed similar principles to the 158 "voiturette" he designed at Alfa Romeo and was entirely conventional for the time: a ladder-frame layout based on longitudinal oval tubes braced by tubular cross members, with a box section at the front. The suspension, too, adhered to common practice, with unequal-length wishbones and a transverse leaf spring up front, and a torsion bar arrangement at the rear, all damped via Houdaille lever-arm shock absorbers. This early design of the damper relied on the resistance of oil against rotary vanes within a cylindrical vessel, and was therefore prone to losing effectiveness as the oil heated up under prolonged duress.

Appearing for the first time at the 1948 Italian Grand Prix in Turin, Alfa Romeo's last before taking a short sabbatical from Grands Prix, the 125 F1 proved sporadically competitive but not consistent front-running material. In its initial form, the engine was massively outgunned—producing in the region of 220 bhp, while the Alfa's made well over 300 bhp—and the gearbox proved temperamental. The car itself was brutally tail happy.

125 F1 SPECIFICATIONS

Engine	1,497 cc 60-degree V-12, dual-stage supercharger	Suspension	Double wishbones (front), swing axle/De Dion beam axle (rear), transverse leaf springs, lever-arm dampers
Power	300 bhp @ 7,000 rpm	Brakes	Drums f/r
Gearbox	Five/four-speed manual	Tires	Pirelli, Englebert
Chassis	Steel tube frame with twin longitudinal beams, aluminum body	Weight	700 kg

←
Peter Whitehead's 125 was the sole Ferrari to contest the 1950 French Grand Prix after the works team decided their new 275s weren't fast enough and withdrew.

↑
Ferrari's first Grand Prix car
was a handful. "Any attempt to
take corners with the power on
resulted in the tail chasing the
front wheels," wrote Raymond
Mays of his experience racing it
at Silverstone in 1949.

By the end of 1949, Colombo had rebodied the 125, lengthened the wheelbase by 10 inches, widened the track by 3.5 inches, replaced the torsion bars with swing axles, and substantially revised the engine. The V-12 now had gear-driven twin overhead camshafts, new cylinder heads with centrally located spark plugs, and a two-stage supercharger. The works team and customers still fielded the short-wheelbase, single-stage 125s at certain events, and the disparity in performance was remarkable.

Ferrari skipped the first World Championship F1 race, at Silverstone in May 1950, because he judged the money on offer insufficient to merit the disruptive effect it would have on preparations for the more lucrative Monaco Grand Prix a week later. There Alberto Ascari finished second in a two-stage 125 to Juan Manuel Fangio's Alfa Romeo. Next time out, in the Swiss Grand Prix at Bremgarten, the 125s appeared with De Dion suspension (and a four-speed gearbox integrated with the final drive) at the rear in place of swing axles, but all the works entries retired. The 125 made just two further world championship race appearances as Ferrari phased it out in favor of naturally aspirated machinery.

Having skipped the 1950 British Grand Prix, Ferrari appeared for the first time in a world championship race at Monaco a week later. The 125s now had two-stage superchargers, but a first-lap shunt at Tabac delayed the Ferrari drivers; Ascari (car No. 40) threaded his way through to finish second.

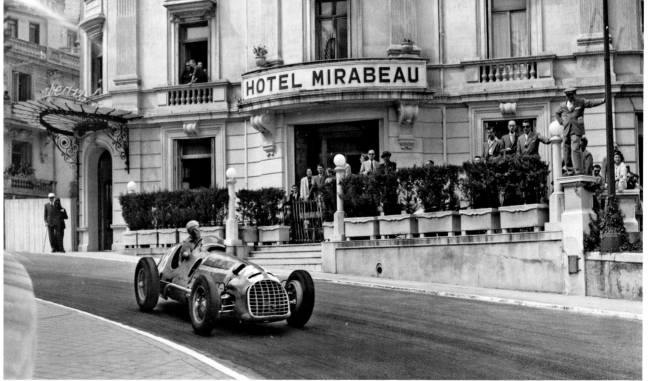

→ Luigi Villoresi charged back into second place at Monaco in 1950 after stalling his 125 while negotiating the aftermath of the famous accident at Tabac, but the car's rear axle broke before the end.

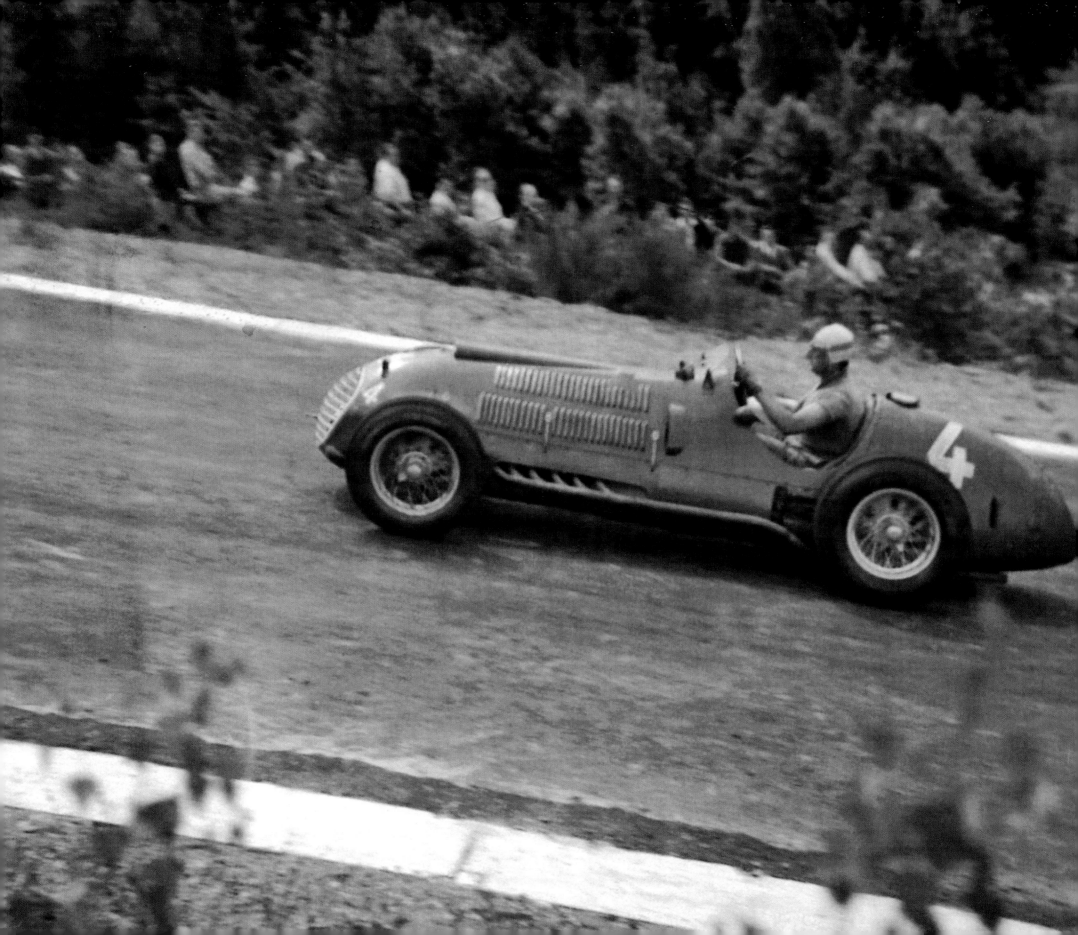

Accounts differ as to why Ferrari switched to natural aspiration when the dominant cars in Grand Prix racing tended to be supercharged. One theory has it that the decision was prompted by the Scuderia's disappointing 1949 Belgian Grand Prix, in which Luigi Villoresi led from the start in a works 125 only to be passed in the pits by Louis Rosier's unblown 4.5-liter Talbot-Lago while the Ferrari's prodigious thirst was being serviced.

It's more likely that Enzo Ferrari's thought processes were influenced by the febrile form of Grand Prix racing at the time. What was initially known as Formula A was coalescing into Formula 1, and a world championship was in the offing, but motor racing's international governing body had yet to alight on a firm set of rules for the future. The present regulations—1.5-liter blown, 4.5-liter unblown—were in effect a fudge to ensure healthy grid sizes.

Aurelio Lampredi, Gioacchino Colombo's assistant at Ferrari, proposed that a larger-capacity, naturally aspirated V-12 would offer a degree of future proofing. Ultimately, his concept proved so successful that he was appointed as technical director and his mentor returned to Alfa Romeo.

Lampredi's V-12 shared its 60-degree angle with Colombo's but architecturally it was very different—5 inches longer overall, with the bore centers further apart, and taller. Though the goal was to reach 4.5 liters, the Lampredi V-12 first saw action in 3.3-liter form. At the Belgian Grand Prix in 1950, Luigi Villoresi drove a 125 while Alberto Ascari gave the 275 its debut. Despite the new designation, it was an existing chassis (one of the long-wheelbase 125s) with the 3.3-liter engine installed. Ascari finished fifth, a lap down on the leading group.

The next round of the World Championship was at the high-speed Reims-Gueux, where Ferrari entered two 275s but withdrew before the race, not expecting to be competitive. The 275 raced again only in non-championship events. It was time for a new chassis as well as a larger engine.

← The short-lived 275—an early 3.3-liter version of Lampredi's V-12 engine fitted into a long-wheelbase 125 chassis—made its race debut in the 1950 Belgian Grand Prix, where Alberto Ascari elevated the ill-handling car to fifth place.

275 F1 SPECIFICATIONS

Engine	3,322 cc 60-degree V-12	Suspension	Double wishbones (front), swing axle (rear), transverse leaf springs, lever-arm dampers
Power	270 bhp @ 7,200 rpm	Brakes	Drums f/r
Gearbox	Four-speed manual	Tires	Pirelli
Chassis	Steel tube frame with twin longitudinal beams, aluminum body	Weight	720 kg

By the end of 1950, Ferrari's definitive naturally aspirated F1 car was ready. Initially raced in the non-championship Swiss Grand Prix with the 340 type number, powered by a 4.1-liter version of the V-12 (achieved by widening the cylinder bores), the new car was based on a revised but still very conventional chassis design. Rectangular tubes replaced ovals for the main longitudinal members and, in an effort to save weight, rather than an elaborate box section up front, a single plate helped provide rigidity and locate the suspension. Another broad beam braced the rear, and the suspension was carried over from the latest iteration of the 125, including the De Dion axle and the four-speed gearbox.

While the performance of the new car had been promising on the Geneva street circuit—only Juan Manuel Fangio in an Alfa Romeo 158 ran ahead of Ferrari's Alberto Ascari—the 340's engine failed before the finish and Ascari's teammate Luigi Villoresi injured himself, badly shunting his 275 on oil. Ferrari didn't enter another Grand Prix until the final world championship round at Monza a month later, by which time the 4.5-liter V-12 was considered ready. Aurelio Lampredi and his engineers created the additional displacement by lengthening the stroke, and in combination with larger twin carburetors, this boosted power to a claimed 330 bhp.

Now known as the type 375—taken prosaically from the swept capacity in cubic centimeters of a single cylinder—the new Ferrari enabled Ascari to take the fight to Fangio and Giuseppe Farina both on single-lap pace and in the race itself. The supercharged Alfa Romeos were unable to shake off Ascari and, because he would need to make fewer refueling stops, he was almost certain to win—until his engine blew with barely a quarter of the race gone. Still, having walked back to the pits and taken over teammate Dorino Serafini's car, he rose from sixth to second place despite a truculent gear change.

This performance, on a circuit where lap times rode on outright power, convinced Alfa to redevelop their 158s over the winter to squeeze yet more grunt from the engine. But this came at the cost of even greater

← Having introduced the 375 at the 1950 Italian Grand Prix, Ferrari entered two of the cars in the non-championship Penya Rhin GP, held on the Pedralbes street circuit in Barcelona, Spain. Test driver Dorino Serafini, pictured here, substituted for the injured Luigi Villoresi.

375 F1 SPECIFICATIONS

Engine	4,494 cc 60-degree V-12	Suspension	Double wishbones (front), De Dion beam axle (rear), transverse leaf springs, lever-arm dampers
Power	350 bhp @ 7,000 rpm	Brakes	Drums f/r
Gearbox	Four-speed manual	Tires	Pirelli, Firestone (in 1952 Indy 500)
Chassis	Steel tube frame with twin longitudinal beams, aluminum body	Weight	720 kg

↑
Alfa Romeo's absence from the non-championship Penya Rhin GP in 1950 meant Ferrari's only meaningful opposition was the temperamental BRM. Alberto Ascari averaged nearly 94 miles per hour on his way to victory over teammate Dorino Serafini in the new 375.

thirst, plus additional weight in the form of larger fuel tanks. Ferrari developed new heads for their V-12 with two spark plugs per cylinder, improving power (Ferrari optimistically claimed an additional 50 bhp) and efficiency. A 375 could perhaps travel 8 miles on a gallon of fuel, while a 158 could barely manage two.

The 1951 World Championship became an epic scrap between Alfa Romeo and Ferrari. Other manufacturers barely figured—which would soon become an existential threat to Formula 1 as a category. Alfa's developments just enabled them to stay ahead of Ferrari until Silverstone, where the pugnacious José Froilán González—a third entry in a single-plug 375—took pole position and an unexpected victory. Pitting from the lead on lap 60, Gonzalez prepared to hand his car to Ascari, whose 375 had halted with gearbox failure. Ascari generously declined and waved him back out.

Ascari won at the Nürburgring and was in contention for the title at the final round, only for Ferrari to squander the opportunity by running smaller-diameter wheels than would have been prudent and suffering a string of tire failures.

← The full 4.5-liter version of Aurelio Lampredi's unblown V-12 didn't appear until the end of the 1950 season. It was immediately competitive, although reliability was questionable early on.

← Roadside fields had to make do as garages at circuits such as Reims-Gueux; this is Luigi Villoresi's twin-plug 375, left briefly unattended during the 1951 French GP weekend.

In the early months of 1952, Formula 1's very future as a category was thrown into doubt. The Fédération Internationale de l'Automobile (FIA) announced a new formula, based on 2.5-liter naturally aspirated or 750 cc blown engines, due to come in to effect in 1954. While that would theoretically give manufacturers adequate time to develop new cars and engines, it presented an immediate cascade of problems: Alfa Romeo had reached the development limit of their car and couldn't afford to create a new one, so they withdrew; no other extant manufacturers had the machinery to challenge Ferrari; and there was little sign of the much-vaunted British Racing Motors (BRM) team. When BRM pulled out of the high-profile non-championship Turin Grand Prix in April 1952, race organizers across Europe fell in line with the promoters of the French Grand Prix, who had already said they would welcome only Formula 2 entries. Accordingly, for the next two years, the world championship Grands Prix were run to F2 regulations.

Ferrari already had a competitive package ready. F2 races were commonplace and featured a significant proportion of private entries, which represented a business opportunity, as well as a competitive one, for Enzo Ferrari. Four-cylinder engines were popular in this 2-liter formula on account of their relative simplicity and greater low-end torque.

Aurelio Lampredi designed a neat 2.5-liter four-cylinder unit with a one-piece block and twin overhead camshafts, sleeved down to 2 liters for F2 use. As

	500 F1	625 F1
Engine	1,984 cc in-line four	2,498 cc in-line four
Power	170 bhp @ 7,500 rpm	250 bhp @ 7,200 rpm
Gearbox	Four-speed manual	Four-speed manual
Chassis	Steel tube frame with twin longitudinal beams, aluminum body	Steel tube frame with twin longitudinal beams, aluminum body
Suspension	Double wishbones (front), De Dion beam axle with trailing arms (rear), transverse leaf springs, lever-arm damper	Double wishbones (front), De Dion beam axle with trailing arms (rear), transverse leaf springs, lever-arm damper
Brakes	Drums f/r	Drums f/r
Tires	Pirelli	Pirelli, Englebert
Weight	560 kg	635 kg

←
Mike Hawthorn got the uncompetitive 625 up to second place in the 1954 Belgian Grand Prix before fumes from an oil leak muddled his senses.

500/625 F1

↑
On a rare off day for Mercedes and the usually dominant Juan Manuel Fangio, José Froilán González hustled his 625 to victory in the 1954 British Grand Prix ahead of Ferrari teammate Mike Hawthorn.

raced by the works team in 1952 and 1953, it had four carburetors and produced a claimed 170 bhp. The type 500 chassis designed to accommodate it took its name from the swept volume of each cylinder, as per Ferrari convention. Customers found that their cars had a lower rev ceiling and produced less power, and only a handful were ultimately sold.

If the collective intention of Europe's race promoters had been to head off the potential of Ferrari dominating the scene, this ambition was thwarted. Against a mixed bag of competitors—chiefly HWM-Altas, Cooper-Bristols,

Gordinis, and Maseratis—the 500 proved dominant in the hands of Alberto Ascari, who won nine consecutive Grands Prix (discounting the anomalous Indy 500s, which counted toward the World Championship) across 1952–53. Ferraris were victorious in all bar one of the World Championship Grands Prix in the F2 era and would have won them all had Ascari not spun out of the lead on the last lap of the '53 Italian Grand Prix.

If Ferrari's first two drivers' championships had arrived with relative ease, the going would get tougher with the rebirth of Formula 1 in 1954. Enzo fell out with

←
Alberto Ascari closed out the 1952 World Championship with a victory in the Italian Grand Prix at Monza. Nowadays the Parabolica turn is better paved and photographers enjoy the safety of a tower.

↓
For the 1954 German Grand Prix, Ferrari evaluated a tweaked engine construction in the cars entered for José Froilán González and Mike Hawthorn, mating the crankcase of the 735 sports car to the block and twin-cam head of the standard 625.

Ascari over money and lost his star driver to Lancia. Ferrari's new car, the 553 "Squalo," endured a difficult genesis, forcing the team to fall back on the existing chassis—now with the 2.5-liter engine and racing under the type number 625.

Ferrari's inability to come to grips with the new formula would eventually cost Lampredi his job and consign the team to the role of makeweights. The 625 would race on until 1955, taking an unlikely victory at Monaco in the hands of Maurice Trintignant.

The 1953 Italian Grand Prix offered a window on Ferrari's F1 future in more than one regard. First, it was supposedly the team's last ever appearance, Enzo having threatened to quit motor racing. It also provided a public debut for Ferrari's new F1 challenger, which rather exposed Enzo's bluff for what it was. The 553 was the most mechanically adventurous Ferrari yet—but like several of the company's racers to come, it would fail to translate that boldness into results.

Nicknamed the "Squalo" (Italian for "shark") on account of its protuberant sides and pronounced tail, the 553 was Ferrari's first attempt at a spaceframe-style chassis. This promised greater rigidity with less weight, though with this construction approach it was challenging for newcomers to achieve the right balance, so the 553 carried a large tubular brace up front to augment the network of small-diameter tubes. Its wheelbase was 2.5 inches shorter than the 500's in an effort to promote greater agility, and the fuel tanks were mounted on each side of the driver rather than behind the rear axle.

For its Monza debut, the 553 complied with F2 regulations by running with the 2-liter Lampredi engine, albeit one with a wider bore and shorter stroke than the 500s. Ferrari fielded six cars, two of which were 553s, but none of the works drivers liked the behavior of the new cars, so they were assigned to juniors.

Having lost Alberto Ascari and Luigi Villoresi, Enzo Ferrari retained the fading Giuseppe Farina and the promising young Briton Mike Hawthorn, and rehired José Froilán González. Though it was not considered to be a lineup out of the top drawer, it would suffice. The 553, however, proved not up to the task, even when fitted with a larger version of the four-cylinder engine for F1.

Reengineered for 1955 with the 555 type number and now nicknamed "Super Squalo," the car continued to underwhelm despite its substantially revised chassis, and it was replaced in several events by the elderly 625.

553/555 F1 SPECIFICATIONS

Engine	2,497 cc in-line four	Suspension	Double wishbones (front), De Dion beam axle with trailing arms (rear), coil springs/ transverse leaf springs, lever-arm dampers
Power	260 bhp @ 7,200 rpm	Brakes	Drums f/r
Gearbox	Four-speed manual	Tires	Pirelli, Englebert
Chassis	Steel tube frame with twin longitudinal beams, aluminum body	Weight	630 kg

553/555 F1

While Enzo Ferrari gratefully received a swag bag of assets as a result of Lancia's financial collapse in late 1955, including its race cars and many of its staff, pride dictated that he immediately begin to set his own stamp upon them. The D50, perhaps even more so than the all-conquering Mercedes W196, was the template for the modern Grand Prix car.

Where the Mercedes was broad, long, and relatively bulky, placing great reliance on its engine, the D50 was built with supreme agility in mind. It was short and relatively narrow, packaged tightly, and used its 90-degree V-8 engine as a partially stressed element of the spaceframe chassis—preempting other developments in that direction by a decade. To neutralize the balance of the car, the engine was angled slightly and the gearbox was at the rear, while the main fuel tanks were located on pontoons between the wheels.

Lancia's chief engineer, Vittorio Jano, had spent over a decade superintending Alfa Romeo's racing efforts, but the D50 was considered to be his tour de force. It had been finished several months behind schedule, though, and missed the 1954 season. Then 1955 was blighted by Alberto Ascari's death, the Le Mans disaster, and Lancia's financial struggles, but the D50 remained a far better car than anything in Ferrari's arsenal.

Not that this dissuaded Enzo from directing that changes should be made. Ferrari obtained the cars in July 1955 and entered them for the season-closing Italian Grand Prix. That race provoked a schism between Enzo and his contracted tire suppliers, Englebert: the D50 had been developed in partnership with Pirelli and, like many short-wheelbase cars, its behavior at the limit could be twitchy. Enzo wanted to run Pirellis at Monza, but Englebert refused, even though their own tires were shedding their treads on the banking. The D50s had to be withdrawn.

Ferrari approached 1956 with a mix-and-match approach, not yet ready to commit fully to the D50 without modifications. Having recruited Juan Manuel Fangio following the withdrawal of Mercedes, Enzo afforded his star driver his choice of machinery. In the first round of the season, in Argentina, Fangio appeared in a much-changed D50, with a tail-mounted fuel tank, a

D50 SPECIFICATIONS

Engine	2,486 cc 90-degree V-8	Suspension	Double wishbones (front), De Dion beam axle (rear), transverse leaf springs, telescopic dampers (f), lever-arm dampers (r)
Power	270 bhp @ 8,000 rpm	Brakes	Drums f/r
Gearbox	Five-speed manual	Tires	Englebert, Pirelli
Chassis	Steel tube frame with twin longitudinal beams, aluminum body	Weight	620 kg

Ferrari-Lancia D50

← Though none of the original D50s survive, during the 1990s a group of wealthy enthusiasts commissioned four re-creations using the original technical drawings and some original spare parts. *James Mann*

→ Health and safety ranked lower in racing priorities during the 1950s; here Alfonso de Portago enjoys a cigarette while sitting in front of a tank of highly flammable fuel.

new rear suspension layout with a conventionally located leaf spring (to lower the center of gravity, it had originally been attached below the differential), and rotary dampers rather than telescopic ones. Ferrari also distrusted the stressed-engine arrangement and added further bracing up front. Fangio's engine blew in the race, but he took over Luigi Musso's unmodified D50 and won.

By the start of the European season, Ferrari's engineers had made over other elements of the car, relocating the fuel tanks between the wheels again but flush to the chassis sides, requiring further sheet metal between the panniers and the chassis. Independent rear suspension via swing axles was tried but abandoned midseason.

Although Fangio claimed another two Grand Prix victories and won the drivers' championship, he felt that the rapidly improving Maserati 250F would be a better bet. That impression was compounded at a jittery final Grand Prix of the season at Monza, where there were more thrown treads and Fangio stopped with a broken steering arm. Though it was customary in this era for senior drivers to take over the running car of a teammate, Luigi Musso refused to give up his D50 and Fangio secured enough points to win the title only when the young Peter Collins handed over his instead.

↑
Wins in Belgium and France elevated Peter Collins to the lead of the 1956 World Championship, but in Britain his car lost oil pressure, although Collins would be credited with second place after taking over teammate Alfonso de Portago's car.

Throughout 1956, Ferrari grappled with the challenges of developing a car that had been designed by another manufacturer. Even with the D50's principal architect, Vittorio Jano, acting as a consultant, Ferrari made little progress and arguably diluted much of what was distinctive and good about the car.

801 F1

While Maserati found clear development paths with their 250F—making it lighter, lowering the center of gravity, shrinking the frontal area, and liberating more power from the engine—the D50's already compact layout was inherently limiting. Where the 250F was stable and predictable, particularly at the limit of adhesion, the D50 was prone to lunging off the asphalt. Ferrari focused on altering elements of the suspension and trying to increase the engine's horsepower, but in the latter department they hit a brick wall. In retrospect, it's easy to say that one of the chief limiting factors in terms of the handling, and one easily remedied, was the Englebert tires.

For 1957, Ferrari built a new chassis based on the original Lancia design, but with larger-diameter longitudinal tubes and a new structure around the engine compartment. They reverted to the original concept of using the engine as a semistressed element of the chassis, removing the bracing that had been added in 1956, but revised the network of small-diameter tubes around it. During the European season, the new chassis were rebodied without side pontoons, and Ferrari tried further suspension changes, including coils up front in place of the transverse leaf spring (in effect, the front end of the older Super Squalo).

The 801s suffered from persistent understeer throughout the season, as well as unreliability. Ferrari failed to win a world championship race, and the 801's inability to improve significantly on its predecessors' lap times moved the team to radical action. The answer had been right there, when Luigi Musso qualified Ferrari's new 156 F2 car on the front row alongside Mike Hawthorn and Collins in 801s at a non-championship race in Naples.

← Peter Collins (pictured) and teammate Mike Hawthorn took turns leading the 1957 German Grand Prix at the Nürburgring, but they failed to spot the looming threat of Juan Manuel Fangio's Maserati until he blew past, breaking the lap record in the process.

800 F1 SPECIFICATIONS

Engine	2,486 cc 90-degree V-8	Suspension	Double wishbones with coil springs and anti-roll bar (front), De Dion beam axle with trailing arms and coil springs (rear), telescopic dampers (f), lever-arm dampers (r)
Power	280 bhp @ 8,400 rpm	Brakes	Drums f/r
Gearbox	Five-speed manual	Tires	Englebert
Chassis	Steel tube frame with twin longitudinal beams, aluminum body	Weight	650 kg

Enzo Ferrari always claimed he was "sold" the idea of developing a V-6 racing engine by his son, Dino, a muscular dystrophy sufferer who died young. Revisionist historians are more inclined to attribute the concept to the influx of Lancia engineers in mid-1955, including Vittorio Jano.

Because the majority of Ferrari's resources were being directed toward curing the problems with the F1 cars, the 246 F2 chassis was in effect a more compact iteration of existing practice derived from previous Ferrari F1 machinery. The semispaceframe chassis and independent front suspension were as per the Super Squalo, and the bodyshell also resembled the F1 cars but for the protuberance of the carburetors through the hood. This, with the engines bored and stroked to increase displacement to just over 2.4 liters, would form the basis of the 1958 F1 car, christened the "Dino" in memory of Ferrari's lost child. Power was now a claimed 275 bhp, but more significantly the engine was ready to go from the very beginning of the season. The same could not be said for Ferrari's key rivals.

BRM and Vanwall were absent from the 1958 curtain-raiser in Argentina in January because they could not persuade their engines to run reliably on the newly mandated Avgas fuel. To score drivers' championship points, Vanwall works driver Stirling Moss ran a privately entered Cooper, but the curious machine with its rear-mounted 2-liter Climax FWA engine was not expected to be competitive. With guile and skill, though, Moss made his way into the lead and hoodwinked the chasing Ferraris into thinking he would need to stop for tires, so they held station until it was too late.

Although another new rule that cut races from three hours to two played into the hands of entrants such as Cooper, the significance of this victory went unrecognized at first. The 1958 season—the first to

← Revealed for the first time at Monaco in 1960, the rear-engined 246P prototype was tested again at Monza ahead of the Italian Grand Prix, where Wolfgang von Trips raced the 1.5-liter Formula 2 variant that would go on to form the basis of the 156 "Sharknose."

	DINO 246	DINO 256	DINO 246P
Engine	2,417 cc 65-degree V-6		
Power	275 bhp @ 8,500 rpm	285 bhp @ 8,500 rpm	275 bhp @ 8,500 rpm
Gearbox	Five-speed manual		
Chassis	Steel tube frame with twin longitudinal beams, aluminum body		
Suspension	Double wishbones (front), De Dion beam axle (rear), transverse leaf springs, telescopic dampers (f), lever-arm dampers (r)		
Brakes	Drums f/r / discs f/r	Drums f/r / discs f/r	Discs f/r
Tires	Englebert / Dunlop	Dunlop	Dunlop
Weight	650 kg	650 kg	650 kg

←
The 246 gained independent rear suspension for the 1959 U.S. Grand Prix, and Phil Hill ran an experimental simplified engine with one camshaft per cylinder bank rather than two.

→

Second place in the 1958 Moroccan Grand Prix was enough for Mike Hawthorn (right) to secure the drivers' championship; future Ferrari champion Phil Hill is pictured on the left.

award a championship trophy to constructors—boiled down to a battle between Ferrari and Vanwall, Maserati having withdrawn as a works force and BRM continuing to be unreliable. Ferrari's Mike Hawthorn edged out Moss for the drivers' title while Vanwall won the constructors', but there was little to celebrate at the end of a season that had claimed the lives of Ferrari's Luigi Musso and Peter Collins, as well as Vanwall's Stuart Lewis-Evans.

Vanwall withdrew and in 1959 the rear-engined British cars began to leave Ferrari standing, as their superior handling and better straightline speed (thanks to having a lower frontal area than the front-engined

cars) outweighed Maranello grunt. Ferrari added disc brakes and independent suspension all around with coils over telescopic shocks, and switched to side-mounted fuel tanks, but this proved insufficient. Boring out the engines a fraction (on cars designated 256) to get closer to the 2.5-liter cap simply made them less reliable.

Ferrari would have to go with the crowd. At Monaco in 1960, Richie Ginther appeared in a hastily constructed Dino-engined prototype designated the 246P and based on a Cooper chassis. Its indifferent performance showed that Ferrari had much to learn.

↑
After first practice for the 1958 Italian GP, the metal air intakes on the noses of the 246s were replaced with plexiglass. Ferrari also evaluated the slightly larger 256 engine, but only Wolfgang von Trips raced it.

CHAPTER 2

Politics would cause Ferrari to underperform for much of the 1960s after Enzo ceased to attend races following the death of his son, Dino. Into this vacuum crept those who would exploit Enzo's absence for their own ends, selectively filtering information back to him as he directed the wider operation from his Maranello office.

Resources also became an issue, as money and material supplies grew tighter. It is a tragedy that, for instance, none of the original "Sharknose" cars exist because, for the most part, they had to be scrapped and recycled to build their replacements. Sports car racing also sapped Ferrari's focus, for it was lucrative in terms of its financial rewards and enabled the company to tap in to the American market in a way Grand Prix racing couldn't. Year in, year out, F1 car development lay fallow until after the Le Mans 24 Hours in June. Ferrari also became caught up in an absurd arms race with Ford at Le Mans after Enzo courted the Blue Oval as a potential buyer and then left the American company standing at the altar.

In an era of unprecedented innovation, of advanced mid-engine concepts and monocoque chassis, time and again Ferrari was left playing catch-up. Too often, the long-suffering engineers took the blame.

←
Internal politics led to John Surtees's premature Ferrari departure but not before he won the World Championship.

Enzo Ferrari had long maintained that a car's engine should be at the front, on the grounds that a horse pulls its cart rather than pushing it. Watching his *rosso corsa* machines being trounced on track during 1959 and '60—and by the improvisational British marques he openly derided at "garagistes"—persuaded him to overturn this piece of sophistry. Without great enthusiasm, he directed his engineers to follow suit.

Ferrari's first effort at a rear-engined chassis, the 246-powered prototype raced by Richie Ginther at Monaco in 1960, was in effect cribbed from the Cooper design being run by Scuderia Centro Sud. The likes of Cooper and Lotus had several years' head start over Ferrari in terms of optimizing a chassis and its suspension geometry around a rear-mounted engine, having followed that philosophy in Formula 3.

While Ferrari faced a steep learning curve—and the 156 would never handle as sweetly as its rivals did—a major change in the rules overturned the advantage the rear-engined pioneers held—to begin with, at least. Ostensibly to promote safety, but chiefly to reduce costs and encourage more entrants, the FIA cut the maximum engine displacement in F1 to 1.5 liters and mandated pump fuel. Rather than embrace the change, the British teams chafed fruitlessly against it.

The result was that Ferrari began the 1.5-liter era at a considerable advantage because the Dino V-6 engine had originally been designed with that displacement in mind. Engineer Carlo Chiti widened the bore and shortened the stroke to alter its power-delivery characteristics, but otherwise it was ready to go. BRM and Climax wouldn't have equivalent-size V-8s running until 1962, and Porsche's flat-8 was also delayed.

The 156 sported sleek bodywork with a distinctive split air intake at the front, leading it to be dubbed the "Sharknose." To mitigate its suboptimal handling, Chiti also proceeded with a new variation of the V-6 in which the cylinder heads were widened from 65 degrees to 120. This gave a more advaantageous balance, lowered the center of gravity, and enabled a lower rear deck to be fitted. Power was a claimed 190 bhp, at least 30 bhp more than any rival could muster.

←

The 156 made its world championship debut in Monaco in 1961. Although Wolfgang von Trips stopped two laps from the end, the battle for the lead had been so intense—and its protagonists so far ahead—that he was credited with fourth.

156 F1 SPECIFICATIONS

Engine	1,496 cc 65-degree V-6 / 1,476 cc 120-degree V-6	Suspension	Double wishbones with coil springs, telescopic dampers
Power	180 bhp @ 10,500 rpm / 190 bhp @ 9,500 rpm	Brakes	Drums f/r
Gearbox	Five / six-speed manual	Tires	Dunlop
Chassis	Steel tube frame with twin longitudinal beams	Weight	460–420 kg

↑
Mauro Forghieri's revised version of the 156 featured new bodywork, including a different nose treatment, and the driving position was more inclined for better aerodynamics. John Surtees finished fourth here in Monaco despite vision problems caused by oil from another car.

Only the genius of Stirling Moss could outweigh Ferrari's power advantage through the world championship races of 1961. In Monaco, he was dazzlingly quick while passing slower cars in his aging privateer Lotus 18, and in Germany he made a better tire choice as rain enveloped the Nürburgring, beating the 156 of home favorite Wolfgang von Trips by 21.4 seconds.

Even so, the drivers' title was the province of the Ferrari drivers, and it fell to the quiet and underrated Phil Hill after the death of von Trips and eleven spectators in an accident at the penultimate round at Monza. Ferrari withdrew from the final race of the season.

Internal strife then undermined Ferrari's efforts for 1962, as Chiti and a group of senior engineers quit. One of the last engineers standing was Mauro Forghieri, who dutifully revised and lightened the 156—and dispensed with the distinctive nose—but rivals had caught up and the Ferrari failed to win a single race.

← Light, compact, and powerful, the 120-degree type 178 V-6 engine gave Ferrari a massive advantage at the beginning of the 1.5-liter era.

→ Enzo Ferrari had the original 156s scrapped but a handful of re-creations exist. This is one of two commissioned by American historic racer Jason Wright and wears the race number Phil Hill's car was carrying in the 1961 Italian Grand Prix. *James Mann*

In 1962 and 1963, it became irksomely clear that the small British marques of which Enzo Ferrari was so dismissive had moved ahead once again. This put Ferrari engineers in a quandary because, while the "Old Man" generally believed that the engine was the most significant performance differentiator in an F1 car, one only had to watch from trackside to observe that the likes of Lotus and BRM were considerably more agile.

So as work progressed at Maranello on a new V-8 and flat-12 to replace the V-6, Mauro Forghieri explored a different chassis philosophy, adopting a semi-monocoque concept similar to BRM's, in which the aluminum bodywork was riveted to a tubular steel structure in order to absorb some of the torsional loads. Like the Lotus 25, the fuel was carried in pontoons on either side of the driver, enabling the seat to be mounted lower and with the driver's body reclined to reduce aerodynamic drag. To save weight, the main structure of the car ended at the bulkhead behind the driver, and Forghieri's original intention was for the V-8 to act as a fully load-bearing member of the chassis with the rear suspension mounted to it and the transmission.

This latter design conceit never quite got over the line. Concerns about the V-8's reliability prompted Ferrari to delay its introduction. When the car appeared for the first time at Monza in 1963 as the 156 "Aero," it had the proven 120-degree V-6 in the back. This engine's crankcase hadn't been designed to carry suspension loadings, so for this application it was mounted in a subframe.

In the run-up to the 158's debut in 1964, Forghieri began to doubt the V-8's ability to act as a fully stressed element of the car. As raced, it would have an adaptation of the subframe used at the end of 1963: a bulkhead around the clutch bellhousing mounted the "tub" via two steel members running below the engine. The rear wishbones and coil-over shock absorbers mounted to this rather than the bellhousing.

John Surtees drove the 158 to victory on its debut at a nonchampionship race in Syracuse in April 1964. The V-8 featured fuel injection, which proved tricky to set up, so throughout the season Ferrari took a mix-and-match approach in which Surtees generally took the V-8 while teammate Lorenzo Bandini persisted (not always happily) with the V-6. Although Surtees retired at Monaco (with gearbox failure), Spa-Francorchamps (the fuel mixture was too weak, which melted a piston),

← Although John Surtees would win the World Championship in the 158 F1, it was unreliable early on. He was running fifth in Monaco when gearbox trouble struck, forcing him to retire from the race.

158 F1 SPECIFICATIONS

Engine	1,489 cc 90-degree V-8	Suspension	Double wishbones with coil springs (f), wishbones with double trailing arms and coil springs (r), telescopic dampers
Power	210 bhp @ 11,000 rpm	Brakes	Discs f/r
Gearbox	Six-speed manual	Tires	Dunlop
Chassis	Aluminum semi-monocoque with tubular steel bracing	Weight	470 kg

←
Despite revisions to the V-8
engine, the 158 F1's issues
continued well into the summer
of 1964. Here, at Rouen,
Lorenzo Bandini nursed his
rough-sounding car home in
ninth place; John Surtees had
already retired after an oil
line sheared.

Rouen (oil leak), and Zeltweg (broken suspension), podium
finishes at Zandvoort and Brands Hatch and wins at the
Nürburgring and Monza put him in contention for the
drivers' championship.

An Enzo tantrum over sports car homologation led to
a brief suspension of Ferrari racing activities, and for
the final two rounds of the season the cars were entered
by the North American Racing Team and painted blue.
Second place at Watkins Glen kept Surtees in the title
hunt and, despite a brief scare at the start of the finale
in Mexico—the thin air at altitude was playing havoc with
the fuel-injection metering—Surtees prevailed and won
the championship when key rival Jim Clark slowed with
an oil leak on the penultimate lap.

With better reliability, Clark had the upper hand over
Surtees in 1965, the final season of the 1.5-liter era. But
this wasn't quite the end for the 158: one chassis was
pressed into service as a stopgap with the old 2.4-liter
Dino V-6 in the opening races of 1966, designated 246
F1-66.

↑
Victorious in the hands of John Surtees at Monza in 1964, 158 chassis 0006 was reused with a 2.4-liter V-6 in a handful of races in 1966. Lorenzo Bandini raced it to second place here in Monaco.

←
The 158 followed the same semi-monocoque design philosophy first seen on the stopgap 156 "Aero," but with the rear suspension mounted to a subframe rather than directly to the gearbox.

Despite the teething troubles with the V-8 through late 1963 and into 1964, Ferrari persisted with development of a flat-12 in parallel. The abiding belief was that the 12-cylinder would ultimately develop more power and that this would be a benefit on flowing, high-speed circuits. But with no time or resources to build a new car—Ferrari was already fighting a war on several fronts, because it also had a sports car program—the 12 would have to be accommodated in the existing "Aero" chassis.

It's perhaps a cliché to liken a small, multicylinder racing engine to a Swiss watch, but the comparison is no less true for being oft repeated. The flat-12 was little longer than the V-8, despite having more cylinders, because many of the ancillaries were located above the block. Each cylinder displaced just 125 cc, breathed through twin-cam heads, and had a stroke of just 2 inches. Considering the failure of BRM's supercharged 1.5-liter V16 engine a decade or so earlier, the project carried a high degree of risk.

Forghieri's team was able to do without the subframe deployed around the transmission of the 158; the flat-12's block was strong enough to take the chassis loadings without extra bracing, and it was mounted to the car's "tub" via a cast-alloy plate that also acted as a fixing point for the rear radius arms. The wheelbase only needed to grow by 0.8 inch. Despite the added mass of the engine and the requirement to carry extra fuel to satisfy its thirst, the 1512 weighed just 25 pounds more than its V-8-engined sibling.

Racing historians dispute Ferrari's strategy in determining which car would be allocated to which driver. Some claim that the 1512 was the better car and that Ferrari team manager Eugenio Dragoni favored Lorenzo Bandini—as an Italian driver—over John Surtees. Indubitably the relationship between Surtees and Dragoni was not characterized by great warmth, but "Il Grande John" was generally faster than Bandini, had Enzo Ferrari's ear, and was a tough character who tended to get what he wanted. By his own admission, he preferred the V-8 until the flat-12 was improved through further development.

← The flat-12 engine was thirsty, prompting Ferrari to fit a supplementary fuel tank above the engine in 1965. This had a negative impact on handling—John Surtees finished a lap down in seventh at Zandvoort.

1512 F1 SPECIFICATIONS

Engine	1,490 cc 180-degree V-12	Suspension	Double wishbones with coil springs (f), wishbones with double trailing arms and coil springs (r), telescopic dampers
Power	225 bhp @ 12,000 rpm	Brakes	Discs f/r
Gearbox	Five-speed manual	Tires	Dunlop
Chassis	Aluminum semi-monocoque with tubular steel bracing	Weight	490 kg

1512 F1

↑
Lorenzo Bandini (17) led the
1965 Monaco Grand Prix in a
1512, ahead of John Surtees
(18) in a 158, but "Mr. Monaco"
Graham Hill (3) barged past
both of them in his BRM P261.

→

Ferrari's intricate 1.5-liter
flat-12 never quite delivered
on its potential, but it did
inform development of the
subsequent—and highly
successful—3-liter flat-12
used in the 1970s.

↓

John Surtees began his racing
career with motorcycles
and remains the only world
champion on two and four
wheels.

As such, it was Bandini who tested the 1512 in public for the first time in practice for the 1964 Italian Grand Prix, but rain prevented him from learning anything useful and he was assigned Surtees's spare V-8 for the race. In the final two rounds of the World Championship in the United States, Bandini raced the 1512, retiring at Watkins Glen and passing Surtees in Mexico City before handing the position back so his teammate could claim the drivers' title.

Through the early races of 1965, Surtees continued to race the 158 in preference to the 1512. The two engines proved to have very similar torque characteristics. The flat-12 made only slightly more power, at a cost of much greater fuel consumption, and the need to carry more juice (in an auxiliary tank above the engine) negated the additional performance. When detuning the engine served only to make the 1512 uncompetitively slow—Bandini was ninth at Spa-Francorchamps—Ferrari engineer Franco Rocchi redesigned the 1512 with new cylinder heads. This was ready in time for Monza, but by then the championship was lost, and the team suffered a further blow when Surtees was injured in a sports car race and missed the last two rounds.

Though much maligned by some—generally the drivers, who felt the cars were underpowered and peaky—the 1.5-liter era promoted inventiveness in chassis and tire technology, as well as enabling new teams and manufacturers to compete. This was a time in which ambitious drivers branched out and became chassis builders in their own right.

Thus Ferrari faced more intensive competition on all fronts just as the company was beginning to struggle for funds. A putative acquisition by Ford in 1963 had fallen through, sufficiently enraging the American company to declare war on the racetrack. By 1966, when Formula 1 became a 3-liter category, Enzo was fighting on several fronts and resources were spread correspondingly thin. When 1.5-liter engines were introduced in 1961, Ferrari enjoyed a competitive advantage over rivals who had wasted time fighting the new regulations. Though the shift to 3-liter engines prompted similar chafing and gnashing of teeth, this time Ferrari wouldn't have it so easy.

Much to the ongoing chagrin of lead driver John Surtees, seasonal F1 development typically lagged until after the Le Mans 24 Hours in June. Paucity of resources prevented chief engineer Mauro Forghieri from developing an all-new 3-liter mill for 1966; instead the new F1 car would be powered by a downsized version of Franco Rocchi's 3.3-liter V-12, which had been competitive in the 275 P2

sports car. Reduced to 2,989 cc via a shorter stroke, it retained the double overhead camshaft heads with two valves per cylinder (three- and four-valve heads arrived after further development). Power was a claimed 360 bhp at 10,000 rpm, but the reality proved to be some way short of that.

In a shift of naming convention, the 312 took its title not from the displacement of a single cylinder but instead it stood for 3-liter V-12. The chassis was a strengthened version of the semi-monocoque "Aero" concept used in the 158 and 1512, but with a subframe for the engine, which was also enclosed in bodywork. Both of these came at the cost of additional weight—and at 604 kilograms in its initial form, the 312 was well over the 450-kilogram minimum.

Surtees—after several months out recovering from his sports car accident—won against a thin field on the 312's debut at a nonchampionship race in Syracuse, but he wasn't impressed with the car's bulk or the engine's

312 SPECIFICATIONS

Engine	2,989 cc 60-degree V-12	Suspension	Double wishbones with rocker-actuated coil springs/dampers (f), wishbones with coil springs/dampers (r)
Power	360 bhp @ 10,000 rpm	Brakes	Discs f/r
Gearbox	Five-speed manual	Tires	Dunlop, Firestone
Chassis	Aluminum semi-monocoque with tubular steel bracing	Weight	600 kg

↑
John Surtees won the 312's first race, the non-championship Syracuse Grand Prix in 1966, but the only serious opposition in the field was Jack Brabham, whose engine cut out on the first lap.

inability to reach peak revs. His stock was beginning to drop within Ferrari as team manager Eugenio Dragoni briefed the "Old Man" against him. Surtees didn't want to race the 312 at the first World Championship round in Monaco, but company pride dictated that he take the latest machine. He retired from the lead when his differential let go, while teammate Lorenzo Bandini finished second in the car Surtees had wanted to drive, a stopgap 2.4-liter Dino V-6-engined 158 chassis.

In miserable conditions in Belgium, Surtees won cleverly, staying out of the spray of Jochen Rindt's leading Cooper-Maserati until the rain had passed before making his move. But allowing a rival Italian marque to enjoy the glory of leading so long led to further political ructions, and at Le Mans Surtees walked out after another dust-up with Dragoni, who in turn was fired at the end of the season.

Ferrari would win just one more race, and second position in the constructors' championship—to runaway leader Brabham—flattered to deceive, because their rivals were in engine-related chaos of their own.

↑
Ferrari introduced a more powerful version of the V-12 for the 1966 Italian Grand Prix that featured three valves per cylinder. Ludovico Scarfiotti led Mike Parkes in a Ferrari one-two—Scarfiotti's only grand prix win.

→
Surtees argued against racing the 312 in Monaco, 1966, but qualified second and led the race before retiring when his car's differential cracked.

Jack Brabham became the first world champion of the 3-liter era, and the first to do so in a car bearing his own name, thanks to his canniness in securing a reliable and adequately powerful engine at the right time. Ferrari, short on funds and in political disarray, had failed to take advantage of being one of the few teams to kick off 1966 with a 3-liter engine. For the next three seasons—across various iterations of the 312—it could never quite manage to take up the slack.

For 1967 the competitive picture would change again, as other engine manufacturers pitched in with increasingly competitive offerings. At the third championship round a game-changer arrived in the form of the Cosworth-built, Ford-badged DFV. Initially an exclusive for Lotus, it was strong enough to act as a fully stressed member of the chassis. Only the shaky reliability of the Lotus-Ford combination prevented the 1967 from being a Jim Clark whitewash. Brabham fitted quad-cam heads to their Repco engines in a bid for more power, but it was the failure of others that enabled his team to snatch the championship double again.

Ferrari had liberated more power from the 3-liter V-12 with new three-valve cylinder heads late in the '66 season, and for 1967 built up four new chassis. Though based on the same fundamental design, these were around 50 kilograms lighter than before, with a lower frontal area and detail revisions to the cooling apertures on the nose. The engine's inlet trumpets were repositioned slightly, as were the exhausts, which now sat in a compact arrangement within the bank of the vee.

New Zealander Chris Amon joined the team alongside Lorenzo Bandini and Ludovico Scarfiotti. Ferrari had skipped the last championship race of 1966 and didn't enter the first of '67—a January round at Kyalami in South Africa—beginning instead with non-championship races in Europe before the Monaco Grand Prix. This race would prove to be disastrous, as Bandini crashed

← For 1967 Ferrari revised the exhaust layout of the 312 so the pipes sat in an asbestos trough within the vee of the engine. Chris Amon finished third here at the Nürburgring.

	312 (1967)	312 (1968)	312 (1969)
Engine	2,989 cc 60-degree V-12	2,989 cc 60-degree V-12	2,989 cc 60-degree V-12
Power	390 bhp @ 10,000 rpm	430 bhp @ 11,000 rpm	450 bhp @ 11,500 rpm
Gearbox	Five-speed manual	Five-speed manual	Five-speed manual
Chassis	Aluminum semi-monocoque with tubular steel bracing	Aluminum semi-monocoque with tubular steel bracing	Aluminum semi-monocoque with tubular steel bracing
Suspension	Double wishbones with rocker-actuated coil springs/dampers (f), wishbones with coil springs/dampers (r)	Double wishbones with rocker-actuated coil springs/dampers (f), wishbones with coil springs/dampers (r)	Double wishbones with rocker-actuated coil springs/dampers (f), wishbones with coil springs/dampers (r)
Brakes	Discs f/r	Discs f/r	Discs f/r
Tires	Dunlop, Firestone	Dunlop, Firestone	Dunlop, Firestone
Weight	550 kg	550 kg	530 kg

←

During 1968 Ferrari lowered
the mounting points of the
V-12 and opened the bodywork
at the front to improve cooling.
Chris Amon led here at Jarama,
Spain, but, as ever, luck wasn't
on his side and he retired.

→
In 1969 Ferrari followed the trend of adding aerodynamic devices, but this and further engine modifications didn't satisfy Chris Amon and he quit. Ernesto Brambilla, pictured here, was drafted in for the Italian Grand Prix but dropped in favor of Pedro Rodriguez.

↓
Chris Amon talks to Ferrari chief engineer Mauro Forghieri in the pits at Mosport Park, near Toronto, Canada.

with fatal consequences. Mike Parkes—the sometime Ferrari sports car driver who had replaced John Surtees in 1966—took Bandini's place but suffered career-ending injuries at Spa-Francorchamps. The combination of these two accidents moved a shaken Scarfiotti to quit motor racing. After this, Amon would be Ferrari's sole representative until the last race of what would be a winless season.

At Monza, Ferrari introduced a revised version of the engine with four-valve heads, and this formed the basis of the team's 1968 effort, with three new chassis featuring slimmer bodies and lower engine mountings. Amon took the first pole position of his career at the second round in Spain, but he retired from the lead at two-thirds distance. New teammate Jacky Ickx retired with a similar fuel pump problem. In all, Amon would retire from seven of the eleven Grands Prix he started.

Like many teams, Ferrari experimented with high rear airfoils (mounted to the engine rather than the suspension uprights) during the year in an effort to combat the growing surfeit of power over grip. Ickx proved his mettle in wet conditions, with victory at Rouen, but it was otherwise a barren year for Ferrari, and Ickx left for Brabham at the end.

Ferrari's acquisition by Fiat in 1969 paved the way for greater investment, but the 312 was a development dead end. Amon drove the first half of the '69 season solo with another pair of new chassis at his disposal, and a new reversed-flow engine with the exhausts outside the vee to lower the center of gravity, but it was rarely competitive. And when it was, it tended to break—such as when Amon was leading the Spanish Grand Prix. When the new 312B wasn't ready in time, Ferrari abandoned midseason and Amon left.

CHAPTER 3

The fallow competitive period of the late 1960s called for nothing less than total change. Successive iterations of the original 312 had failed to keep pace with rival developments, chiefly because the V-12 engine—originally built for sports cars—was overweight and overcomplicated in comparison with Ford's standard-setting V-8. The Cosworth-built DFV, bankrolled by Ford, was Lotus-exclusive in its first year, but from 1968 onward it became the default choice for any team wishing to win Grands Prix—unless that team was committed to building its own engines.

As Mauro Forghieri led the planning for a new flat-12 engine, following principles he explored first in the 1.5-liter era, he knew it would have to be good. Fiat's investment in Ferrari unlocked development funds, but neither the new engine nor the bespoke chassis designed for it would be ready to race in '69.

Although this engine would go on to power Ferrari to three drivers' championships and see the team through the entire 1970s, the initial auguries were not great. During track testing in late 1969 it repeatedly suffered catastrophic seizures and messy bottom-end failures. Taken in combination with the increasing unreliability of the V-12-engined 312, this was enough to prompt a dispirited Chris Amon to call time on his career with Ferrari and look elsewhere for 1970. Amon would later come to be regarded as one of the greatest F1 drivers never to win a Grand Prix; had he kept the faith with Ferrari, that might not have been the case.

←

Niki Lauda joined a resurgent Ferrari in 1974 and led the team to two drivers' championships and three constructors' titles.

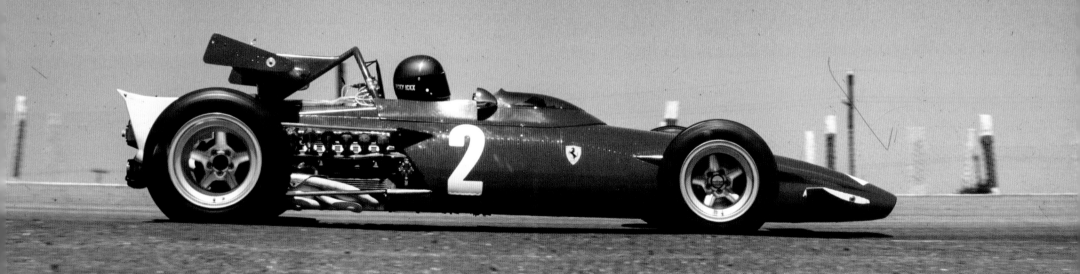

The 312B designation would cover four very different cars, one of which would never even race. Ferrari's internal politics and wavering commitment to F1 militated against this generation of car achieving its potential. Forghieri's initial 312B was probably the strongest of the genre, and the best-integrated piece of engineering. Taking his lead from the Lotus 49—which had seen three seasons but was still the definitive 3-liter F1 car at this point—Forghieri focused on packaging the 312B's ancillaries as neatly as possible within a wind-cheating profile. The nose was wide and relatively flat, with a slim cooling aperture feeding a conventional front-mounted radiator, but further back it remained true to the conventions of the cigar-tube F1—just as Lotus's new 72 ushered in the era of the wedge shape.

Having a minimal frontal area remained important in the 3-liter formula, even though aerodynamic priorities had shifted toward assisting the rear axle now that grunt was exceeding grip. Most racing teams had a relatively rudimentary understanding of aerodynamics, and wind tunnel research was in its infancy, so the proliferation of airfoils that appeared on the cars from 1968 onward owed more to intuition and faith than science. By the time the 312B was on the drawing board, the FIA had outlawed the more outlandish designs and settled on clear regulations governing size, shape, and location. Besides the 312B's inherent lower center of gravity, the

←
The neat 312B made its second appearance in the 1970 Spanish Grand Prix at Jarama, but Jacky Ickx's car was destroyed by fire after an accident.
	312B	312B2	312B3
Engine	2,992 cc flat-12	2,992 cc flat-12	2,992 cc flat-12
Power	450 bhp @ 11,500 rpm	480 bhp @ 12,500 rpm	485 bhp @ 12,500 rpm
Gearbox	Five-speed manual	Five-speed manual	Five-speed manual
Chassis	Aluminum semi-monocoque with tubular steel bracing	Aluminum semi-monocoque with tubular steel bracing	Aluminum monocoque
Suspension	Double wishbones with rocker-actuated coil springs/dampers (f), wishbones with coil springs/dampers (r)	Double wishbones with rocker-actuated coil springs/dampers (f), lower wishbones and upper rocker arms with inboard coil springs/dampers (r)	Double wishbones with rocker-actuated coil springs/dampers (f), lower wishbones and upper radius arms with inboard coil springs/dampers (r)
Brakes	Discs f/r	Discs f/r	Discs f/r
Tires	Firestone, Goodyear	Firestone	Goodyear
Weight	540 kg	560 kg	580 kg

312B B2/B3

lower profile of the flat-12 enabled Forghieri to locate the wing on a longitudinal beam, which also acted as part of the engine's mounting to the chassis, an elegant engineering solution.

The engine failures that prevented the 312B from making its debut in 1969 were generally a result of oil starvation but also because the multielement crankshaft spun within just four roller bearings, a design decision taken to save weight and reduce frictional losses compared with a V-8. Because the cylinders were "oversquare"—78.5 by 51.5 millimeters—this was naturally a high-revving engine that proved too much for the reciprocating parts at first. Forghieri's team would exorcise the flat-12's demons by swapping two of the roller bearings for conventional inserts, replacing the crankshaft with a one-piece cast unit, and fitting rubber cushion couplings at the flywheel end of the crankshaft to damp torsional stresses. Fiat's investment later yielded a tilting dyno that enabled Ferrari to resolve the oil-surge issues.

Ferrari's flat-12 derived from a collaboration with the Franklin aircraft company, which wanted an engine that could be housed within an airplane wing. The 3-liter version powered Ferrari's F1 cars for a whole decade.

The 312B2 of 1971 was wider and flatter from the nose backwards, following the trend for wedge shapes set by the Lotus 72, but its unusual rear suspension arrangement proved problematic.

The 312B chassis itself followed the semi-monocoque philosophy in which Ferrari felt confident, with rocker arms actuating inboard-mounted springs and dampers at the front and conventional wishbones at the rear. As per new regulations, the fuel tanks were rubber bags. The 312B was certainly neat and strong, but the Lotus 72 proved aerodynamically superior and better able to put down its power, thanks to a more rearward weight bias gained by moving the radiators to a position just ahead of the rear wheels. Like the 312B, it had teething

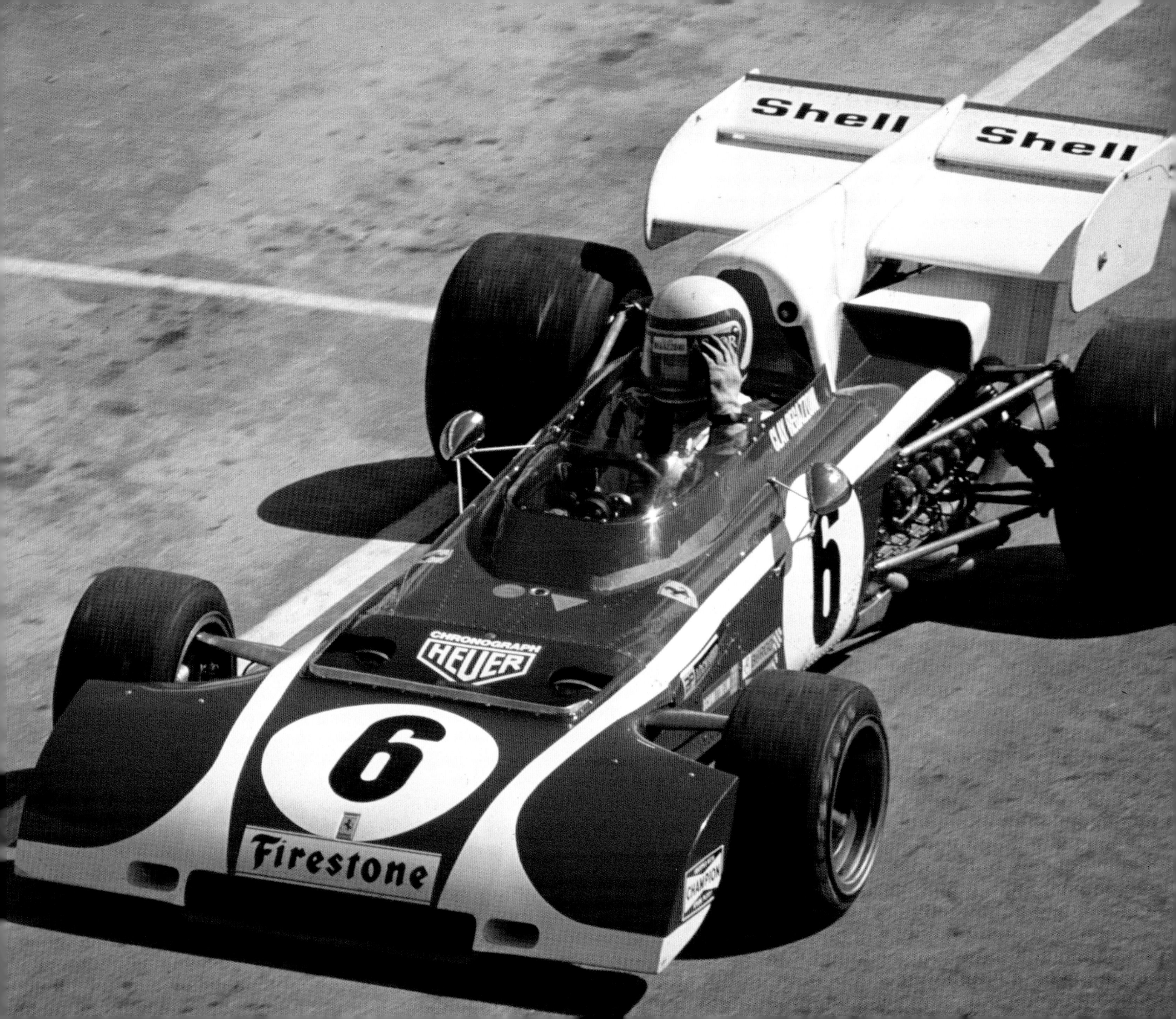
Shell
Shell
6
6
CHRONOGRAPH
HEUER
Firestone
CHAMPION

←

For the 1972 South African
Grand Prix, the 312B2s were
modified to feature a streamlined
nose, similar to that used by
the rival Tyrrell team.

→

Jacky Ickx led the 1970 French
Grand Prix from the pole
position until a cracked valve
seat forced him to retire.

troubles, but Lotus could fall back on the proven 49C.

Ferrari didn't win a race until August. Changes to the rear wing, front suspension, and brakes enabled Amon's replacement, the returning Jacky Ickx, to build a late run of form and finish second in the driver's standings behind posthumous champion Jochen Rindt, whose Lotus crashed with fatal consequences at Monza.

Over the winter, Ferrari revised the engine again, returning to full roller bearings and adjusting the bore and stroke to 80 by 49 millimeters to enable a higher rev ceiling. New rules mandating thicker-gauge bodywork called for a new car, designated 312B2, with 16-gauge aluminum sheeting forming part of the conventional semi-monocoque chassis. Its wedge shape echoed the Lotus 72's, and while the suspension remained the same up front, at the rear Forghieri tried to reduce unsprung weight by installing inboard brakes in tandem with spring-damper units mounted almost horizontally.

Vibrations from the new low-profile Firestone tires, and twitchy handling, proved insurmountable during the 1971 season and Ferrari emerged from it with just two victories, only one of which was claimed by a 312B2. Ditching the inboard rear suspension for '72 yielded an improvement, but not enough to rival the dominant Emerson Fittipaldi's Lotus 72.

Faced with this—and new rules mandating deformable impact structures—Ferrari determined that a new car was required, as well as a new tire supplier, Goodyear. The disappointments of the preceding seasons had caused Forghieri's political stock to fall, and when his unusual-looking 312B3—a short-wheelbase car with a central weight bias and an extreme wedge shape—failed to impress Ickx and Arturo Merzario during testing, Ferrari banished Forghieri to the special projects department.

Forghieri's B3, witheringly christened the "Spazzaneve" ("snowplough"), was consigned to a distant corner of the factory. The B3 that actually raced was based on a monocoque chassis built in England by TC Prototypes. New technical manager Sandro Colombo took the unusual step of outsourcing production to a specialist, partly because of Ferrari's lack of experience in monocoques and partly because of ongoing industrial strife in Italy. The B3 was initially a flop—it was bulky by the standards of the time and the front-mounted radiators were a retrograde step—which prompted Ickx to leave and Ferrari to temporarily withdraw until the car's problems were solved.

Forghieri was recalled to reengineer the car, and with new aerodynamics and different weight distribution and suspension geometry—and Niki Lauda at the wheel—it would become a race winner in 1974.

Although his personal relationship with Enzo Ferrari had been terminally damaged by his temporary exile to the special projects department, Mauro Forghieri remained industrious through 1974 as he juggled ongoing refinements of the 312B3 with work on a new car for '75. Convinced that the B3's development potential was spent, Forghieri pursued a very different concept—much to the bafflement and chagrin of Niki Lauda, who wondered why Ferrari would junk a well-known philosophy for an unproven one. But once Lauda was on board with the notion, and had lent his considerable development expertise to it, the new car would mature into a championship winner.

While the construction of the chassis signified a return to Ferrari convention—a semi-monocoque with what was essentially an aluminum spaceframe strengthened by stress-bearing steel panels—mechanically it was more adventurous. The "T" in the model designation stood for "trasversale" (often incorrectly written as "transversale"), for in this car the gearbox was mounted transversely, with the gear cluster ahead of the rear axle line, to achieve a more central weight distribution.

Working from a clean sheet enabled Forghieri to package the ancillaries and cooling systems better than in the B3, where he had been modifying an existing design.

← The 312T5 was cripplingly slow in a straight line and not much better around corners. At Monaco in 1980, Jody Scheckter (pictured) quit the race after 27 laps.

	312T	312T2	312T3	312T4	312T5
Engine	2,992 cc flat-12	2,992 cc flat-12	2,992 cc flat-12	2,992 cc flat-12	2,992 cc flat-12
Power	485 bhp @ 12,500 rpm	500 bhp @ 12,000 rpm	500 bhp @ 12,000 rpm	515 bhp @ 12,000 rpm	515 bhp @ 12,000 rpm
Gearbox	Five-speed manual	Five-speed manual	Five-speed manual	Five-speed manual	Five-speed manual
Chassis	Aluminum semi-monocoque with tubular steel bracing				
Suspension	Double wishbones with rocker-actuated coil springs/dampers (f), lower wishbones and upper radius arms with coil springs/dampers (r)	Double wishbones with inboard coil springs/dampers (f), lower wishbones and radius arms with coil springs/dampers (r)	Double wishbones with rocker-actuated coil springs/dampers (f), parallel links and radius arms with rocker-actuated coil springs/dampers (r)	Double wishbones with rocker-actuated coil springs/dampers (f), wishbones and radius arms with rocker-actuated coil springs/dampers (r)	Double wishbones with rocker-actuated coil springs/dampers (f), wishbones and radius arms with rocker-actuated coil springs/dampers (r)
Brakes	Discs f/r	Discs f/r	Discs f/r	Discs f/r	Discs f/r
Tires	Goodyear	Goodyear, Michelin	Michelin	Michelin	Michelin
Weight	575 kg	575 kg	580 kg	590 kg	595 kg

312T T2/T3/T4/T5

Niki Lauda was reluctant to move to an all-new car design in 1975 but changed his mind after driving the new 312T. Here at the Nürburgring he would have won but for a puncture.

Niki Lauda talks to team manager Daniele Audetto during practice for the 1976 Japanese Grand Prix. Rain on race day prompted him to withdraw.

The radiators remained behind the front axle line but were now more neatly integrated. This, along with a new front suspension layout mounted to a thicker but narrower front bulkhead, enabled the front of the car to have a slimmer profile for similar or better structural rigidity than before.

Although early testing suggested the 312T had delivered on its mandate of having a more neutral handling balance than the understeery B3, some snappiness had to be dialed out, and Lauda did not give the new car its debut until the South African Grand Prix, the third round of the 1975 season. That race yielded a distant fifth for Lauda and a DNF for Clay Regazzoni, but afterward Lauda's engine was found to be down on power because of a problem with the fuel injection. Not that this washed with the ever-critical Italian press, who gained further ammunition when Lauda and Regazzoni collided with each other at the start of the Spanish Grand Prix.

Lauda silenced the critics by winning from pole in the wet at Monaco, the beginning of a three-race winning streak. Two more victories underlined his superiority and, in a year when only one other driver won more than a single race, he tied up the championship with third place at Monza in front of Ferrari's delighted home crowd.

New rules for 1976 banned the unsightly airboxes from May 1—halfway through the Spanish Grand Prix weekend, by which time a new rear suspension layout based on a De Dion axle with tubular locating linkages had been tried on the incoming 312T2 and discarded. The new car was 2.2 inches longer in the wheelbase and slightly lighter, but the chief visual difference from its predecessor was the pair of NACA ducts that induced air into the engine.

Lauda had already won twice before the 312T2 made its World Championship debut at Jarama. Lauda was declared the winner of that—despite racing with cracked ribs after a skiing accident—when James Hunt's McLaren was thrown out at scrutineering, but Hunt would be reinstated later amid growing rancor between McLaren and Ferrari. Wins in Belgium, Monaco, and Britain

made Lauda the runaway championship leader, but his fiery accident at the Nürburgring meant he failed to score at three Grands Prix. And then upon his return at Monza, still bandaged and bleeding, he found Enzo Ferrari had recruited Carlos Reutemann to replace him. Lauda plugged on but lost the championship to Hunt at the final round, when he withdrew from the dangerously wet Japanese Grand Prix at Fuji. This did not endear him to the Italian public and further soured his relationship with Ferrari.

Driving a B-spec 312T2 featuring revised bodywork, several iterations of front and rear wing, and a more powerful engine, Lauda won three of the seventeen races in 1977 to claim his second World Championship. Then he abruptly left Ferrari for Brabham. But the real emergent threat to Ferrari was the resurgent Lotus.

After finding several dead ends trying to better the 72, Lotus happened upon a cunning aerodynamic technique to boost aerodynamic grip with airfoils concealed in large sidepods. As others rushed to copy, Ferrari

struggled in subsequent seasons because the layout of the flat-12 militated against maximizing airflow through underbody venturi.

The 312T3 for 1978, to be driven by Reutemann and Gilles Villeneuve, featured a redesigned semi-monocoque and chassis geometry to take advantage of the switch to Michelin radial tires. The car was noticeably more angular than its predecessor, but it was also heavier, and it was no match for the new Lotus 79. It was prone to understeer, too, despite experiments with a wider front track. Reutemann departed for Lotus at the end of a season of fighting for scraps.

With no alternative but to keep on with the flat-12 engine, Forghieri turned to Pininfarina's wind tunnel for assistance in shaping the 312T4, which featured a smooth upper body tapering to a sharp cutoff above a narrow nose from which the front wing hung. Under the skin, Forghieri had worked to narrow the load-bearing structure of the semi-monocoque as much as possible to maximize airflow through the sidepods. Even the

UNITED STATES GRAND PRIX WEST

$2.50

Long Beach, California – March 26, 27, 28, 1976

→

Ferrari struggled to
comprehend "ground effect"
aerodynamics produced by
sculptured sidepods, not
helped by the flat-12 engine
configuration.

←

For the 312T4, Ferrari narrowed
the chassis around the cockpit
and moved the fuel tank
behind the driver to improve
aerodynamics. *James Mann*

fuel tank was mounted behind the driver, facilitated by
another marginal increase in wheelbase.

The 312T4 wasn't always the fastest car in the 1979,
field but it enjoyed reliability and a level of consistency
its rivals lacked. Villeneuve and new teammate Jody
Scheckter took three wins apiece and, while Alan
Jones won four races in the second half of the season,
Scheckter's greater consistency enabled him to claim
what would be Ferrari's last drivers' championship for
twenty-one years.

As rivals found better reliability and exploited "ground
effect" aerodynamics better, time was running out for
the flat-12. The 1980 312T5, featuring new bodywork
and suspension geometry and a narrower chassis "tip"
at the front, was a flop, and Ferrari quickly switched to
developing a more compact turbocharged engine.

CHAPTER 4

In the era of the Space Shuttle, the video recorder, and the mobile telephone, Ferrari embraced modernity in a rush. The team became the last to adopt monocoque chassis design, nearly twenty years after Lotus made the philosophy essential, and did so in step with the widespread adoption of carbon fiber. Believed to be an unsafe voodoo substance at first, this composite material became de rigueur within two seasons of McLaren introducing it in 1981.

Ground-effect aerodynamics had rendered Ferrari's cherished flat-12 engine unworkable, because its cylinder heads occupied space where airflow needed to be channeled. Enzo Ferrari needed little prompting to green-light a new turbo engine, his team's first blown Formula 1 unit since the 1950s. Turbocharging, along with increasingly exotic fuels and additives, would take power figures into the stratosphere by the middle of the decade.

As peaky, short life span engines producing 1,000 bhp became essential in qualifying, motor racing's governing body moved to rein in power during the 1980s and finally ban turbocharging entirely. But not before Ferrari and its rivals had produced some iconic—if challenging—powertrains.

Power came at a cost, though, and for Ferrari this would be a decade of frustration as either the cars or the engines—and sometimes both—came up short on reliability. Tragedy would come into play too. And by the end of the decade, a new corporate structure loomed as Enzo Ferrari succumbed to the ill health that accompanied his advancing years.

←
Gilles Villeneuve was the kind of driver Enzo Ferrari loved: loyal, committed, and capable of squeezing results from subpar machinery—as demonstrated here in the 1981 Monaco Grand Prix, a race the ill-handling 126CK ought not to have won.

The 126 model designation—returning to the old Ferrari tradition of relating to the swept volume of a single cylinder—encompassed four very different cars powered by variants of the same engine as the Scuderia rushed to come to terms with the changing shape of Formula 1. Rather too much of the initial design was rooted in the past, however: the aluminum semi-monocoque chassis concept could trace its ancestry back to Mauro Forghieri's "Aero" concept first launched in 1963; the 120-degree layout of the new alloy-block turbocharged V-6 was also a nod to the early 1960s; the rocker-arm suspension was rather early 1970s; and the bodywork of the first 126CK bore a close resemblance to its immediate predecessor, the 312T5. The transverse gearbox was also familiar.

	126CK	126C2	126C3	126C4
Engine	1,496 cc 120-degree twin-turbocharged V-6	1,496 cc 120-degree twin-turbocharged V-6	1,496 cc 120-degree twin-turbocharged V-6	1,496 cc 120-degree twin-turbocharged V-6
Power	540 bhp @ 12,000 rpm	580 bhp @ 11,000 rpm	600 bhp @ 11,000 rpm	660 bhp @ 11,500 rpm
Gearbox	Five-speed manual	Five-speed manual	Five-speed manual	Five-speed manual
Chassis	Aluminum semi-monocoque with tubular steel bracing	Aluminum honeycomb monocoque with carbon fiber panels	Carbon fiber monocoque	Carbon fiber monocoque
Suspension	Rocker arms with coil springs/dampers (f/r)	Rocker arms with coil springs/dampers (f/r), double wishbones with pullrod-actuated coil springs/dampers (f), double wishbones with rocker-actuated coil springs/dampers (r) from French Grand Prix	Double wishbones with pullrod-actuated coil springs/dampers (f), double wishbones with rocker-actuated coil springs/dampers (r)	Double wishbones with pullrod-actuated coil springs/dampers (f/r)
Brakes	Discs f/r	Discs f/r	Discs f/r	Discs f/r
Tires	Michelin	Goodyear	Goodyear	Goodyear
Weight	620 kg	595 kg	595 kg	540 kg

←
The 126CK was a handful, so the sight of Gilles Villeneuve on opposite lock was a familiar one during 1981. Here in Canada, rain on race day was the leveler that enabled Villeneuve to ascend from 11th to 3rd in front of his home crowd.

↑
Harvey Postlethwaite's input enabled Ferrari to design and build its first "in-house" monocoque chassis for 1982. The 126C2 might have brought home both championships but for tragedy on track; winning the constructors' title was scant consolation.

It was, therefore, largely the noise that distinguished the 126CK when Gilles Villeneuve drove it in public for the first time during practice for the 1980 Italian Grand Prix, held at Imola rather than Monza that year. Though he lapped 0.6 seconds faster than he managed in the 312T5, it was considered too early to race the car.

Over the winter, Ferrari evaluated two different methods of forced induction with a view to eliminating turbo lag, a lull in power delivery caused by the turbo's compressor losing momentum as the exhaust gases drop in volume when the driver comes off the throttle. The

Brown Boveri company's Comprex system, a mechanically driven supercharger that might have eliminated lag entirely, was tried but eventually dropped in favor of twin KKK turbochargers mounted in the vee of the engine.

Power was not a problem initially but reliability was, and neither Villeneuve nor new teammate Didier Pironi finished the first three Grands Prix of the 1980 season. Handling was also an issue because the car was overweight and Ferrari had yet to properly come to grips with ground-effect aerodynamics. Most teams had begun to augment their underbody venturi with sliding

→
The "B" specification on the 126C2, shorn of its underbody venturi to comply with new technical rules, was competitive during the first half of 1983 before being replaced by the C3. Patrick Tambay won in San Marino while teammate René Arnoux won in Canada on its final outing.

↓
Gilles Villeneuve's incandescent talent was snuffed out at Zolder in 1982, when he suffered a fatal accident in his 126C2 during qualifying for the Belgian Grand Prix.

skirts that, in effect, sealed the underfloor, boosting downforce. But many within Ferrari—Forghieri included—still clung to a belief that the better handling enjoyed by their rivals arose from clever differential design. For 1981, the FIA banned skirts and mandated a minimum ride height—but because this was measured in the pits, the Brabham team cleverly circumvented it by fitting their car's body on pneumatic struts, which held it at the legal level while at rest but compressed under load.

Brabham's Nelson Piquet duly won the championship as Ferrari labored to cure the 126CK's ponderousness by experimenting with different wheelbase lengths and suspension pickup points. Its prodigious power enabled Villeneuve to claim remarkable victories in Monaco and Spain, on circuits where overtaking is difficult.

Enzo recruited British engineer Harvey Postlethwaite to oversee the design of the 126C2 and bring full monocoque design to Maranello for the first time since the anomalous British-built 312B3. The FIA had given up trying to police the ride-height rules, so it grudgingly permitted fixed side skirts to be used, with the unforeseen consequence of pushing teams to set their cars up stiffly for maximum aerodynamic benefit.

Ferrari adopted carbon fiber construction for the 126C3. René Arnoux won two races after its introduction at the 1983 British Grand Prix, but failing to score in the final two rounds ruled him out of the drivers' championship.

→ Ferrari's turbocharged V-6 was undoubtedly powerful, but increasing restrictions on fuel brought frugality into the competitive mix, and by 1984 the Ferrari engine was too thirsty.

They were both faster and horrendously difficult and unpleasant to drive.

Pironi and Villeneuve might have been within a shout of the drivers' title—they finished one-two in the controversial San Marino Grand Prix, during which Villeneuve felt his teammate had reneged on a prerace agreement—but both would suffer appalling accidents during the season. Villeneuve's was fatal, while Pironi broke both his legs. Ferrari took the constructors' title but felt the loss of Villeneuve deeply.

McLaren had made carbon fiber construction a must, so Postlethwaite's 126C3 used this material for the first time, albeit in a two-piece molding for the monocoque that was then bonded together. A last-minute rule change

mandating that all cars should have flat bottoms—that is, no skirts or underbody venturi—forced the team to begin the season with a B-spec version of the C2, but the engine now featured the Agip-patented "Emulsistem," a device that sought to improve combustion by injecting fine droplets of water into the fuel mix. René Arnoux and Patrick Tambay were still able to claim four wins between them. A spin and a failure to finish in the last two rounds meant Arnoux fell short of the drivers' title, but Ferrari claimed the constructors' championship— their last for sixteen years.

The advent of the flat-bottom rules produced a slew of arrow-shaped cars with large front and rear wings to claw back lost downforce and retain traction. Given a

year's experience, the more aerodynamically advanced teams, such as McLaren, approached 1984 with tidier and more efficient designs. The 126C4, though, essentially doubled down on crudeness and relied on allying huge power to a vast rear wing, to the benefit of traction but at great cost in fuel efficiency. This was particularly damaging given the new rules banning refueling and mandating a maximum tank size of 220 liters.

Time and again in 1984, Arnoux and new teammate Michele Alboreto would qualify well but then have to ease off during races to conserve fuel, while McLaren's parsimonious TAG-Porsche-powered cars eased to victory.

Politics came to define Ferrari's 1985 as Mauro Forghieri was banished to the research and development department before the close of the '84 season, leaving Harvey Postlethwaite in sole charge of the chassis and ex-Fiat man Ildo Renzetti overseeing the engine. There would be rancor in the garage too, as René Arnoux was dismissed after one race, replaced by Stefan Johansson.

Postlethwaite's 156/85 was a ground-up redesign, and the first Ferrari F1 car to be completed using computer-aided design (CAD/CAM). Most significantly, the monocoque was now formed using a one-piece molding rather than two bonded together. For better stability, the wheelbase was lengthened slightly and the suspension redesigned, while new aerodynamic regulations forbidding endplate-mounted "winglets" dictated a new rear deck and wing configuration. During the season, Ferrari also introduced carbon brake discs for the first time.

The fifth generation of the 120-degree V-6 was plumbed very differently than before, with a view to better reliability and a more aerodynamically optimized body shape. The twin KKK turbochargers were relocated from the vee of the engine to either side of the block, as they were on McLaren's all-conquering MP4/2. A delay in implementing a planned reduction in fuel tank size from 220 liters to 195 (the change required a unanimous vote that the FIA didn't achieve) got Ferrari off the hook in terms of consumption, which was still an area in which McLaren's TAG-Porsche engine reigned supreme,

courtesy of its more advanced Bosch fuel-metering systems. Even so, during the season, Ferrari was able to drop the "Emulsistem" (saving 15 kilograms in weight) as Agip produced a new fuel blend and Marelli introduced a new injection system.

The 156/85 looked strong early in the season, as Michele Alboreto picked up a string of podium finishes, then led Johansson home in a one-two finish in Canada. He also put the car on pole for the Belgian Grand Prix, but that race was canceled and rescheduled for later in the year after the newly laid track surface broke up during the support race. These results, plus a commanding win in Germany, enabled Alboreto to stay in the lead of the drivers' championship, ahead of McLaren's Alain Prost, until midseason.

Abruptly, the 156/85's relatively respectable reliability departed. After Germany, Alboreto claimed just one more points finish in the remaining six rounds. Prost overtook him in the title race and, although Alboreto clung on to second place, much more had been expected given Ferrari's form early in the season.

← Stefan Johansson (right) joined Michele Alboreto in Portgual after René Arnoux was fired just one round into the season. Alboreto finished second to Ayrton Senna in this wet and attritional race and was in contention for the championship until the 156/85 hit reliability problems.

156/85 F1 SPECIFICATIONS

Engine	1,496 cc 120-degree twin-turbocharged V-6	Suspension	Double wishbones with pullrod-actuated coil springs/dampers (f/r)
Power	800 bhp @ 11,500 rpm	Brakes	Discs f/r
Gearbox	Five-speed manual	Tires	Goodyear
Chassis	Carbon fiber monocoque	Weight	540 kg

Harvey Postlethwaite's 156/85 was a one-piece carbon fiber molding and was the first Ferrari to feature carbon brakes. Michele Alboreto led here in Monaco, then had to fight back into contention after sliding on an oil spill, only to suffer a puncture and drop back to second.

For 1985 Ferrari relocated the turbochargers from the inside of the engine's vee to the outside.

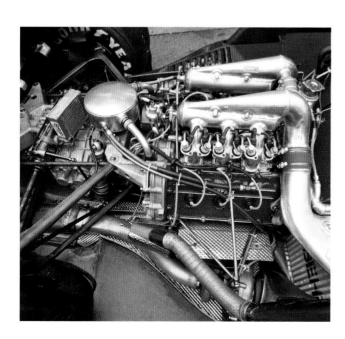

Fire-spitting turbos defined the look of 1980s Formula 1 cars. Michele Alboreto led teammate Stefan Johansson in a Ferrari one-two here in Canada.

While the key visual difference between the F1-86 and its predecessor was the incorporation of the roll hoop into the main bodywork, creating a bulge behind the driver's head, the chassis design followed a new concept in order to remove some of the flex-related issues suffered in 1985. The central carbon fiber "tub" was molded as an inverted *U* shape with the floor bonded on later. Although the car looked bulkier, it actually had a smaller frontal area than the 156/85.

In an effort to limit horsepower gains, the FIA used fuel consumption as a lever, reducing the maximum permitted tank size from 220 liters to 195. Ferrari recruited Jean-Jacques His from Renault to spearhead engine development, with a mandate to improve reliability while minimizing power losses. He increased the compression ratio, specified new butterfly valves in the turbo plumbing to reduce lag, reprofiled the cylinder heads, and modified the electronic engine management software. Ferrari also swapped from KKK to Garrett turbochargers from the Belgian Grand Prix onward, and there were several changes in exhaust design over the course of the season.

Reliability proved to be poor—and the failures were generally of the one-off variety in ancillary mechanical areas, such as the brakes and wheel bearings. Nor was the car fast enough to challenge the dominant Williams and McLaren chassis. Stefan Johansson finished third on four occasions, while Michele Alboreto was second in Austria—but that position was an inherited one, after Keke Rosberg's McLaren suffered an electrical problem.

By mid season, Enzo Ferrari resolved to make changes, sidelining Postlethwaite and recruiting Austrian designer Gustav Brunner to create a clean-sheet car for 1987. Enzo also began courting McLaren technical director John Barnard to head up the entire engineering organization.

↑
Michele Alboreto hustled his F1-86 to fourth on the grid at Monaco in 1986, but a turbo failure eliminated him from the race at mid-distance.

←
Despite a stiffer chassis design and theoretically better aerodynamics than the 156/85, and further engine revisions, the F1-86 lacked speed and reliability. Ferrari slid to fourth in the constructors' championship.

F1-86 SPECIFICATIONS

Engine	1,496 cc 120-degree twin-turbocharged V-6	Suspension	Double wishbones with pullrod-actuated coil springs/dampers (f), pushrod-actuated coil springs/dampers (f)
Power	850 bhp @ 11,500 rpm	Brakes	Discs f/r
Gearbox	Five-speed manual	Tires	Goodyear
Chassis	Carbon fiber monocoque	Weight	540 kg

To reassert Ferrari's preeminence in the engine bay, as well as to address the latest FIA measures to control power outputs (mandatory pop-off valves in the turbos to limit boost pressure to 4.0 bar), Jean-Jacques His's team developed an all-new V-6 for 1987. This carried over the 120-degree engine's bore and stroke dimensions but at a narrower angle—90 degrees—and with an iron block as opposed to an aluminum one, though it was cast using advanced techniques pioneered by another Fiat-owned company, Teksid. The new unit proved to be a little heavier than the old one and a new Marelli ignition system contributed to improved efficiency; quoted maximum power was 880 bhp, but Enzo Ferrari subsequently said that by the end of the season it was producing up to 960 bhp in qualifying races.

Aerodynamic efficiency was another key driver behind the move to a narrower vee angle, and in tandem with this Ferrari reverted to a longitudinal gearbox design in order to make the bodywork at the rear narrower, reducing blockages between the rear wheels. Although John Barnard arrived too late in the F1-87's gestation to influence its overall layout, this is an area he had demonstrated as being of critical importance to rear-wing efficiency on his McLaren MP4-2 designs. The entire F1-87 was narrower, owing to Brunner's focus on minimizing frontal area: even the mirrors and "periscope" air inlets were smaller than before and positioned differently. Brunner also returned to a pullrod rear suspension setup.

Barnard, renowned for his singular and uncompromising approach, would later say there were various elements he would have done differently. But he had a lot of work on his hands: Ferrari was so keen to pry him away from McLaren that he was able to name his terms, among

	F1-87	F1-87/88C
Engine	1,496 cc 90-degree twin-turbocharged V-6	1,496 cc 90-degree twin-turbocharged V-6
Power	880 bhp @ 11,500 rpm	650 bhp @ 12,000 rpm
Gearbox	Six-speed manual	Six-speed manual
Chassis	Carbon fiber monocoque	Carbon fiber monocoque
Suspension	Double wishbones with pullrod-actuated coil springs/dampers (f/r)	Double wishbones with pullrod-actuated coil springs/dampers (f/r)
Brakes	Discs f/r	Discs f/r
Tires	Goodyear	Goodyear
Weight	540 kg	542 kg

←

The quest for aerodynamic efficiency meant Gustav Brunner's F1-87 featured narrower bodywork and pullrod rear suspension, together with a new 60-degree V-6 engine. New recruit John Barnard would contribute several detail changes over the course of the season.

The F1-87 was revised to compete for a second season in 1988 when internal politics delayed progress on an all-new car. *James Mann*

→
The new V-6 was cast in iron rather than aluminum, but thanks to advanced casting techniques, it was barely heavier than its predecessor.

which was that he would remain based in the UK and establish a design and manufacturing facility there. He would be pulled in to work on developments of the F1-87, including a suspension, braking, and aerodynamic update introduced at the San Marino Grand Prix, but one of the biggest calls on his time was setting up what became known as the Guildford Technical Office, located on the Broadford Park industrial estate in the village of Shalford, England.

The F1-87 was sporadically fast but also fragile. Michele Alboreto and Gerhard Berger notched up nineteen retirements between them over the course of the sixteen-race season. The car's longer wheelbase induced understeer at first but, once this had been dialed out, Berger was regularly qualifying among the front-runners in the second half of the year, picking up victories in Japan and Australia.

Because turbo boost was to be reduced to 2.5 bar in 1988, and blown engines banned thereafter, Barnard wanted to press on with developing an advanced car powered by a naturally aspirated V-12 for that season. But delays in setting up GTO, and internal politics in Maranello, stymied those plans, and Ferrari had to compete throughout 1988 with a development of the '87 car. Honda built an entirely new engine for McLaren and that partnership dominated the season, though Ferrari picked up a fortuitous one-two finish on home ground in Italy shortly after Enzo's death that summer.

Delays plagued the development of John Barnard's putative 1988 Ferrari, code-named 639; only two were eventually built, and they were used as test mules for the advanced and troublesome semiautomatic transmission mated to the new naturally aspirated 3.5-liter V-12 engine. Setting up Barnard's remote UK design and manufacturing headquarters accounted for some of that lag, as did teething troubles with the new V-12—not helped by Jean-Jacques His returning to Renault in mid-1988. But there were other, deeper problems in the Ferrari organization that finally came to a head in the months before Enzo Ferrari's death in the summer of '88.

Frustrated by lack of feedback from the aerodynamicists in Maranello, Barnard investigated and found that a faction involving Harvey Postlethwaite and chief aerodynamicist Jean-Claude Migeot, operating with the say-so of Enzo's illegitimate son Piero Lardi Ferrari, was unilaterally working on its own design. A bust-up ensued in which Barnard emerged the unlikely victor, and Piero was exiled to a distant corner of the Ferrari empire. But Barnard would have to fight again after Enzo's death, this time as the new managers drafted by Fiat got cold feet about the troublesome new gearbox.

Removing the conventional gearshift mechanism, Barnard believed, would unlock a virtuous chain of benefits: the monocoque itself could be narrower because there was no need to route a mechanical shift mechanism through it or make room in the cockpit for a gearstick; shift times would be shorter; there was less chance of shifting down into the wrong gear; and an electronic limiter could be fitted to prevent the driver from over-revving the engine.

Having made the decision to run the 639 as a mobile test bed only, Barnard was able to refine the mechanical layout and aerodynamics further for the 640, which made its debut on schedule in 1989. Exchanging conventional springs and dampers for torsion bars at the front enabled the nose to be distinctively flat and narrow. Whereas many rivals were still channeling the majority of the hot air from the radiators from the side or top of the sidepods, disrupting airflow to the rear wing, the 639

←

John Barnard's beautiful and genre-defining 640 had a troubled start. Nigel Mansell contested the 1989 Monaco Grand Prix solo after a front wing failure caused teammate Gerhard Berger to crash out of the previous race, suffering burns and broken ribs.

640 SPECIFICATIONS

Engine	3,498 cc 65-degree V-12	Suspension	Double wishbones with pushrod-actuated torsion bars/dampers (f), coil springs/dampers (r)
Power	650 bhp @ 12,500 rpm	Brakes	Discs f/r
Gearbox	Seven-speed semiautomatic	Tires	Goodyear
Chassis	Carbon fiber monocoque	Weight	510 kg

→ The 640's tall but narrow sidepods ducted the airflow from the radiators to an outlet under the rear wing.

← Nigel Mansell won the 640's first race, the 1989 Brazilian Grand Prix, against all expectations—the new semiautomatic transmission had been problematic throughout testing.

→
Torsion-bar front suspension
enabled the 640 to have a
distinctively flat nose.

and 640's distinctive-looking sidepods ducted the entire flow within the car to an outlet below the wing (in hotter locations, a small side exit was required).

The semiautomatic transmission continued to be problematic through testing and into the season. At the opening race in Brazil, Gerhard Berger and new signing Nigel Mansell qualified third and sixth. So poor were the cars' prospects of finishing that team manager Cesare Fiorio lobbied Barnard to start the race with just a fraction of the fuel required, so that they could at least put on a good show before they broke. Barnard resisted and, against all odds, Mansell won—even though his steering wheel bolts fell off, forcing him to stop for a spare to be fitted.

Neither car finished a race again until midseason, by which time the transmission issue had been traced to the engine: crankshaft vibrations were dislodging the alternator pulley, robbing the control electronics of power. The 640 won two further races, but Barnard had grown tired of Maranello politics and took up an offer with the Benetton team.

CHAPTER 5

Optimism bookended Ferrari's decade, but between those competitive flourishes lay a wasteland of failure. Politics undermined virtually every effort to bring the Formula 1 project forward, but the underlying problems ran deeper than that. Ferrari's very philosophy was flawed: the company was grasping for magic-bullet solutions and then flying into a panic when new approaches failed to deliver race wins right away.

The level to which Ferrari had fallen is illustrated by how long it took from making one of the key decisions that began the recovery to actually delivering a tangible result. Luca di Montezemolo hired Jean Todt, one of the most astute managers in the business, to run Ferrari's competitions department in 1993—but it took six further years to alight upon the correct technical approach and build a fighting unit capable of winning Grands Prix consistently.

In hindsight, it's easy to see that designing the car remotely in England and then building it in Maranello was a fundamentally flawed process, but it's the arrangement Todt inherited when he arrived. Poaching Michael Schumacher to drive delivered an immediate competitive uplift, and then luring Ross Brawn and Rory Byrne from Benetton to lead a new in-house development program set the team on the road to recovery. Even then it would take time to bed in the new wind tunnel and build a technical team capable of making state-of-the-art race cars: in the 1990s and beyond, only strength and depth across all departments would deliver championship wins.

←
The 1990s began full of promise as Alain Prost joined and came close to winning the World Championship for Ferrari in his first year with the team.

Ferrari hired Enrique Scalabroni from Williams to replace John Barnard, and he was joined late in 1989 by Steve Nichols, one of the McLaren engineers responsible for the seminal 1988 MP4/4. Nichols joined at the behest of Alain Prost, who had quit McLaren for Ferrari after his working relationships with teammate Ayrton Senna and team boss Ron Dennis collapsed.

Prost therefore brought the coveted number one plate to Maranello, and Ferrari was determined to win straight away, though the factory remained riven by internal politics. Barnard's 640 design was so radical that it seemed to have plenty of development road left; furthermore, it was very quick, so the natural course to take for the 641 was evolution, with a focus on sorting out the reliability.

The basic body shape and suspension layout remained, but Scalabroni and Nichols redeveloped the cooling architecture and raised the level of the leading edge of the sidepods slightly, giving it a more rounded profile than before. The seven-speed semiautomatic gearbox was redesigned with an emphasis on better reliability, and the engine air intake scoop above the driver's head was enlarged. A bigger fuel tank was included to account for the increased thirst of forthcoming engine designs, including the short-block version of the V-12 scheduled to be introduced at Imola.

Despite the focus on reliability, the 641 was beset by a variety of small but inconsistent problems. Both Ferrari drivers retired from the season-opening U.S. Grand Prix at the unloved Phoenix circuit, Prost with an oil leak and Nigel Mansell with clutch failure. Prost began to harbor reservations about the way Cesare Fiorio was running the team, and the way politics rather than pragmatism seemed to govern important decisions. Many years later he would describe a test session in which he had tried to focus on setup evaluations, only to be asked to drop that in favor of a performance run to match a qualifying simulation time set by Mansell—the reason being that if Mansell was seen as the quicker driver, the team would begin to focus on him.

This never came to pass, and in fact it was Mansell who came to regard himself as the neglected man as the season progressed. Prost claimed an important victory at round two in Brazil, a win significant not only because it demonstrated a useful virtue of the 641 on

641 SPECIFICATIONS

Engine	3,498 cc 65-degree V-12	Suspension	Double wishbones with pushrod-actuated torsion bars/dampers (f), coil springs/dampers (r)
Power	680 bhp @ 12,800 rpm	Brakes	Discs f/r
Gearbox	Seven-speed semiautomatic	Tires	Goodyear
Chassis	Carbon fiber monocoque	Weight	510 kg

bumpy circuits such as Interlagos—the semiautomatic gearbox meant the drivers didn't have to take a hand off the wheel—but also because Prost had defeated Senna on home ground. Senna had been leading from Prost before suffering a damaging clash with a backmarker.

Although Senna won in Monaco and Canada, Prost surged through from thirteenth on the grid to serve another reminder of the 641's prowess on bumpy tracks. Mansell drove around the outside of Berger at the notoriously dangerous Peraltada corner to claim

Ferrari's first one-two finish in eighteen months. Prost also won next time out, in France, to secure Ferrari's 100th Grand Prix victory, and again at Silverstone. But here the win was overshadowed by Mansell suffering his fifth retirement of the season and, in front of his distraught home crowd, theatrically announcing his retirement.

Ferrari introduced a launch-control system for the Portuguese Grand Prix, but Mansell declined to use it—and picked up too much wheelspin at the start,

chopping across Prost's path and letting both McLarens
by. Though he fought back and won, with Prost third, the
outcome of the championship might have been different
but for these events.

Prost won in Spain, but at the penultimate round, in
Japan, Senna took both himself and Prost out at the
start, settling the drivers' title in his favor.

Following Enrique Scalabroni's departure for Lotus during 1990 and aerodynamics chief Henri Durand's move to McLaren, the 642 was chiefly the work of Steve Nichols and represented another evolution of the John Barnard 640 concept. The nose and radiator inlets had a more rounded profile, and the sidepods sloped down toward the rear to improve the airflow to the rear wing. While the suspension layout was similar, the geometries were different and the wheelbase was slightly longer. In hindsight, an entirely new concept would have been preferable.

Although the 642 was among the pacesetters in preseason testing, the 1991 season began disappointingly. Alain Prost qualified in second place for the first round in Phoenix but couldn't challenge Ayrton Senna in the race. New signing Jean Alesi retired. In Brazil, the 642 proved too stiffly sprung and Prost and Alesi were more than a second off the pace in qualifying. Come round three in San Marino, Prost spun off in the wet on the formation lap.

Prost began to step up his machinations for the removal of team manager Cesare Fiorio, with whom relations had been frosty since Prost was made aware of Fiorio's attempts to lure Ayrton Senna to Ferrari. At the fourth round of the season, in Monaco, Prost and Alesi qualified a miserable seventh and ninth, once again more than a second off polesitter Senna's pace. Prost might have finished second but for a problematic pit stop, and Alesi salvaged third, but behind the scenes Nichols and the returning chief aerodynamicist Jean-Claude Migeot had already begun to work on a much-revised

car. Prost got his wish, and Fiorio departed. The 642 would see service in just two more Grands Prix, failing to finish both.

↑
Mercurial and super-committed, just like Gilles Villeneuve, Jean Alesi was the archetypal Ferrari driver, but he tended to drive around a car's problems rather than solve them.

←
Another evolution of the 640 concept, the 642 lacked agility and speed. Here in San Marino, Prost spun off in the wet on the formation lap of the race.

642 SPECIFICATIONS

Engine	3,499 cc 65-degree V-12	Suspension	Double wishbones with pushrod-actuated torsion bars/dampers (f), coil springs/dampers (r)
Power	700 bhp @ 13,500 rpm	Brakes	Discs f/r
Gearbox	Seven-speed semiautomatic	Tires	Goodyear
Chassis	Carbon fiber monocoque	Weight	510 kg

Hurriedly designed and rushed into service at the French Grand Prix in 1991, the 643 was only ever an interim car as Steve Nichols and Jean-Claude Migeot developed an all-new car for the 1992 season. The 643 carried over much of the architecture of the 642 but with a focus on greater reliability and more sympathetic behavior over bumps. While Jean Alesi, the young firebrand of the team, was of a mind-set to climb in any car and just drive around its weaknesses, Alain Prost believed that optimizing a car's potential would ultimately yield better results.

Prost had found the 642's stiff-leggedness over bumps far too compromising because it often bounced the wheels partially off the ground and made for poor traction, especially in the wet. It also exacerbated the tendency of ancillary components to break. Accordingly, Nichols redrew the suspension geometry in an effort to soften the ride without inducing too much pitch or squat, which would impair aerodynamic efficiency. Within the constraints of the existing architecture, Migeot raised the nose slightly to improve airflow under the car toward the diffuser. The engine cover was also reshaped and the sidepod apertures moved back slightly.

In concert with further engine-development steps, the 643 provided a small upturn in performance, but it remained outclassed by the McLaren and Williams cars. Prost and Alesi took two podium finishes each, but when Prost compared the deportment of his car unfavorably with that of a truck after laboring to fourth place at Suzuka, the three-time world champion was summarily fired and replaced for the final round by test driver Gianni Morbidelli.

↑
Hurriedly introduced in the seventh round of the 1991 season, the 643 proved marginally more competitive than the 642 but not a race winner. Jean Alesi claimed third place here at Hockenheim.

←
Alain Prost's relationship with Ferrari deteriorated during 1991 and he was fired before the end of the season after making uncomplimentary remarks about the 643.

643 SPECIFICATIONS

Engine	3,499 cc 65-degree V-12	Suspension	Double wishbones with pushrod-actuated torsion bars/dampers (f), coil springs/dampers (r)
Power	700 bhp @ 13,500 rpm	Brakes	Discs f/r
Gearbox	Seven-speed semiautomatic	Tires	Goodyear
Chassis	Carbon fiber monocoque	Weight	510 kg

The fallout from the catastrophic 1991 season resulted in change at the very top of Ferrari as Luca di Montezemolo was lured back to become president of the entire company. He rehired Harvey Postlethwaite to replace Steve Nichols, who departed over the winter for the new Sauber team after supervising the design of the new F92A, and would later bring in Niki Lauda as a consultant and team figurehead. But the 1992 season would bring further pain, as the new car concept failed to translate theory into practice.

The F92A was a bold piece of thinking but, in prioritizing aerodynamics over all other aspects of the car, Ferrari was asking for trouble. Following a suggestion by Nichols to mount the radiators at an angle to create room for a sidepod undercut that would enable more air to flow around the body, chief aerodynamicist Jean-Claude Migeot drew a car with an entirely separate second floor. Wind tunnel research suggested this would yield a huge increase in downforce with relatively little drag penalty, but it would prove impossible to reproduce this on track.

At the front, the F92A signified its departure from previous concepts with a rounded and raised nose, from which the front wing hung from a pair of pylons. As with other high-nose cars such as Migeot's Tyrrell 019, John Barnard's Benetton B191, and Adrian Newey's Leyton House CG901 and Williams FW14, the aim here was to direct air under the car where it would eventually reach and be accelerated by the diffuser between the rear wheels. The F92A's twin floor aimed to maximize this effect. To keep the nose as narrow as possible, the front suspension featured an unusual monoshock arrangement in which both sides of the front suspension actuated a single horizontally mounted spring-damper unit. The oval-shaped air intakes and rounded sidepods attracted comparisons with fighter jets.

Behind the driver sat an all-new V-12 that had been designed to provide greater torque than before in order for the gearbox to be more compact and feature six ratios rather than seven. But right from the start of testing it proved to be insufficiently powerful and prone to seizures brought on by oil starvation while cornering.

	F92A	F92AT
Engine	3,499 cc 65-degree V-12	3,499 cc 65-degree V-12
Power	700 bhp @ 13,500 rpm	700 bhp @ 13,500 rpm
Gearbox	Seven-speed semiautomatic	Seven-speed semiautomatic
Chassis	Carbon fiber monocoque	Carbon fiber monocoque
Suspension	Double wishbones with pushrod-actuated monoshock/damper (f), coil springs/dampers (r)	Double wishbones with pushrod-actuated monoshock/damper (f), coil springs/dampers (r)
Brakes	Discs f/r	Discs f/r
Tires	Goodyear	Goodyear
Weight	510 kg	540 kg

←
The revolutionary twin-floor aerodynamic concept of the dramatic-looking F92A failed to deliver its theoretical gains and saddled the car with ponderous handling.

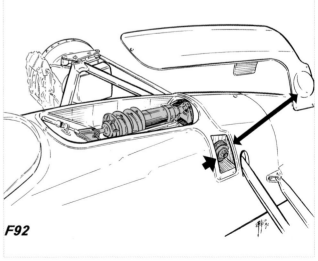

An interesting monoshock arrangement facilitated an aerodynamically advantageous narrow nose, but it proved challenging to set up properly and transmitted very little feeling for available grip.

F92

Ferrari introduced the F92AT, featuring a seven-speed transverse gearbox and front suspension revisions, at the Belgian Grand Prix—but only for Jean Alesi. Ivan Capelli (pictured), one of the scapegoats for the car's underperformance, didn't get the revised car until Monza.

→
The new V-12 prioritized torque so that the longitudinal gearbox could have six ratios rather than seven, enabling it to be more compact. But it wasn't powerful enough and was compromised by oil system problems.

New signing Ivan Capelli would later say that when he tested the new car back-to-back with the previous year's 643 and reported his reservations about the F92A, he was simply ignored—because Jean Alesi had declared it the best car he had ever driven. Alesi's capacity to take a car by the proverbial scruff of the neck and drive around problems enabled him to notch up points finishes in the early races of 1992, between reliability-related failures, while Capelli's confidence evaporated.

The monoshock front suspension gave very little feeling for the available grip, but mechanical flaws further aft also compromised performance. The twin-floor arrangement made the car heavier than its rivals, and it had an inherently higher center of gravity. Most vexingly, the F92A had more aerodynamic drag than expected and the twin floor worked effectively only when the car was perfectly flat to the ground; while cornering, braking, or accelerating, the downforce just wasn't there.

A transverse seven-speed gearbox was added from the Belgian Grand Prix, along with active suspension, and the revised car was designated the F92AT. But while the active system theoretically maintained the car flat to the road, enabling the twin floor to work more effectively, it was temperamental and brought a 30-kilogram weight penalty. At Lauda's urging, Montezemolo rehired John Barnard midseason and facilitated his wish to set up another design office in the UK. The benighted Capelli, meanwhile, was fired with two rounds remaining.

The situation at Maranello remained febrile during the gestation of the F93A as Luca di Montezemolo and Niki Lauda scrambled to build a new organization. They believed it would be possible to permit John Barnard to work under his own terms—overseeing a research and design facility with limited manufacturing capability near his home in Godalming, England—while Harvey Postlethwaite superintended in-season development and race operations in Maranello. The first obstacle to this plan was that Ferrari had already sold their Guildford Technical Office (established by Barnard during his previous stint with Scuderia) to McLaren, who were using it for production of their road-going F1 supercar.

F93A

Barnard set up a new facility, Ferrari Design and Development, on the same industrial estate as GTO on the banks of the River Wey in the village of Shalford. While it was the initial plan for him to focus on development of the 1994 car, he would soon become embroiled in the ongoing work on the 1993 chassis after Postlethwaite left to return to the Tyrrell team. Operational dysfunction of this magnitude would prove particularly damaging at a time of rapid technological change in Formula 1.

The year 1993 was arguably the point at which the age of electronic driver assistance reached its peak, when the dominance of the Williams team made such technologies as active suspension, traction control, and launch assistance de rigueur. Ferrari's active program

was well behind the curve, and even when it had finally been introduced on the F92AT late in 1992, the system was immature.

The F93A was essentially a stopgap car during a period of personnel change. Jean-Claude Migeot, the principal architect of the F92A, took the fall for its failure and departed on the eve of the 1993 season. Clearly an evolution of the previous car, the F93A featured a similar mechanical layout but without the twin floor, enabling the powertrain and all its ancillaries to be mounted lower for a more optimal center of gravity. The sidepods were also more conventional in appearance and terminated slightly further back than before, and the front track was 5.9 inches narrower, in line with new regulations

← Gerhard Berger had an eventful return to action at Ferrari thanks to the F93A's temperamental active suspension, qualifying only 15th in South Africa. So few cars finished the race that he was classified sixth despite suffering an engine failure three laps from the flag.

F93A SPECIFICATIONS

Engine	3,499 cc 65-degree V-12	Suspension	Double wishbones with pushrod-actuated and electronically governed torsion bars/dampers (f/r)
Power	700 bhp @ 13,500 rpm	Brakes	Discs f/r
Gearbox	Seven-speed semiautomatic	Tires	Goodyear
Chassis	Carbon fiber monocoque	Weight	510 kg

↑
The F93A was a tidied-up version of the F92AT, with a conventional single floor, enabling the cooling architecture to be repackaged and the sidepods set further back.

introduced (along with narrower rear tires) to reduce cornering speeds. Under the skin, the F93A was suspended by torsion bars with electronically actuated damping.

Ferrari's engine program also lagged behind the state of the art, and the 65-degree V-12 retained its five-valve cylinder head design. A pneumatic-valve version would not arrive until midseason.

Although the F93A was more competitive than its predecessor, F1 continued to be dominated by Williams throughout the 1993 season. Only Benetton and McLaren poached victories, and Ferrari faced the double ignominy of not recording a single win while the driver they had fired in 1991, Alain Prost, waltzed away with the drivers' championship.

Gerhard Berger joined Jean Alesi on the driving roster, but neither pilot enjoyed the F93A experience. The active suspension system proved extremely temperamental; even when stationary, the car often appeared to be suffering a fit of St. Vitus's dance. Suspension failures eliminated both drivers from several races, most dangerously when Berger was leaving the pits during the Portuguese Grand Prix. As Berger engaged maximum throttle, the rear suspension essentially dropped the car onto the ground, and he spun across the track in the face of oncoming traffic before crashing into the barrier. The FIA wisely banned active suspension and other such driver aids for the following season.

↑
After a troubled start to the season, Jean Alesi delivered the F93A's first podium position in Monaco. Teammate Berger crashed while attacking second-placed Damon Hill.

←
Ferrari rehired three-time champion Niki Lauda as a consultant, and he in turn persuaded John Barnard (right) to come back on board. Barnard's hopes of not getting embroiled in race operations were dashed midseason when Harvey Postlethwaite left for the Tyrrell team.

The next year, 1994, offered the opportunity for a reboot at Ferrari as the FIA banned the electronic driver aids that had caused lap times to tumble for teams who had perfected such technologies. The 412T1 was the first new Ferrari in John Barnard's second era at the Scuderia and benefited from the presence of another returning Ferrari employee, Gustav Brunner, at Maranello to supervise the engineering of the designs Barnard transmitted from his UK base. Osamu Goto, formerly the head of Honda's F1 development, joined over the winter and began work on a brand-new V-12. Another key hire by company president Luca di Montezemolo had arrived in mid-1993 to take control of the race organization: Jean Todt, formerly head of Peugeot's rallying and sports car programs.

That the 412T1 was a clean-sheet design was obvious, for it had nothing in common with its flawed predecessor apart from its initial powertrain spec. Barnard specified an aero-efficient dart-shaped design with very tall and slim sidepods, rakishly angled. The suspension was now passive, with pushrod-actuated torsion bars all round.

At the season-opening round in Brazil, Jean Alesi qualified third, but the gap to polesitter Ayrton Senna's Williams was telling: 1.4 seconds. Alesi got by Michael Schumacher's Benetton at the start (this in spite of claims that Benetton was illegally using traction control and launch control) but had no answer to Senna's pace as the Brazilian streaked away in front of his home crowd. Once Schumacher got by, Alesi slipped backward, but salvaged a podium finish after Senna spun off. Alesi then suffered a back injury while testing at Mugello and had to sit out the next two rounds while Nicola Larini substituted for him. One of those was the tragic weekend at Imola where Roland Ratzenberger and Ayrton Senna lost their lives, prompting immediate regulatory changes; Larini finished second to Schumacher, but nearly a minute in arrears.

	412T1	412T1B
Engine	3,499 cc 65-degree V-12	3,498 cc 75-degree V-12
Power	700 bhp @ 13,500 rpm	800 bhp @ 15,000 rpm
Gearbox	Seven-speed semiautomatic	Seven-speed semiautomatic
Chassis	Carbon fiber monocoque	Carbon fiber monocoque
Suspension	Double wishbones with pushrod-actuated torsion bars/dampers (f/r)	Double wishbones with pushrod-actuated torsion bars/dampers (f/r)
Brakes	Discs f/r	Discs f/r
Tires	Goodyear	Goodyear
Weight	510 kg	540 kg

← Nicola Larini, substituting for the injured Jean Alesi, finished second in the San Marino Grand Prix and brought some succor to the home crowd on a day marred by the tragic death of Ayrton Senna.

412T1 412T1B

↑
Alesi returned to the cockpit
in Monaco and finished fifth,
but cooling issues continued to
afflict the car until midseason.

In the aftermath of Imola and another accident in Monaco, the FIA ordered front wings and rear diffusers to be reduced in size (from Spain onward), that engine power be reduced via holes in the airbox and cockpit protection be improved (from Canada), and that all cars had to be fitted with a wooden "plank" underneath the floor to prevent ride heights being set too low (from Germany). Barnard also had to debug the 412T1's cooling issues, which were harming reliability and power. He would later assert that the engine department had gotten its figures wrong for the V-12's cooling demands, and that the majority of the coolant was flowing through a smaller radiator rather than the main one. The 412T1 therefore appeared with several different configurations of sidepod even before the B-spec car was introduced at the French Grand Prix.

In the German Grand Prix, the new Tipo 43 engine was raced for the first time, having been introduced for qualifying sessions from San Marino onward. Designed by Goto in collaboration with Claudio Lombardi, the new

←
The ban on driver aids such
as active suspension for 1994
dictated a return to passive
springing and damping, a
development that pleased both
drivers who had toiled with
Ferrari's troublesome active
system the previous season.

↓

Until the B-spec car was
introduced in Germany, the
412 T1 went through many
iterations of radiator inlet
profile. John Barnard later
asserted that the problem
was rooted in the engine
department getting its
figures wrong.

V-12 had a slightly wider vee (75 degrees as opposed
to 65), with a shorter stroke to mitigate the additional
width of the block. Claimed output rose to 750. Berger
qualified on pole and went on to win the race, challenged
only by Schumacher, who eventually fell back with a
sickly engine. This would be Ferrari's only win of the
year but, coming at a circuit where engine power and
reliability generally dictated the outcome, it was a sign
that Maranello was back in the game.

During the final months of the 1994 season, Paolo Martinelli was appointed as head of the engine department in place of Claudio Lombardi, and one of his first acts was to begin a research project into future engine architectures. By now Ferrari was the only team to persist with V-12 engines, this being seen as a key pillar of the brand. But Williams had dominated the World Championship in recent years with a Renault V10, and Michael Schumacher claimed the 1994 drivers' title (albeit narrowly) with a Ford V-8 ahead of his Benetton team switching to Renault power in 1995. There was also an FIA-mandated reduction in engine size to 3 liters looming.

Martinelli opted to begin development of a V10 for 1996 while approaching '95 with a downsized version of the existing V-12 concept, enabling Barnard to continue with an evolution of the 412T family. The T2 had a lower nose and a shorter wheelbase than its predecessor, with shorter, more sharp-edged sidepods. From this season on, the driver was factored into the overall calculation of the car's minimum weight, which was increased to 595 kilograms.

The new car was competitive enough to deliver at least one of its drivers onto the podium for the first six rounds of the year. Jean Alesi took what would prove to be the only win of his F1 career in Canada, on his thirty-first birthday, but that would be Ferrari's only victory of the season. It was on this weekend, too, that rumors began to circulate of Michael Schumacher's imminent move to Maranello.

↑
On his 31st birthday, Jean Alesi registered the only win of his F1 career. This victory, in Canada, was Ferrari's only win of the 1995 season.

←
The 412 T2 was the last Ferrari F1 car to use a V-12 engine.

412T2 SPECIFICATIONS

Engine	2,998 cc 75-degree V-12	Suspension	Double wishbones with pushrod-actuated torsion bars/dampers (f/r)
Power	690 bhp @ 16,800 rpm	Brakes	Discs f/r
Gearbox	Seven-speed semiautomatic	Tires	Goodyear
Chassis	Carbon fiber monocoque	Weight	595 kg

John Barnard would later describe his final Ferrari design as "a bit of a wobble" and it would prompt a further revolution in the design arrangements at Maranello—one that would ultimately yield the team's richest streak of victories. Ground zero for this change was the F310, a car that epitomized Barnard's constant urge to innovate.

Aerodynamically, the F310 was intriguing and unusual, eschewing the fashionable high nose for a low one, and with rounded sidepod apertures that harked back to the failed F92A of 1992. But in chasing unusual solutions, Barnard had failed to identify loopholes in the regulations that others would exploit to their advantage. The most obvious area was around the cockpit, where Barnard's team had interpreted the new rules requiring raised side-impact cushions for the driver's head rather too literally. The majority of the other teams had realized they could satisfy the wording by shaping these structures in the form of a ramp that rose to the specified height and then fell away, leaving a channel between it and the airbox. The F310's padding was designed such that it was flush to the side of the cockpit, rising almost to the level of the airbox and forming part of the greater area of the engine cover. It made the car look portly compared with its rivals and impeded the flow of air to the rear wing.

Williams had also exploited a loophole in the wording of the rules regarding the underfloor plank, enabling them to increase the size of the diffuser and enjoy a substantial downforce boost. Their car was almost untouchable during 1996, and the championship boiled down to a fight between their drivers, Damon Hill and Jacques Villeneuve.

But Ferrari now had Michael Schumacher. Having tested the 412T2 before the F310, he expressed a preference for the power of the V-12 engine, but Ferrari was now committed to the new car and its V10. The new engine produced more vibrations than its predecessor, enough to crack the gearbox casing, and in the early races Ferrari had to revert to a previous transmission design that had different suspension pickup points, compromising the suspension geometry.

This, in combination with aerodynamics that proved extremely pitch-sensitive, made the F310 difficult to

← Double world champion Michael Schumacher joined Ferrari for 1996 and worked his magic to notch up three wins in the F310, a car that required many major changes during the season, including a whole new nose concept.

	F310	F310B
Engine	2,998 cc 75-degree V10	2,998 cc 75-degree V10
Power	715 bhp @ 15,500 rpm	730 bhp @ 16,000 rpm
Gearbox	Seven-speed semiautomatic	Seven-speed semiautomatic
Chassis	Carbon fiber monocoque	Carbon fiber monocoque
Suspension	Double wishbones with pushrod-actuated torsion bars/dampers (f/r)	Double wishbones with pushrod-actuated torsion bars/dampers (f/r)
Brakes	Discs f/r	Discs f/r
Tires	Goodyear	Goodyear
Weight	595 kg	595 kg

F310 F310B F310B

drive. Nevertheless, Schumacher hauled it onto the podium several times, including three wins—one of which, in the wet in Spain, is considered one of his finest performances.

Team principal Jean Todt reached the conclusion that the team's design practices—Barnard essentially faxed his work over from the UK page by page to Maranello, where the blueprints then had to be reassembled—were no longer working. He issued Barnard with a take-it-or-leave-it proposal to move to Italy full time, which Barnard declined. At Schumacher's suggestion,

Todt poached Benetton's chief designer, Rory Byrne, and technical director, Ross Brawn, to rebuild the design function at Maranello.

This would not be the work of a moment, and would require Todt to act as a lightning rod for criticism during the rebuilding process. Following Barnard's departure, Byrne and Brawn revised the F310 into a B-spec to compete in 1997. The F310B was outwardly very different from its predecessor, with a raised nose and squarer sidepod apertures—which were now blended into the side of the tub rather than protruding forward. The area

around the cockpit was also substantially revised. At the rear, the powertrain had been developed for better power and reliability, and in the hands of Schumacher—less so in the hands of his number two, Eddie Irvine—the F310B was very competitive.

Schumacher won five races and entered the final round of the year a point ahead of Jacques Villeneuve, but disgraced himself with a clumsy attempt to take out the Williams driver and failed to make the finish.

Schumacher's extraordinary
win in sodden conditions in
Barcelona is considered to be
one of the finest drives of his
career. Fighting back from
a poor start, the result of
clutch problems, he remained
sure-footed as others spun
or crashed.

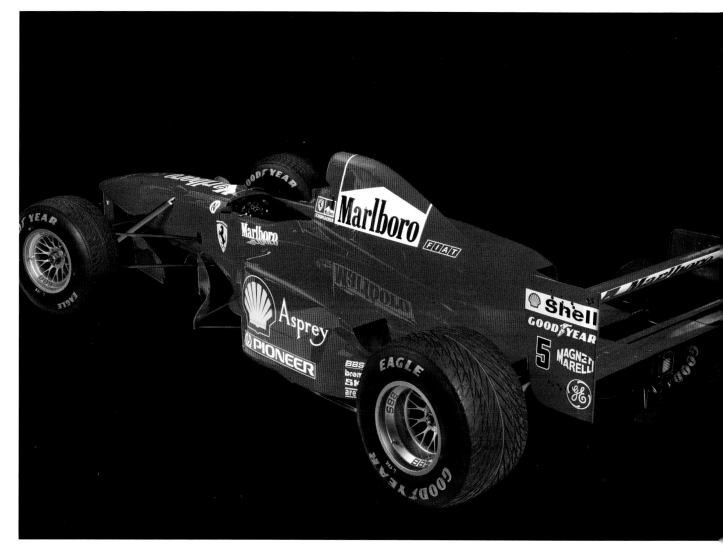

←
The incoming technical team
led by Ross Brawn extensively
revised the F310B. *James Mann*

←
The F310's high cockpit
sides interpreted the new
safety regulations too
literally—rivals had exploited
loopholes that gave them an
aerodynamic benefit.

The F300 was the first Ferrari designed under the auspices of what would become the definitive technical structure for the following nine seasons, with Ross Brawn as technical director and Rory Byrne as chief designer working from Maranello, and team principal Jean Todt acting as a firebreak between them and the hostile forces without. Pressure from the Italian media and the upper echelons of Fiat Group management were unceasing—indeed, one of Brawn's first moves upon taking up his post had been to ban newspapers from the technical office, viewing their negativity as bad for morale.

Again the FIA stepped in to put the brakes on increasing car performance, this time mandating that all cars have a 7.9-inch narrower track front and rear. In tandem with new grooved tires—essentially meaning less rubber in contact with the track surface—this was intended to exercise the greatest effect on cornering performance. The grooved tires were never popular because their tendency was for the raised sections in the center to deform under duress, a phenomenon known as "graining," which reduced both the available grip and the driver's feel for what remained.

As with any reset of the technical regulations, the change favored those teams best prepared for it. The previously dominant Williams team, having lost star designer Adrian Newey to McLaren, would endure a steep fall in 1998 as the Newey-penned McLarens proved to be the class of the field. Ferrari's offering was Maranello's most competitive car in several seasons, but it was not quite enough to bring home the championship silverware.

At first glance, the F300 closely resembled the F310B, but it was different in detail. The front wing endplates were squarer in profile, the bargeboards were mounted horizontally, and the entire rear end of the car had been redesigned around a new aerodynamic philosophy. After wrestling with several different exhaust and cooling configurations, the design team fixed upon a novel solution in which the exhausts exited through the top of the rear deck. Introduced at the start of the European season, this was less aerodynamically effective than directing them through the "Coke-bottle" area of the bodywork between the rear wheels, but it resolved many heat-related problems. The shorter exhaust pipe lengths this entailed also reduced the engine's sensitivity to throttle inputs, improving drivability. Relocating the exhausts also enabled Ferrari to experiment with different aerodynamic furniture on the rear three-quarters of

← Michael Schumacher spins his rear tires as he exits the pit box in Hockenheim. The grooved tires introduced in 1998 to peg back cornering speeds were never popular with drivers.

F300 SPECIFICATIONS

Engine	2,997 cc 90-degree V-10	Suspension	Double wishbones with pushrod-actuated torsion bars/ dampers (f/r)
Power	790 bhp @ 16,300 rpm	Brakes	Discs f/r
Gearbox	Seven-speed semiautomatic	Tires	Bridgestone
Chassis	Carbon fiber monocoque	Weight	595 kg

↑
Ugly high-mounted "x-wings" briefly became a design trend early in the 1998 season. They were banned—on safety rather than aesthetic grounds—the day after Schumacher and teammate Eddie Irvine finished second and third here at the San Marino Grand Prix.

the car to condition the airflow around and over the rear wheels.

In Australia, for the opening round of the season, Michael Schumacher qualified third on the grid but was an ominous 0.7 second off the pace of Mika Häkkinen's polesitting McLaren. He then retired with engine failure as the McLarens dominated the race. The pattern of McLaren superiority was repeated in Brazil, but in Argentina Ferrari demonstrated a tactical acuity that would become a hallmark in the coming seasons: Schumacher ran an aggressive two–pit stop strategy

that enabled him to leapfrog the one-stopping Häkkinen. Five more wins over the course of the season took Schumacher to the final round still in contention for the drivers' title with Häkkinen, who had won eight races but scored slightly less consistently.

Having qualified on pole position for the final round, at Suzuka, Schumacher inexplicably stalled at the start and had to fight his way through the field. He rose to third place but then suffered a high-speed blowout that eliminated him from the race, enabling Häkkinen to secure the championship.

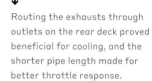

← Schumacher had a difficult Monaco weekend in 1998, suffering a breakdown in practice and then finishing 10th after colliding with another car.

↓ Routing the exhausts through outlets on the rear deck proved beneficial for cooling, and the shorter pipe length made for better throttle response.

After running McLaren close for both championships in 1998, Ferrari chose an evolutionary path for the following season. Time and again in '98, astute calls from the pit wall had enabled Ferrari to gain the upper hand over McLaren's mechanically superior cars, so the F399 was built around what technical director Ross Brawn called a "small tank" philosophy: to make more frequent pit visits but to be as fast as possible between them.

Power-assisted steering made the F399 easier to drive, but despite the addition of this system, it was 20 kilograms lighter than the F300, enabling the engineers to add ballast strategically to optimize its weight distribution for different circuits when bringing it up to the minimum weight. The front suspension was a new design featuring a third damper to control "heave," and the aerodynamics were reworked from tip to tail: the front wing endplates were more sculptured and the bargeboards more sophisticated, while the sidepods were more tightly packaged and featured a small undercut. The exhaust configuration remained, but the hot air outlets from within the sidepods had been relocated and tidied up and the aerodynamic furniture around them adjusted to suit.

Once again McLaren appeared to have the faster car, but it was also fragile. Both McLarens retired from the season-opening Australian Grand Prix after annexing the front row in qualifying, but Michael Schumacher was in no position to take advantage because he had been forced to start from the back after his engine stalled

on the grid. Teammate Eddie Irvine won, albeit by only one second from the Mugen-Honda-powered Jordan of Heinz-Harald Frentzen.

Schumacher won in San Marino when Mika Häkkinen made an unforced error while leading, while in Monaco he grabbed the lead at the start from second on the grid, then controlled the remainder of the race. But Häkkinen dominated in Spain from pole and Schumacher crashed out of the Canadian Grand Prix after leading from pole—then broke his right leg below the knee when he crashed out of the British Grand Prix.

Schumacher was forced to sit out six rounds while Mika Salo deputized for him and Irvine took on the unexpected role of team leader and title contender. Irvine won three further Grands Prix—though his victory in Germany was a result of Salo obeying team orders—and he arrived at the Suzuka finale in mathematical contention for the drivers' title.

Irvine's journey was not without controversy, as developments to the F399 attracted the attention of rival teams and the scrutineers. Nor was Schumacher keen

← Michael Schumacher put his F399 on pole for the 1999 Canadian Grand Prix but was one of four drivers to hit the wall at turn 13—henceforth known as the Wall of Champions since three of those drivers were world champions.

F399 SPECIFICATIONS

Engine	2,997 cc 90-degree V-10	Suspension	Double wishbones with pushrod-actuated torsion bars/dampers (f/r)
Power	805 bhp @ 17,300 rpm	Brakes	Discs f/r
Gearbox	Seven-speed semiautomatic	Tires	Bridgestone
Chassis	Carbon fiber monocoque	Weight	595 kg

← Aerodynamically the F399 resembled its predecessor, but with reconfigured furniture ahead of the rear wheels as the design team cultivated a better understanding of the concept's characteristics.

↓ Inside the nose, the F399's front suspension featured a third shock absorber, known as a heave spring, to control roll, while the steering arms were aerodynamically shaped and located directly ahead of the wishbone to minimize disturbance of the airflow.

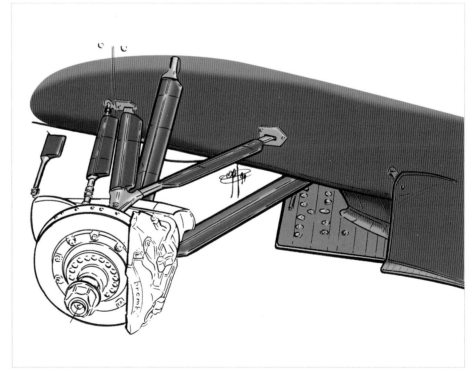

to return to the cockpit just to act as a rear gunner for his teammate; he tested at Monza late in the season but reported that his leg was too sore to contemplate racing. When he arrived in Kuala Lumpur for the Malaysian Grand Prix, word circulated that he had been compelled to do so after Luca di Montezemolo telephoned for a status update and was informed by Schumacher's daughter that "Daddy is out playing football."

In Malaysia, Schumacher infuriated McLaren by holding Mika Häkkinen behind him as Irvine pulled clear to win. After the race, Ferrari's bargeboards were declared illegally large and Irvine's win was struck off—only to be reinstated a week later.

This paved the way for a showdown at Suzuka, where Schumacher qualified on pole. Häkkinen, keen to make a point, passed him as soon as possible while Irvine circulated a distant and irrelevant third, over a minute and a half behind at the checkered flag. It was not enough to win the drivers' championship, but it did bring the constructors' championship to Maranello for the first time since 1983.

↑
Returning from injury for the Malaysian Grand Prix in 1999, Schumacher boosted teammate Eddie Irvine's prospects of grabbing the drivers' title by holding McLaren's Mika Häkkinen behind him.

CHAPTER 6

At the turn of the decade, Jean Todt's Ferrari matured into a fighting unit that achieved dominance in all areas of Formula 1. In Michael Schumacher they had the best driver of his generation, and under Ross Brawn's leadership the technical team delivered class-leading cars year after year. Crucially, Brawn's pit-wall operation was the sharpest in motor racing, consistently outfoxing their rivals even when Ferrari looked vulnerable.

But in becoming unbeatable, Ferrari would develop a peculiar relationship with the sport's governing body. After years of being riven by internal politics, the team would become a key player in F1's wider wranglings as FIA president Max Mosley fought to maintain his preeminence against a background of F1's motor manufacturers flexing their muscles.

This was an era in which big manufacturers jumped in and spent huge sums—and wanted some return on their investment. Honda, Toyota, and BMW would all acquire teams during this period and then pull out in a panic when the global economy crashed in 2008. In the interim, they fought Mosley and F1 ringmaster Bernie Ecclestone for control. Ferrari, a team steeped in F1 history and vital to the brand, knew its power and was unafraid to wield it.

In the twisting, arcane wranglings over the years, Ferrari sometimes appeared to be favored by the governing body, sometimes not. There were those who joked that FIA stood for Ferrari International Assistance. Equally in other periods, Ferrari's dominance was seen as toxic to F1's interests and rules were rushed in to reel in that superiority.

←

After an overhaul in the late 1990s and the recruitment of Michael Schumacher, Ferrari was virtually unbeatable in the first half of the new decade; the F2002 remains one of the most successful F1 cars of all time.

In their battle with McLaren through 1998 and 1999, the resurgent Ferrari had been lacking in two key areas: aerodynamics and engines. The new Renzo Piano–designed wind tunnel at Maranello had come on line in 1997, but it had taken Ross Brawn more than one season to recruit and build a functional design team after several years in which the factory had merely built and assembled cars from drawings produced in the UK. The '98 and '99 cars had benefited from good in-season development, but not enough to regain ground lost early in the season. Similarly, Ferrari was being outdone by McLaren's Ilmor-built Mercedes V-10, which featured exotic materials such as beryllium.

But the Ferrari design group was now stable and mature. Brawn set the tone for the 2000 season at the launch of the F1-2000, saying, "I think we've probably had the best car we have ever had at the beginning of the season since the present group has been working together here at Ferrari."

The F1-2000 was clearly an evolution of its predecessor, but it featured a much bolder front-end treatment in which the underside of the nose was higher than before, enabling greater airflow under the car. Structurally, it was a very difficult to engineer in terms of crash-test compliance, and it required the driver's body and legs to be more steeply angled, but the aerodynamic benefit was significant.

Within the sidepods, the radiators had been relocated and reduced in size to reduce aero blockage. Ferrari also retained the philosophy of directing the exhaust pipes along the top deck of the sidepods, requiring detail engineering to protect against heat damage.

Elsewhere the focus was on lowering the center of gravity, which was a trend across the grid in this third season of the narrow-track regulations. The brake calipers were rotated to sit at the bottom of the discs rather than at the front, an approach that lowered weight but required clever engineering to recoup lost braking performance and overcome structural issues. Like several other engine manufacturers, Ferrari widened the angle of its V-10 from 75 to 90 degrees in order for the cylinder heads to be lower.

Ferrari therefore began the season with a car well capable of fighting for wins. And if Schumacher's victories in the opening rounds were assisted by the fragility of

← McLaren annexed the front row at the opening round of the 2000 season in Melbourne, Australia, but both cars broke down, enabling Michael Schumacher and Eddie Irvine to run unchallenged to a Ferrari one-two.

F1-2000 SPECIFICATIONS

Engine	2,997 cc 90-degree V-10	Suspension	Double wishbones with pushrod-actuated torsion bars/dampers (f/r)
Power	805 bhp @ 17,300 rpm	Brakes	Discs f/r
Gearbox	Seven-speed semiautomatic	Tires	Bridgestone
Chassis	Carbon fiber monocoque	Weight	595 kg

↑
Häkkinen versus Schumacher was the defining battle of the 2000 season, and here in Brazil Ferrari's different approach delivered the race win; running with less fuel meant having to make one more pitstop than McLaren but made Schumacher's car lighter and faster.

the new McLaren car (Mika Häkkinen set pole position in Australia and Brazil but retired with engine failure), his win in San Marino was a strategic master class. Häkkinen led Schumacher at Imola, and the McLaren MP4/15 seemed to have pace in hand over the Ferrari. But Ferrari overturned the deficit by putting more fuel in at Schumacher's first pit stop, and he was then able to match Häkkinen's pace over a long middle stint before executing a much quicker second stop, because he required less fuel.

Häkkinen and his McLaren teammate David Coulthard claimed a victory apiece in the following two rounds before Schumacher hit back to win at the Nürburgring. After retiring from Monaco, Schumacher won again in Canada, round eight of seventeen, to lead Coulthard by 22 points. But he retired from the next three rounds, leaving the field to McLaren, and entered the Belgian Grand Prix two points behind new championship leader Häkkinen.

←
The F1-2000 delivered Ferrari's first drivers' championship in over 20 years. *James Mann*

↓
From midseason Ferrari reconfigured the exhaust system to exit via faired chimneys rather than being flush with the rear deck.

That deficit extended to 6 points (with McLaren 8 points ahead in the constructors' championship) after Belgium, where Häkkinen mugged Schumacher for the lead as they lapped the BAR of Ricardo Zonta. But Schumacher then won the final four rounds, clinching the title with a race to spare: it was Ferrari's first drivers' championship in two decades.

Winning the drivers' and constructors' championships in 2000 gave Ferrari confidence and momentum as they prepared for the following season. They also anticipated being on par with Mercedes on engine performance, having successfully lobbied the FIA for beryllium to be banned; McLaren technical director Adrian Newey would later say that Mercedes entered 2001 with no more power than they had in 1998.

Ferrari also successfully scuttled McLaren's plans to run a gearbox with a torque-biasing differential. To comply with regulations, the British team ran their design by the FIA, which cleared it because it was technically legal, but Ferrari then successfully argued that it was illegal on principle. This was a major political victory and one with significant performance connotations, too, because it forced McLaren to compromise their car design by using the previous season's transmission.

Though much of the F2001 was evolutionary, its front-end aerodynamic treatment was different owing to new regulations mandating that the front wings be 3.9 inches above the ground rather than 1.57 inches. This rule had been brought in to reduce aerodynamic performance—and it did, though it also made the front wings more sensitive to disrupted air from cars ahead. Ferrari's approach here was novel, and Rory Byrne was among the first designers to exploit a loophole in the wording of the regulations, adding a spoon-shaped section in the center of the wing that was below the 3.9-inch level. In tandem with these changes, Ferrari

changed to a drooping nose design, while maintaining an aggressively scooped undercut below the driver's feet.

More exacting impact regulations led to a marginal increase in chassis weight, but Ferrari mitigated this with wide-ranging changes to the engine and suspension design, shaving weight off in fractions across many components.

There had been mutterings within the paddock since the middle of the 2000 season that Ferrari had found a clever way to circumvent the ban on traction control by using sophisticated control software to mimic its effects. Rival teams employed acoustic analysis specialists in an attempt to catch them out. Those same rivals continued to lobby the FIA to take action. In the absence of compelling evidence of such systems, but certain that they were being used by at least one team, FIA president Max Mosley had to capitulate and rescind the ban on the grounds that it could not be policed.

Traction control was permitted again as of the Spanish Grand Prix, by which time Michael Schumacher had already won the first two rounds of the season. He won

← The F2001 proved so competitive that Ferrari continued using it in the first races of 2002 while work on its successor was still being completed.

F2001 SPECIFICATIONS

Engine	2,997 cc 90-degree V-10	Suspension	Double wishbones with pushrod-actuated torsion bars/dampers (f/r)
Power	825 bhp @ 17,300 rpm	Brakes	Discs f/r
Gearbox	Seven-speed semiautomatic	Tires	Bridgestone
Chassis	Carbon fiber monocoque	Weight	595 kg

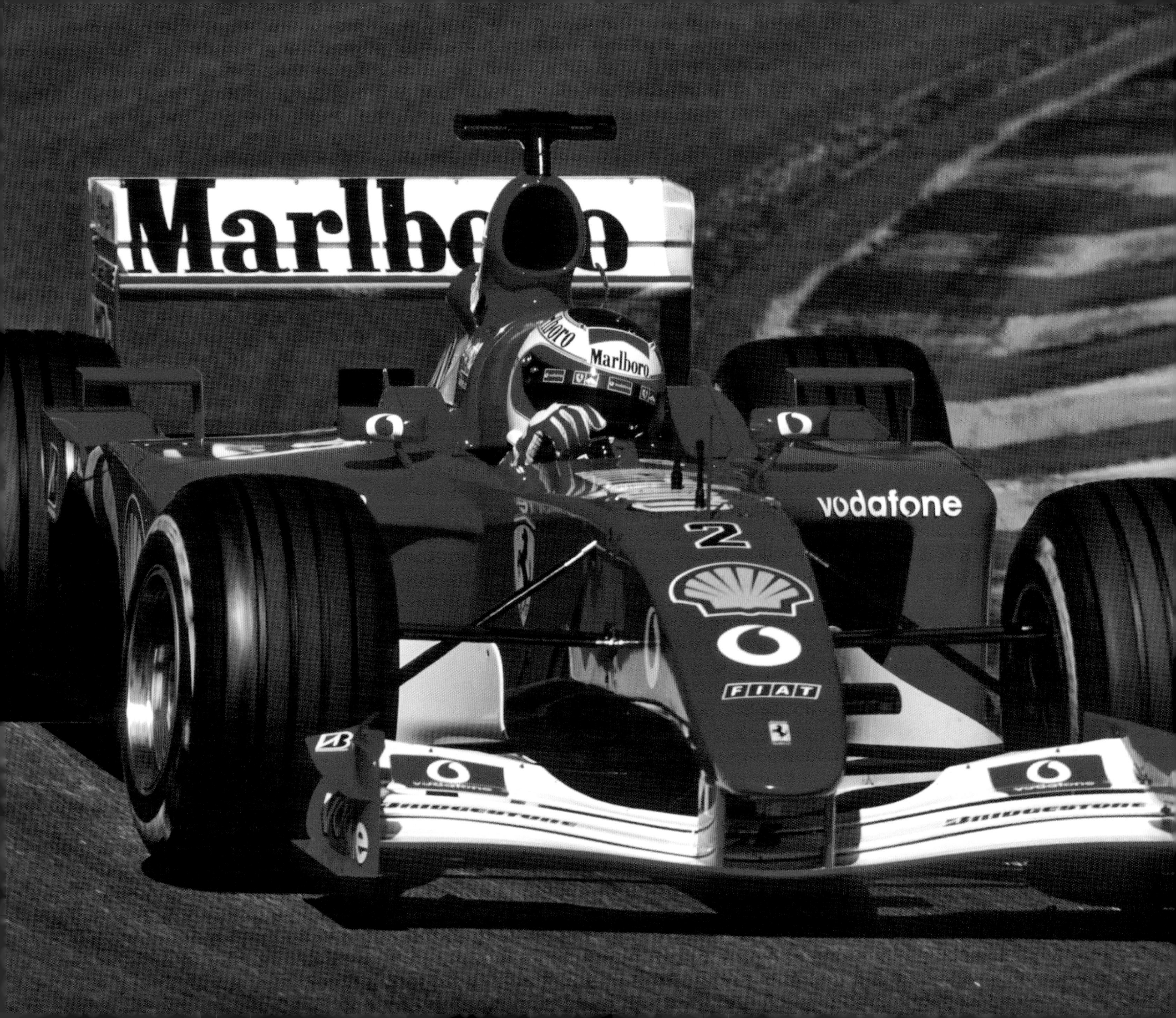
Marlboro
vodafone
2
FIAT

←
New rules mandated a higher front wing for 2001, which prompted Ferrari's designers to move from a high nose cone to a drooping one as they sought to recoup lost downforce.

←
Rubens Barrichello qualified his F2001 on pole position for the 2002 season opener but tangled with the Williams of Ralf Schumacher at the first corner.

in Spain, too, and the legalization of traction control did nothing to hamper Ferrari for the remainder of the year. Mercedes struggled to implement the system reliably, causing the McLarens of Mika Häkkinen and David Coulthard to stall on the grid on more than one occasion and have to start from the back; the increasingly demotivated Häkkinen announced that he was going on sabbatical at the end of the season. The Williams-BMWs of Ralf Schumacher (Michael's brother) and Juan Pablo Montoya took four wins over the course of the season but were not reliable enough to compete with Ferrari.

Nine wins for Michael Schumacher and a consistent run of podium finishes by his teammate Rubens Barrichello made this season a rout as Ferrari finished with 179 points to McLaren's 102, and Schumacher claimed the drivers' title once more.

When the F2002 wasn't deemed ready for the start of the 2002 season, the F2001 was rolled out again for the opening rounds.

←
The 2001 Australian Grand Prix set the tone for the season—Michael Schumacher led throughout from pole position.

Although doubts over its reliability meant the F2002 made its debut later than anticipated in the 2002 season, this profoundly innovative car would become Ferrari's most successful Grand Prix car since the 500, which dominated the World Championship in 1952–53. The keys to its success were Ferrari's deepening relationship with Bridgestone—whose supremacy had come under assault from the returning Michelin in 2001—along with an aggressive lightweighting program. Ferrari also continued to enjoy the benefits of virtually limitless testing at the Fiorano track opposite the factory gates in Maranello.

The 90-degree V-10 retained the architecture of its predecessor but was manufactured using a new casting process, and all the internals were revised to save weight and minimize rotating masses. It transmitted power through an all-new titanium-alloy gearbox that was smaller and stronger than the previous unit.

Aerodynamically, the F2002 represented an aggressive shift in concept. The nose was raised slightly compared with the 2001 car, the bargeboards were longer and lower, the furniture between the rear wheels and the sidepod was less fussy in appearance, and the rear suspension layout was also redesigned to tidy the airflow. Most significantly, the sidepods themselves were radically downsized as a consequence of Ferrari angling the radiators forward from the vertical; this enabled them to effectively maintain the same cooling surface but with less aerodynamic drag. New periscope-style exhausts exited from the rear deck behind curved fairings.

Changes to the design and manufacture of the suspension components yielded a chain of further weight savings. The net effect was a car that was well under the minimum weight, enabling the trackside engineers to add ballast strategically to tune its handling for different circuits.

Michael Schumacher won the first round of the season in the B-spec F2001, then finished third in Malaysia before swapping to the F2002 in Brazil. At Interlagos, the leading Michelin-equipped teams—McLaren and Williams—appeared to have the advantage, and in qualifying Schumacher's was the only Bridgestone-shod car in the top seven. From second on the grid, Schumacher took the lead at the first corner, survived a collision with Juan Pablo Montoya's Williams, and

Michael Schumacher gave the F2002 its debut in Brazil, the third round of the 2002 season, and won from second on the grid.

F2002 SPECIFICATIONS

Engine	2,997 cc 90-degree V-10	Suspension	Double wishbones with pushrod-actuated torsion bars/dampers (f/r)
Power	835 bhp @ 17,800 rpm	Brakes	Discs f/r
Gearbox	Seven-speed semiautomatic	Tires	Bridgestone
Chassis	Carbon fiber monocoque	Weight	595 kg

↑
The entire cooling architecture
was repackaged in the F2002,
with the radiators angled
forwards within the sidepods
to make this area of the car
dramatically lower. Upswept
winglets on each side helped
steer air over and around the
rear wheels.

then drove at a controlled pace that conned his rivals into believing he was running a two pit-stop strategy. By the time they realized he wasn't, it was too late: Schumacher had track position and the longevity of the Bridgestone rubber on his side.

This would be the first of ten wins for Schumacher in the F2002 that season, and teammate Rubens Barrichello would add four more. Schumacher finished every race on the podium. Remarkably, Ferrari remained cautious throughout the season, expecting to be wrong-footed by Michelin at any point. This was emphasized when they imposed team orders at round six in Austria, when Schumacher already had four wins in the bag and a commanding championship lead: calling upon Barrichello to cede the race lead and the win to Schumacher while they ran one-two provoked a storm of protest and led to the FIA imposing a ban on team orders. Five races later Schumacher won in France, securing the title with six rounds remaining.

The F2002 was competitive enough to be deployed over the first four rounds of 2003, taking one more win in Schumacher's hands.

↑
The prodigiously successful F2002 was also competitive in the first few rounds of 2003, although here in Brazil, Rubens Barrichello (pictured) retired with a fuel system failure.

←
Chimneys on the F2002's rear deck vented hot air from the radiators and used the hot exhaust gases to accelerate the flow, drawing out more air.

Three seasons of Ferrari superiority had proved fatiguing for those not bound in with the Maranello cause, and as such the FIA came under pressure to tweak the F1 regulations to improve the show. The headline change was a new points system that rewarded the top eight rather than the top six finishers and gave a slightly narrower spread of points. There was a change, too, to the qualifying system: each driver would now have just one flying lap in order to set a time. The idea here was to make the Saturday session a more compelling TV spectacle by adding a greater element of jeopardy.

Another change, introduced too late in the day for its effects to be factored in to car design, was a more subtle one: immediately after qualifying, each car entered *parc fermé* and could not be worked upon. That meant no components could be moved or swapped out, and no fuel could be added—each car would begin the race as it finished qualifying. The FIA's intention was to prevent teams from building cars that were in effect "qualifying specials" to gain advantage in the new qualifying format, but a side effect of the change was that teams could no longer adjust ballast to optimize the car's handling for race conditions. This would prove particularly problematic for the F2003-GA (named after the recently deceased Fiat magnate Gianni Agnelli) because its wheelbase was 2 inches longer than its predecessor. Weight distribution became a challenge at every round as Ferrari was forced to compromise between race pace and one-lap speed.

The fundamentals of the F2002 remained, with even more aggressively packaged sidepods now featuring an undercut that encouraged airflow attachment around the base of the body and steered to between the rear wheels. An even smaller gearbox mated to a redesigned and more compact V-10 to maximize rear-end performance.

Michael Schumacher already had one win on the board before the F2003-GA made its debut one round later than planned, in Spain. By then, McLaren's Kimi Räikkönen was leading the championship even though McLaren had been forced to delay the introduction of their radical new car, the MP4-18. Schumacher won the Spanish Grand Prix from pole in the new car, then again in Austria—though this time it was an inherited win after Räikkönen retired from the lead. He won again in Canada but for the next five rounds labored even to get near the podium.

F2004-GA SPECIFICATIONS

Engine	2,997 cc 90-degree V-10	Suspension	Double wishbones with pushrod-actuated torsion bars/dampers (f/r)
Power	845 bhp @ 18,300 rpm	Brakes	Discs f/r
Gearbox	Seven-speed semiautomatic	Tires	Bridgestone
Chassis	Carbon fiber monocoque	Weight	595 kg

← A midseason dip in results made the 2003 championship tougher for Michael Schumacher, but he put his season back on track with victories in Monza and here in Indianapolis.

F2004-GA

↑
One of the key differences between the F2003-GA and its predecessor was its 2-inch-longer wheelbase.

The fundamental problem of adjusting the F2003-GA's weight distribution under the new rules took the edge off its performance. But more than that, the tire war was becoming nasty. Michelin now undoubtedly had the upper hand, but that was about to change. The French rubber was much more square-shouldered than that of its rivals as a consequence of a different sidewall construction philosophy. Ferrari and Bridgestone argued—and won, supplying photographic evidence—that Michelin's front tires exceeded the maximum permitted tread width once they had started to wear down.

From the Italian Grand Prix onward, the FIA announced it would measure the tires after the race as well as beforehand, forcing the Michelin-supplied teams to adjust their setups—such as camber settings, pressures, and toe-in—to remain compliant. This cost performance, and Schumacher romped to victory at Monza and Indianapolis, retaking the lead in the drivers' championship. He sealed the deal in the final round at Suzuka, a peculiarly scrappy race in which he finished eighth in a car beset by vibrations after an earlier tire lockup.

↑
Aggressively undercut sidepods became a design trend in this era, facilitated by changing the shape and mounting angle of the radiators. The goal was encouraging smooth airflow around the base of the sidepod.

←
Shorter exhaust pipes than before helped to reduce weight, allied to an even lighter new engine block.

Having been caught out by the *parc fermé* rules introduced on the eve of the 2003 season, Ferrari entered the following year with a car that followed evolutionary principles while erasing the F2003-GA's weaknesses. Chiefly these arose from the '03 car's long-wheelbase concept, which gave a rearward weight bias that proved destructive to Ferrari's Bridgestone tires. The Bridgestones typically had stiffer sidewalls than their Michelin rivals, which made for more tread movement and therefore higher temperatures and more wear. The F2003-GA's balance had exacerbated this tendency, with a deleterious effect on race performance and strategy.

With this in mind, Ferrari shortened the wheelbase once more and redesigned the rear suspension in order to be gentler on the tires, while lowering the car's center of gravity. The F2004 followed the same fundamental aerodynamic principles of the cars from the previous two seasons but developed them further, with a more aggressive undercut around the sidepods and exhaust outlets mounted nearer the center line. The larger, simpler two-plane rear wing was a response to new regulations banning multielement setups.

Launch control systems were banned, a result of teams lobbying the FIA; Renault's starts had been noticeably excellent the previous season and nobody else had been able to set their systems up as effectively. But the most significant change was a new rule that all engines had to last for a complete race meeting; any engine change would result in a ten-place grid drop. This was another of FIA president Max Mosley's initiatives to reduce the costs of competing in F1 because manufacturer involvement over the course of the decade had prompted what amounted to an arms race.

Despite the attempted cap on engine performance, the 2004 season proved to be the peak of the V-10 era and generated many lap records that would stand for many years. Michael Schumacher won five consecutive races at the start of the year and then, after a brief interruption in service (a bizarre accident in the Monaco Grand Prix, where he locked his wheels behind the safety car and was struck from behind), he won the following seven. It was a crushing display of dominance; the F2004 won fifteen of the eighteen rounds, including eight one-two finishes.

← The F2004 was miles ahead of its rivals—as illustrated here at Spa-Francorchamps, where Michael Schumacher is already accelerating out of the La Source hairpin while the other drivers still negotiate the corner.

F2004 SPECIFICATIONS

Engine	2,997 cc 90-degree V-10	Suspension	Double wishbones with pushrod-actuated torsion bars/dampers (f/r)
Power	865 bhp @ 18,300 rpm	Brakes	Discs f/r
Gearbox	Seven-speed semiautomatic	Tires	Bridgestone
Chassis	Carbon fiber monocoque	Weight	600 kg

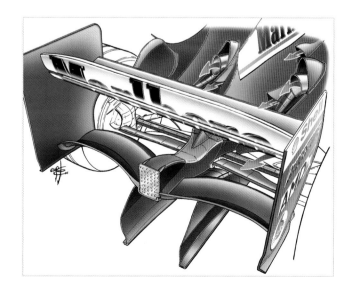

←
Ferrari one-two finishes continued as a regular sight throughout the 2004 season.

This would be Schumacher's seventh and final drivers' championship and Ferrari's sixth consecutive constructors' title. At the end of the season, Rory Byrne announced his intention to step back from front-line design duties and hand over more responsibility to his deputy, Aldo Costa, ahead of Byrne's planned retirement in 2006.

The F2004 would go on to see service in the first two round of 2005 before its replacement was ready. It also enjoyed a peculiar second life as the basis for the spec chassis in the A1 Grand Prix Championship, which launched in 2005 as a competition between national teams (theoretically, at least). After two seasons with Lola chassis, the championship reached a deal with Ferrari to adopt a new car based on the look of the F2004 but with a less sophisticated engine and chassis.

↑
Technical director Ross Brawn, test driver Luca Badoer, Rubens Barrichello, team principal Jean Todt, president Luca di Montezemolo, Michael Schumacher, chief designer Rory Byrne, and engine chief Paolo Martinelli look confident at the launch of the F2004.

←
This Giorgio Piola illustration shows how the hot air from the exhausts and radiators (orange arrows) is exploited by the aerodynamically shaped rear wishbone and the complex lower rear-wing element.

Ferrari's victory streak ended dramatically in 2005, as new technical regulations erased the key advantages of their car concept. The rules package included a move to smaller diffusers and wings, along with another change to the qualifying format: now the grid would be set by aggregate times from two different sessions. In practice this format was widely despised, and F1 returned to the previous format as of the European Grand Prix.

F2005

The key change was a ban on in-race tire stops except for compelling safety reasons. Because Ferrari's entire car philosophy had been based around running the smallest fuel tank possible and turning each race into a set of intermediate sprints, this represented a major hurdle. It was a challenge, too, for Bridgestone, whose products had been optimized around multiple changes. The company went too conservative in response to the new regulations and the tires lacked grip in comparison with Michelin's.

All this became apparent in the opening races of 2005, as the Michelin-shod Renault R25s left Ferrari standing. The F2005 was rushed into service in Bahrain, two rounds earlier than planned, after a catastrophic Malaysian Grand Prix in which excess tire wear caused Rubens Barrichello to retire and Michael Schumacher to limp home in seventh.

The F2005 was the first Ferrari credited to Aldo Costa, but it was essentially a nuanced reworking of the F2004 in terms of its aerodynamics, and its principal innovation was its carbon fiber gearbox casing. Engines now had

to last for two races rather than one, but reliability was generally not Ferrari's problem in 2005.

Schumacher managed one victory, but it was an empty one: at the U.S. Grand Prix in Indianapolis, the Michelin teams were forced to withdraw after a string of tire failures, and only the six Bridgestone runners started the race.

↑
Schumacher labored to 10th place in the 2005 Italian Grand Prix, a minute and a half behind the McLaren of race winner Juan Pablo Montoya.

←
Ferrari's struggles through 2005 are summed up by the Japanese Grand Prix—where Renault's Fernando Alonso passed Michael Schumacher twice .

F2005 SPECIFICATIONS

Engine	2,997 cc 90-degree V-10	Suspension	Double wishbones with pushrod-actuated torsion bars/dampers (f/r)
Power	865 bhp @ 18,300 rpm	Brakes	Discs f/r
Gearbox	Seven-speed semiautomatic	Tires	Bridgestone
Chassis	Carbon fiber monocoque	Weight	600 kg

After the competitive blip of the 2005 season, Ferrari regrouped in 2006 as a fresh batch of regulatory changes offered new opportunities. The widely disliked ban on in-race tire changes was rescinded on safety grounds after a number of high-profile failures the previous season. A cap on the number of sets of tires each driver could use each weekend maintained a focus on efficient use of resources, though, and it came with a new three-stage qualifying format in which the slowest cars in the first two sessions were eliminated in groups, leaving the remaining ten to engage in a shoot-out for pole position. Teams would now have to be much more strategic in their tire use all through the weekend.

The greatest change of all was an entirely new engine format. Now, 2.4-liter V-8s replaced the V-10s, with a mandatory 90-degree vee angle and a cap of four valves per cylinder. Downsized engines created room for aerodynamic maneuver and the new 248 F1 was much narrower than the F2005 around the engine and transmission cover, creating a large expanse of bare floor behind the sidepod.

The three-element front wing had a more pronounced "spoon" section at the center, with the endplates sweeping in at an angle. The bargeboards were more elaborate, and to the rear of the sidepod a secondary horizontal element at midheight swept up toward the back tire, with a secondary winglet mounted above it. The mirrors were relocated from the cockpit sides to the front corner of the sidepods.

Michael Schumacher and new teammate Felipe Massa picked up nine wins between them, but Renault's Fernando Alonso beat Schumacher to the title by 134 points to 121.

↑
Schumacher's last race before retirement was marred by a puncture that put him almost a lap down.

248 F1 SPECIFICATIONS

Engine	2,398 cc 90-degree V-8	Suspension	Double wishbones with pushrod-actuated torsion bars/dampers (f/r)
Power	750 bhp @ 18,500 rpm	Brakes	Discs f/r
Gearbox	Seven-speed semiautomatic	Tires	Bridgestone
Chassis	Carbon fiber monocoque	Weight	605 kg

Michelin's withdrawal at the end of 2006 ended Formula 1's debilitating tire war and promised a level playing field of sorts. Also, 2007 was the first year in which engine development was theoretically frozen—limited changes were permitted, provided manufacturers could build a case that they were for reliability or safety. Naturally, this led to a below-the-radar arms race, but principally the key performance differentiator besides the engine would now be aerodynamics. There were also marginal gains to be found in minimizing gearshift times through "seamless-shift" transmissions, which became another area of considerable investment.

The year 2007 marked the beginning of a new epoch at Ferrari, as team principal Jean Todt stepped away and handed over the reins to Stefano Domenicali, technical director Ross Brawn went on sabbatical, and former chief designer Rory Byrne completed his handover to Aldo Costa and new chief designer Nikolas Tombazis. There was change in the cockpit, too, as Kimi Räikkönen replaced Michael Schumacher, who went into retirement not entirely willingly.

Although the F2007 carried over many elements of the 248 F1, it represented a step change in aerodynamic philosophy. For several seasons a number of Ferrari's rivals had been experimenting with "twin keel" front suspension setups in which the lower wishbones mounted to slim vertical extensions of the nose. This enabled the main section of the underside of the nose to be higher, expediting airflow under the car. But it also came with trade-offs in rigidity. Byrne had kept faith with a single keel extending below the nose and mounting the wishbones to this, sacrificing maximum aero performance for a more rigid chassis. Now Ferrari embraced what was known as the "zero keel," in which the bottom wishbones were mounted further up the hub carrier than before, and both wishbones angled upward to meet the nose rather than being parallel with the ground.

To spice up the spectacle, Bridgestone had been compelled to supply two tire variations for each Grand Prix, one softer than the other and theoretically faster but less durable. Drivers had to use both in each race, and the softer variant was marked with a white band around one of the grooves. In testing it became apparent that the rear tires were very sensitive while the fronts

← Teamwork made the dream work for Ferrari as Felipe Massa moved over for teammate Kimi Räikkönen in Brazil, enabling him to win the World Championship on a day McLaren self-destructed.

F2007 SPECIFICATIONS

Engine	2,398 cc 90-degree V-8	Suspension	Double wishbones with pushrod-actuated torsion bars/ dampers (f/r)
Power	780 bhp @ 19,000 rpm	Brakes	Discs f/r
Gearbox	Seven-speed semiautomatic	Tires	Bridgestone
Chassis	Carbon fiber monocoque	Weight	605 kg

F2007

↑
Räikkönen was third in the points going into the season finale at Interlagos but came away with the title by a single point.

were a little too hard and difficult to bring up to working temperature. As such, a number of teams, including Ferrari, began to add aerodynamic furniture to the front of their cars to work the front axle harder.

Having built their cars around a rearward weight bias for better traction while being Michelin's preferred partner, Renault abruptly fell from the sharp end of the grid and the season became a battle between Ferrari and McLaren. Räikkönen won the first round

of the year but then didn't stand on the top step of the podium again until midseason, by which time teammate Felipe Massa had won two of his own and the McLaren pairing of Fernando Alonso and Lewis Hamilton also had two apiece.

Against the background of this finely balanced four-way battle for the drivers' championship, a more disturbing narrative developed. It emerged that Ferrari's chief mechanic, Nigel Stepney, had grown disenchanted with

←
Sloping radiators enabled a greater surface area within the F2007's sidepods. Note how the short, high exhausts are placed to energize airflow over the rear deck. *James Mann*

↓
The F2007 signaled a change in design philosophy at Ferrari, using a higher nose with a zero-keel attachment for the lower front wishbones.

his career prospects and passed a dossier of sensitive technical information to McLaren designer Mike Coughlan. McLaren would later be fined and have their constructors' championship points revoked.

Räikkönen was third in the points going into the final round in Brazil, but as McLaren's race dissolved into a series of blunders, the advantage swung his way. Victory at Interlagos brought him the title by a point from Hamilton and Alonso.

The F2008 was born into a political landscape of abject bitterness: Ferrari, having won both the drivers' and the constructors' championships in 2007, remained angry at the theft of their intellectual property during that season's spying scandal. Equally there were those who felt that the $100 million fine levied against McLaren was disproportionate given how few within the organization had access to Ferrari data. Regardless of sensitivities, the British team had to submit to several forensic inspections of their 2008 designs by FIA watchdogs in order to prove themselves free of Ferrari influence.

For the Ferrari engineering team, the key tasks would be to sharpen up in several areas in which the F2007 had been found wanting. Reliability could have been better, as could performance in slower corners and chassis dynamics over bumps. There were small but significant regulatory changes, too: gearboxes had to last for four races on pain of a five-place grid penalty and more padding around the drivers' heads had become mandatory. But the most far-reaching technical change was the removal of electronic driver aids, such as traction control, via a homologated Engine Control Unit (ECU). This item was standardized across the whole grid and enabled manufacturers and teams to exercise a degree of freedom in terms of engine mapping, but it was in effect a sandbox. Its introduction was not without controversy because the single supplier that had won the bid was McLaren Electronic Systems, a subsidiary of Ferrari's reviled enemy.

The suspension layout of the F2008 was virtually identical to the 2007 car but for a 0.5-inch trim to the wheelbase, achieved by repositioning the front wishbones slightly. To add compliance over bumps, the carbon fiber layup of the suspension components and the damping were adjusted.

While the F2008 was evolutionary in terms of its aerodynamics, the nose cone was slightly more challenging in terms of driver comfort, taking the shrink-wrapped approach to extremes. It was narrower in width and height than before, with a greater space underneath. The undercut now ran all the way back to the main part of the tub, with a small bulge to accommodate the base of the driver's seat in the hip area.

The season-opening Australian Grand Prix was a disappointment: Felipe Massa qualified only fourth, while a fuel pump issue consigned Kimi Räikkönen to sixteenth on the grid, then both retired from the race

F2008 SPECIFICATIONS

Engine	2,398 cc 90-degree V-8	**Suspension**	Double wishbones with pushrod-actuated torsion bars/dampers (f/r)
Power	820 bhp @ 19,000 rpm	**Brakes**	Discs f/r
Gearbox	Seven-speed semiautomatic	**Tires**	Bridgestone
Chassis	Carbon fiber monocoque	**Weight**	605 kg

←
Felipe Massa won six races in 2008 and became Ferrari's focus as Kimi Räikkönen's title defense faded midseason.

→
The so-called s-duct became a design trend in this era, creating a channel between the upper and lower surfaces of the nose cone and relieving potential aerodynamic blockages behind the front wing.

with engine failure. But they won the next four races between them as McLaren's MP4-23 demonstrated a tendency to spin up its rear wheels while accelerating out of slow corners, damaging its tires. McLaren's Australian Grand Prix winner Lewis Hamilton picked up a valuable victory in Monaco when a puncture forced him into a strategic gamble that paid off, and he emerged as the main championship challenger to the Ferrari drivers. From midseason onward, Räikkönen's bid to retain his title faded after he failed to finish in Canada (where Hamilton accidentally drove into the back of him in the pit lane) and then a broken exhaust cost him victory in France. After a rancorous Belgian Grand Prix, where Hamilton was penalized for cutting a chicane while passing Räikkönen (who crashed a lap later) for the lead, handing Massa the win, it was Massa who established himself as Ferrari's strongest candidate for the drivers' title.

After Massa failed to finish in Singapore, having left his pit box with the fuel hose still attached, Hamilton regained the initiative in the points. In a dramatic final round in Brazil, Massa crossed the line first and thought he'd won the championship—only for Hamilton to pick up a position on the final lap and beat him to the silverware by one point.

→
Massa showed tremendous sportsmanship on the day he won his home grand prix from pole but lost the World Championship to Lewis Hamilton by one point.

The year 2009 was meant to be a fresh start for Formula 1, as it embraced wide-ranging changes with a view to improving overtaking. Grands Prix certainly proved to be a lot different in terms of who was fighting whom for victories; in the scramble to develop their cars while battling for the 2008 championship, Ferrari and McLaren neglected to advance their new designs adequately and were caught out.

For two seasons the FIA's Overtaking Working Group had been evaluating and refining the new rules to be introduced in 2009. History now judges these to be a failure because they were fundamentally flawed and contained loopholes that certain teams were permitted to exploit for political purposes. To improve overtaking—theoretically—slick tires replaced the much-hated grooved rubber, front wings were wider and lower and featured flaps that could be adjusted from the cockpit, and the rear wings were higher and narrower. Aerodynamic paraphernalia such as winglets and bargeboards were outlawed, though flow conditioners were still permitted in a limited area by the sidepod openings.

Maximum engine revs were reduced from 19,000 to 18,000 rpm, and drivers were limited to eight engines per season. Kinetic energy recovery systems (KERS) were introduced as an option; these devices reclaimed energy that would otherwise have been dissipated as heat under braking and enabled it to be recycled into a driver-controlled power boost of 80 bhp for 6.5 seconds per lap. Experience would demonstrate that this was barely enough to compensate for the additional weight, and many teams opted to run without.

The unfortunate irony of these costly changes arriving during the worst global economic crisis in decades was not lost on the competitors. Ferrari team principal Stefano Domenicali used the launch of the F60 as a platform to denounce the expense involved in implementing the new rules package. One could argue that this was mildly disingenuous because the teams had combined to frustrate FIA president Max Mosley's attempts to implement a budget cap, and the new rules did include measures to reduce track testing and limit the scope of wind tunnel simulations.

The regulatory change required a complete change in aerodynamic philosophy, which made the F60 very different from its predecessor. A raised nose and shorter splitter aimed to increase airflow under the car, mitigating the loss of aerodynamic furniture up front, and the Ferrari design team had focused on exploiting the wording of the rules in the sidepod area to create relatively intricate flow conditioners in which the mirrors were integrated.

← New rules for 2009 mandated lower, wider front wings and higher, narrower rear wings. The results were rather ugly and failed to deliver the anticipated improvements in overtaking.

F60 SPECIFICATIONS

Engine	2,398 cc 90-degree V-8 with kinetic energy recovery system	Suspension	Double wishbones with pushrod-actuated torsion bars/dampers (f/r)
Power	760 bhp @ 18,000 rpm	Brakes	Discs f/r
Gearbox	Seven-speed semiautomatic	Tires	Bridgestone
Chassis	Carbon fiber monocoque	Weight	605 kg

↑
Kimi Räikkönen had a
lackluster season and fell
out of favor with Ferrari—
though he won here at Spa-
Francorchamps, one of the
great drivers' circuits.

But they missed two key areas of exploitation at the front and rear.

Under the leadership of former Ferrari technical director Ross Brawn, Honda had abandoned development of their flawed 2008 car early and threw all their resources at 2009. Though Honda withdrew from F1 that winter, Brawn and his management team acquired the organization and ran it on a shoestring with a Mercedes V-8 shoehorned into the back of the car. This vehicle dominated the first half of the 2009 season for two reasons: Brawn's team had discovered and exploited the ability to use the front wings' subsidiary planes to wash air outside the front wheels, and they had identified a loophole in the diffuser regulations that enabled them to add a second plane inside it.

Ferrari were among several teams to protest the "double diffuser," but their objections, controversially, were rejected, forcing them to adopt the design themselves. The shape of the F60's transmission meant Ferrari's version carried inherent compromise.

After a huge development push—including a new floor—the F60 gained some performance late in the season, enabling Kimi Räikkönen to win in Belgium.

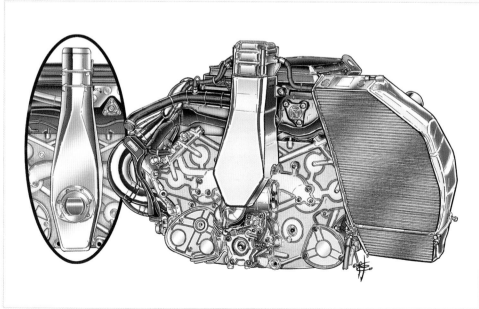

↑
Whether by adhering too closely to the letter of the law (which now demanded less sophisticated aerodynamics) or by overfocusing on in-season development during 2008, Ferrari missed several loopholes in the design of the F60.

←
The F60's kinetic energy recovery system (inset) was centrally mounted on the engine and integral to the weight balance of the car, which made it impossible for Ferrari to follow the lead of other teams in dropping the disappointing technology.

CHAPTER 7

After the breakup of the team that had generated so much success in the 1990s—Michael Schumacher and Rory Byrne into retirement, Jean Todt into politics as president of the FIA, Ross Brawn into a team leader in his own right—Ferrari slid back into old bad habits. Management began to wilt under the onslaught from above and from the Italian media, and relations between the different departments in Maranello soured in a morass of backstabbing.

Ferrari would burn through three team principals in five years, one remaining in the position for but a handful of months. It was a similar tale of revolving doors in the factory as designers and technical directors came and went.

Two teams achieved dominance in this decade, and they were not Ferrari. Red Bull achieved mastery of sophisticated aerodynamics during the homologated-engine era and Ferrari failed to stay in step. When engines became a performance differentiator with the introduction of hybrid powertrains in 2014, once again Ferrari lagged. This was particularly shameful: to Enzo Ferrari, the engine was the most important element of the car—of greater significance than the driver.

But Ferrari would end the decade with arguably the most powerful engine in F1, even if they fell short of winning championships. That at least would have yielded some satisfaction for the company founder, had he been alive to witness it.

←

Few pictures capture the extent to which Ferrari went off the rails in the 2010s quite as much as this. The team began 2017 with a competitive car, but Sebastian Vettel's title challenge imploded late in the season. This collision with teammate Kimi Räikkönen was just one of several disasters.

Having prudently decided to shelve ongoing development of the fundamentally flawed F60 during 2009, Ferrari returned to form in the first season of the new decade. While the F10 carried over a number of design features from its predecessor, including the fundamentals of the suspension layout, the outboard rearview mirrors, and the slim, protuberant nose tip, it differed greatly in detail.

While many of the changes were necessary to comply with new technical regulations for 2010, others were clean-sheet design responses to innovations Ferrari's competitors had introduced the previous season. The F10 was noticeably longer than the F60, both overall and in terms of its wheelbase; in-race refueling had been banned, which meant all cars had to accommodate larger fuel tanks, and the minimum car weight was raised to 620 kilograms.

In a rare bout of consensus, F1's teams had agreed to drop the widely disliked kinetic energy recovery systems until they could be implemented properly and in a way in which their performance justified the additional bulk. Other changes to the regulatory regime included narrower front wheels (down from 11 inches to 9.6 inches), a new scoring system that allocated points to the top ten finishers, and a tweak to the knock-out qualifying format.

Following Gilles Simon's departure to a senior job with the FIA, Luca Marmorini rejoined from the defunct Toyota F1 project as engine and electronics director. Although engine development remained theoretically frozen, mapping would prove to be a key battleground in the coming seasons.

The F10's engine and transmission were inclined upward toward the rear, at 3.5 degrees from the horizontal, in order to accommodate an extreme interpretation of the double-diffuser concept. To reduce weight, the exhausts were shortened and the outlet located further forward. At the front, the wing endplates adopted the outwash philosophy, and the rest of the aerodynamic furniture downstream of this was shaped to exploit this effect. Ferrari cleverly circumvented the wording of new rules banning aerodynamic wheel shrouds, fitting a pair of concentric rings to the rims of both front wheels, but elsewhere they were once again caught out by rivals' innovations.

Late in preseason testing it became apparent that Red Bull was using low-mounted exhausts to boost the effect of their car's diffuser and had disguised this to an extent by painting fake outlets in the conventional position. Arguably cleverer still was McLaren's "f-duct," a device that channeled air from an intake at the front of the car, through a tube in the cockpit, then on through

F10 SPECIFICATIONS

Engine	2,398 cc 90-degree V-8	Suspension	Double wishbones with pushrod-actuated torsion bars/dampers (f/r)
Power	800 bhp @ 18,000 rpm	Brakes	Discs f/r
Gearbox	Seven-speed semiautomatic	Tires	Bridgestone
Chassis	Carbon fiber monocoque	Weight	620 kg

↑
Massa returned from injury in 2010 but increasingly became treated as the number two to Alonso.

the engine cover to the rear wing. By selectively covering a hole in the tube with their leg, the driver could in effect stall the rear wing, reducing drag and enabling the car to reach a higher top speed. Because no moving parts were involved, this did not run afoul of rules barring movable aerodynamic devices.

Ferrari's new signing Fernando Alonso and Felipe Massa finished one-two in the season-opening Bahrain Grand Prix, but only after the leading Red Bull of Sebastian Vettel was stymied by a spark plug failure. The F10 would become a genuine threat only by midseason,

after Ferrari copied the Red Bull exhaust layout and developed a variation of the f-duct. There were a number of controversies, as Ferrari was accused of running wings that flexed at high speed and, like several other teams, they were hit by a ban on outboard-mounted mirrors. Still, Alonso won four more Grands Prix and arrived at the final race of the year in contention for the championship—but Ferrari squandered the opportunity with a mistimed pit stop that mired Alonso in traffic and consigned him to seventh place at the flag.

Braking systems on modern F1 cars are incredibly complex—and compact, since they must be packaged entirely within the wheel or harm the delicate aerodynamic balance. Teams will change the size of the air inlet duct depending on circuit configuration.

By midseason Ferrari had adapted the F10 to feature a Red Bull–style exhaust layout, as well as a version of McLaren's "f-duct," a drag-reducing aerodynamic device.

The F150—named to celebrate the 150th anniversary of Italy's unification—was barely out of the blocks when it had to be rebranded as the 150° Italia as Ford threatened legal action over the name, which was already taken by the Blue Oval's pickup. It was an inauspicious beginning for a car that would enjoy little success.

While overtaking—or the lack thereof—had provoked much consternation during the previous season, so too had technical innovations such as McLaren's f-duct. The FIA banned such systems for 2011, along with double diffusers, and imposed new crash-protection regulations that had far-reaching effects on chassis design. Minimum weight rose again, to 640 kilograms, as KERS was reintroduced alongside the drag reduction system (DRS)—in effect a safer and legally defined development of the f-duct. The DRS aimed to boost overtaking by enabling drivers to drop the main plane of their rear wing in specified areas of the track.

The biggest change of all was F1's move to a new tire supplier, Pirelli, briefed to develop products that would lose performance abruptly after a finite amount of use.

New tires required different geometry, and the 150° Italia's chassis was a major step change from its predecessor. The monocoque and nose were much taller, requiring the front wishbones to be angled upward, and the rear wishbones were also more acutely profiled in plan view.

Ferrari struggled to get the most out of the new tires, but they were also caught out by Red Bull's trick engine mapping, which maintained a flow of hot gas to the diffuser by burning fuel in the exhausts when the driver was off the throttle. Fernando Alonso won just one race all year and technical director Aldo Costa was fired midseason, replaced by former McLaren man Pat Fry.

↑
The floor area at the rear of F1 cars became a focus of development as designers looked to use hot flow from the exhaust to accelerate airflow and boost downforce. Note the Ferrari's wide and flat exhausts mounted flush to the floor.

←
A change of tire supplier for 2011 required new suspension geometry and a change of concept. Ferrari opted for a taller, narrower nose treatment with angled wishbones.

150° ITALIA SPECIFICATIONS

Engine	2,398 cc 90-degree V-8 with kinetic energy recovery system	Suspension	Double wishbones with pushrod-actuated torsion bars/dampers (f/r)
Power	800 bhp @ 18,000 rpm	Brakes	Discs f/r
Gearbox	Seven-speed semiautomatic	Tires	Pirelli
Chassis	Carbon fiber monocoque	Weight	640 kg

Bruised by a miserable 2011 season, Ferrari promised that the first car designed under Pat Fry's technical leadership would be less conservative. The F2012 certainly looked very different, although its rather ugly stepped nose wasn't unique: new rules had reduced the maximum height of the nose from 24.5 inches to 22 inches beyond the front bulkhead, and the majority of the field adopted this letter-of-the-law solution.

Other rule changes sought to rein in the practice of using hydraulically actuated reactive ride-height systems, along with the use of exhaust gases to augment the effects of the diffuser. This entailed a higher mandatory exhaust height and a ban on exotic throttle mapping, but this area would continue to prove controversial throughout the season.

The front of the F2012 was most striking, featuring a very thin nose and long, angled pillars supporting the wing. Behind that the front suspension was pullrod actuated, enabling a lower center of gravity because the springs and dampers were below their conventional positions.

Seven different drivers won the first seven races, and it was only at round eight, in Valencia, that Ferrari's Fernando Alonso became the second double winner. But the F2012 lacked pace in qualifying and was down on cornering performance compared with its rivals from McLaren and Red Bull. McLaren had found a way to circumvent the blown-diffuser regulations using what is known as the Coanda effect, the tendency of liquids or gases to follow a curved surface. It proved singularly difficult to copy effectively and exposed shortcomings in

the wind tunnel that forced Ferrari to close its facility for upgrades and temporarily move into Toyota's tunnel in Cologne, Germany.

This hamstrung development but, thanks to various misfortunes afflicting his rivals, Alonso remained in the hunt for the drivers' championship until the final round, falling three points short of Red Bull's Sebastian Vettel.

↑
The F2012's ugly stepped nose was typical of this year's crop of F1 cars, the result of poorly phrased technical regulations. Pullrod-actuated front suspension offered a lower center of gravity in this crucial area.

←
Ferrari opted for a more aggressive design approach in 2012, feeling that conservatism was creeping in to the detriment of competitiveness.

F2012 SPECIFICATIONS

Engine	2,398 cc 90-degree V-8 with kinetic energy recovery system	Suspension	Double wishbones with pullrod-actuated torsion bars/dampers (f/r)
Power	800 bhp @ 18,000 rpm	Brakes	Discs f/r
Gearbox	Seven-speed semiautomatic	Tires	Pirelli
Chassis	Carbon fiber monocoque	Weight	640 kg

F2012

The consequences of another disappointing season manifested themselves in the form of another reorganization of the technical team over the winter of 2012, this time adding resources to remove some of the load from chief designer Nikolas Tombazis. Having focused on development of the F2012 until season's end, Ferrari's aim was to split its design team with one group directing in-season development and another working exclusively on the following year's chassis. This was particularly important at this point, given the widespread changes coming in 2014.

Since the Maranello wind tunnel was offline for an upgrade throughout its development, the F138 was researched entirely in the Toyota wind tunnel in Cologne, Germany. Though it was a nuanced evolution of the F2012, the new car continued to exhibit signs of lack of correlation between the wind tunnel results and on-track behavior—particularly after Pirelli was compelled to abandon their new steel-belt radial tires midseason.

The F138 retained pullrod-actuated suspension front and rear and featured a dummy panel to conceal the step in the nose. But while it initially appeared competitive, and Fernando Alonso won in China and Spain, it became clear that the F138's strengths lay in it being relatively easygoing on the sensitive new Pirelli rubber. Successive aerodynamic upgrades failed to yield the anticipated gains in performance and, when a string of dramatic delaminations prompted Pirelli to revert to Kevlar-Aramid belt construction from the Hungarian Grand Prix onward, Ferrari's key advantage was gone. Red Bull were now able to work their tires harder, unlocking aero performance in their car (particularly from the Coanda-effect exhausts blowing the diffuser). Sebastian Vettel won the last nine races of the season to claim the championship, 155 points clear of Alonso.

↑
With its own wind tunnel offline for upgrades, Ferrari had to hire the Toyota facility in Cologne, Germany. It struggled to get the most out of the difficult-to-perfect Coanda exhaust concept.

←
The F138 was sympathetic to its tires, a key advantage as Pirelli's new range proved fragile, and Fernando Alonso won in China and here at home in Spain. A midseason reversion to the previous season's tire construction then eliminated one of the car's strengths.

F138 SPECIFICATIONS

Engine	2,398 cc 90-degree V-8 with kinetic energy recovery system	Suspension	Double wishbones with pullrod-actuated torsion bars/dampers (f/r)
Power	800 bhp @ 18,000 rpm	Brakes	Discs f/r
Gearbox	Seven-speed semiautomatic	Tires	Pirelli
Chassis	Carbon fiber monocoque	Weight	642 kg

F138

In 2014, a year later than originally planned, Formula 1's biggest shift in powertrain philosophy since the 1960s was implemented. Hoping to remain in step with movements in the wider automotive world, and with the explicit aim of enticing more manufacturers to join, the championship embraced the philosophy of downsized turbocharged hybrid engines augmented by electrical motors.

The new mandatory powertrain represented an enormous shift in thinking. Each car could carry no more than 100 kilograms of fuel—previously they would have started races with around 160 kilos—and the flow of that fuel to the engine (monitored by an optical system giving continuous reports to the FIA) was capped at 100 kilos per hour. The internal combustion engine within each car was a 1.6-liter V-6 fed by a single turbocharger and a group of electrical mechanisms that were an evolution of the kinetic energy recovery systems that had been in use since 2011. These had been allowed to produce a driver-controlled boost of 80 bhp for 6.7 seconds per lap; now they could output 160 bhp for 33 seconds. The amount of energy that could be recovered was also increased. Under the new regime, the hybrid systems went from having only a marginal impact on lap time to being significant performance differentiators—but to accommodate them, the minimum weight limit rose from 642 kilos to 690.

Reliability traps lurked because the motor generator unit technology was new: the MGU-H (for "heat") recycled heat from the exhaust to keep the turbo compressor spinning, theoretically eliminating lag, while the MGU-K (for "kinetic") was a development of the kinetic energy recovery system (KERS) that could recover (through braking) or deploy energy via the rear axle. Each element was subject to the same five-per-season limit as the internal combustion engine. Problems in these areas would come to define Ferrari's year.

The FIA also sought to reduce aero performance, as well as the risk of injury in T-boning incidents, by mandating further reductions in the height of the nose (from 22.8 inches above the car's floor to 5.3 inches) and the front of the chassis (from 24.6 inches to 20.6).

As such, the 2014 generation of cars were curious-looking beasts that generally had sharply sloping nose cones beyond the bulkhead, with peculiar protuberances at the tip. Ferrari's solution with the F14 T was among the least aesthetically disagreeable of the crop.

The new noses, plus a small reduction in front wing width and the move to a single high-mounted exhaust outlet, dictated a change in aerodynamic philosophy and,

←
By the Brazilian Grand Prix, Fernando Alonso had already fallen out with team principal Marco Mattiacci (the second of three people to hold that role at Ferrari in 2014) and decided to leave.

F14T SPECIFICATIONS

Engine	1,600 cc 90-degree turbocharged hybrid V-6	Suspension	Double wishbones with pullrod-actuated torsion bars/dampers (f/r)
Power	790 bhp @ 15,000 rpm	Brakes	Discs f/r
Gearbox	Eight-speed semiautomatic	Tires	Pirelli
Chassis	Carbon fiber monocoque	Weight	690 kg

↑

Poorly phrased technical
regulations made the front end
of the 2014 cars aesthetically
disagreeable, but the SF14
T's drooping snout was by no
means the ugliest.

like the rest of the 2014 field, the SF14 T was rather bulky. Packaging the hybrid power units and allowing for their cooling requirements was still an inexact science.

It rapidly became clear that the new power units had become the chief arbiter of performance where once aerodynamics had ruled supreme—and, not only that, Mercedes's package was the most powerful, reliable, and thoroughly developed. Ferrari's lacked both top-end power and drivability; it was very abrupt in its action, as was the car's brake-by-wire system (mandatory at the rear this season because of the way the MGU-K affected the rear axle).

Fernando Alonso and the returning Kimi Räikkönen simply could not compete with their Mercedes-engined rivals, and managed just one podium between them. The F14 T was the first Ferrari not to win a race since 1993, and chaos ensued: team principal Stefano Domenicali fell on his sword in April and his replacement, Marco Mattiacci, was sacked at the end of the season after falling out with Alonso, who quit. Technical director Pat Fry and engine director Luca Marmorini were shown the door in summer.

↑
The new formula for 2014 mandated a single high-mounted exhaust outlet, intended to eliminate the practice of using exhaust gas flow to blow the diffuser.

←
The diffuser remained a key area of development; teams routinely used flow-vis paint on aerodynamic surfaces such as this to verify airflow patterns during practice sessions.

Fiat Chrysler Group CEO Sergio Marchionne, having added the position of Ferrari president to his résumé over the winter following the departure of Luca di Montezemolo, quickly made his presence felt in the form of pressure behind the scenes. New team principal Maurizio Arrivabene—a curious choice for the role, given his former life as a Marlboro PR and marketing executive—announced at the launch of the SF15-T that Ferrari's target for 2015 was to win at least two races. A humble target for such a historic team, perhaps, but not given the prevailing circumstances in F1.

Mercedes's dominance of the new hybrid engine era was a result of them having started development of the concept in 2011, when the change was first discussed, and the FIA placing tight constraints on development (in the form of a system of limited tokens) once the powertrains were introduced. Hence Mercedes felt able to adopt the variable-length inlet plenums now permitted for 2015. Ferrari did not, because they were still focusing on debugging their energy-recovery systems and reducing the engine's cooling demands.

Ferrari also felt the time was not yet right to adopt Mercedes's game-changing split turbo design in which the intake and compressor were mounted at the front of the engine and the exhaust-driven turbine at the rear, with the MGU-H packaged within the vee. Cooling, bearing loads, and torsional stresses on the shaft made this concept difficult to perfect. Instead they worked on refining the cylinder head design to improve structural rigidity and combustion efficiency and introduced new control electronics midseason as part of a package of hybrid system upgrades. The oil tank was also relocated from within the gearbox housing to the front of the engine, the exhaust pipe shapes were refined, and the turbocharger was fitted with a larger turbine in an effort to cure the energy-harvesting issues that had plagued the team the previous season.

New technical director James Allison, formerly Pat Fry's deputy and a Maranello man of old before a sojourn with Renault and Lotus, opted for evolution elsewhere on the car—apart from the markedly different nose. The FIA had reacted to the aesthetic abominations of 2014 by tidying up the regulations governing the crash structures at the front. Ferrari's solution was a round-edged shape that drooped low and projected ahead of the front wing. Further aft the pullrod suspension concept was retained, though

Kimi Räikkönen spent much of his second Ferrari tenure being chided by chairman Sergio Marchionne for underperforming, but late in 2015 he registered a podium finish in Singapore, followed by fourth here at Suzuka.

SF15-T SPECIFICATIONS

Engine	1,600 cc 90-degree turbocharged hybrid V-6	Suspension	Double wishbones with pullrod-actuated torsion bars/dampers (f/r)
Power	830 bhp @ 15,000 rpm	Brakes	Discs f/r
Gearbox	Eight-speed semiautomatic	Tires	Pirelli
Chassis	Carbon fiber monocoque	Weight	690 kg

Four-time world champion
Sebastian Vettel joined Ferrari
for 2015 and claimed two race
victories in a car that still
wasn't the fastest in the field.

Revisions to the technical
regulations governing the nose
enabled Ferrari to develop
a less ugly front end for the
SF15-T.

↑
Vettel's win in Hungary was
a fine opportunist smash-
and-grab as he passed the
dominant Mercedes and then
held on for victory.

Ferrari adopted the aerodynamic wishbone shapes pioneered by Mercedes in 2014 and took advantage of the lower nose to angle the wishbones less steeply. The body itself was more tightly packaged than the SF14 T's, thanks to more angled radiators that also permitted smaller cooling apertures. It was also heavier because the weight limit had been increased to 702 kilograms as a consequence of complaints that the previous limit had been too low, and several drivers had been forced on to extreme diets.

The SF15-T proved much more competitive in the hands of Ferrari's new lead driver, the four-time champion Sebastian Vettel. If Vettel's victory in race two, at Sepang in Malaysia, owed more than a little to Ferrari making better decisions during an early safety car deployment, then his two further victories that season underlined Ferrari's improving performance. In Hungary, he overtook both Mercedes at the start and held on tenaciously to win, while in Singapore he led throughout from pole position—Ferrari's first pole since 2012.

Having regained momentum through 2015 with a relatively conservative car, Ferrari—urged on by company president Sergio Marchionne, whose demands to be bolder grew increasingly strident—approached 2016 with a package that was altogether more daring. Engine performance continued to be a key differentiator, but there were still gains to be found in aerodynamics and in extracting the most from the delicate Pirelli tires, especially now that the company had introduced a fifth dry-weather compound that was softer than before.

Although the outline of the SF16-H was similar to that of its predecessor, particularly around the flanks, it was very different in aerodynamic detail and beneath the skin. The nose was reprofiled to resemble the most common solution across the grid, with a short, stubby "thumb-tip" protuberance providing compliance with the regulations. Channels on either side, between the wing pylons, aimed to maximize airflow under the car, and the furniture elsewhere on the front wing was reprofiled with more vertical fences to generate a greater outwash effect. There were also detail changes to the sidepod winglets and rear wing, and the entire engine cover was tighter. The suspension layout also received a wide-ranging review as Ferrari reverted to pushrods at the front and the wishbones themselves were mounted at a less steep angle.

It was the powertrain, however, that received the biggest overhaul. The FIA had loosened the constraints on power-unit development in response to pleas from Renault and Honda, which had fallen well behind. Ferrari also enjoyed the benefits of greater freedom, adopting variable-length inlet plenums as well as relocating various ancillaries such as the intercooler. The MGU-K moved away from the gearbox to a position beside the engine block, enabling the new gearbox case to be much narrower. Above the transmission, the exhaust was now split into three in response to an FIA diktat: having fielded complaints about the lack of noise from the lower-revving engines, the governing body mandated that the outlet be separated so the turbo wastegate breathed out from a different pipe.

Technical director James Allison suffered a family bereavement just before the first race of the season, requiring him to spend more time in the UK, and he departed the team in July. Marchionne took the opportunity to execute a change in management

←

Kimi Räikkönen had an eventful 2016 Chinese Grand Prix, surviving an early clash with teammate Sebastian Vettel as they dodged the errant Red Bull of Daniil Kvyat and passing the Mercedes of Lewis Hamilton to finish on the podium.

SF16-H SPECIFICATIONS

Engine	1,600 cc 90-degree turbocharged hybrid V-6	Suspension	Double wishbones with pushrod-actuated torsion bars/dampers (f), pullrod-actuated torsion bars/dampers (r)
Power	870 bhp @ 15,000 rpm	Brakes	Discs f/r
Gearbox	Eight-speed semiautomatic	Tires	Pirelli
Chassis	Carbon fiber monocoque	Weight	690 kg

philosophy, installing Mattia Binotto—formerly head of the engine department—as technical director with a mandate to encourage a less top-down approach. Head of aerodynamics Dirk de Beer also left.

Bolder design was what Marchionne wanted, but it was the edgier aspects of the SF16-H that proved to be its undoing. The new turbo was a major weak point, eliminating Kimi Räikkönen from the first round. Sebastian Vettel failed to make the start in Bahrain when his engine failed, and Ferrari had to resort to detuning the engine until solutions could be found. Vettel and Räikkönen secured a handful of podium finishes between them, but it was Red Bull, not Ferrari, that presented Mercedes with the biggest challenge in 2016. The Scuderia dropped to third in the constructors' championship, having finished second in 2015.

← Front wings increased in sophistication during the decade thanks to the increasing power of computational fluid dynamics. Complex profiles on the wing plate sought to generate vortices that accelerated airflow away from the front wheels.

← Rules limiting the size of the diffuser led to innovative means of circumvention, such as additional flaps outside the restricted areas—and even aerodynamic fins on the rear brake ducts.

← The 2016 Mexican Grand Prix ended controversially as Vettel launched into an expletive-laden rant over the team radio, frustrated by his attempts to pass the Red Bull of Max Verstappen. Vettel was later stripped of his podium position.

Formula 1's technical regulations underwent another wide-ranging shake-up in 2017 in a knee-jerk reaction by senior stakeholders to Mercedes's dominance. F1 ringmaster Bernie Ecclestone had led the demands for cars to be faster and more aggressive looking—though by the start of the 2017 season the new owners of F1, Liberty Media, had shifted him upstairs to a chairman emeritus role.

SF70H

The controversial turbocharged hybrid power units remained, despite calls to revert to V-8s, and the token system that constrained development was dropped. Now engine builders enjoyed much greater freedom, but the opportunities to introduce upgrades remained limited: the number of engines permitted for each driver had been reduced from five to four.

Cars could now carry 105 kilograms of fuel, but efficiency remained important—these wider cars were also heavier and incurred more aerodynamic drag. Minimum weight went up again from 702 kilograms to 728, as the cars grew from 70.9 inches wide to 78.7 inches. More significantly for overall car performance, aerodynamics became a vital part of the mix again, as the permitted front wing width grew from 65 inches to 70.9 inches. The rear wings were lower (by 5.9 inches) and mounted 7.9 inches further back, while diffuser performance was boosted by it being taller and wider. Tires grew wider by 2.4 inches at the front and 3.1 inches at the rear.

Despite the disarray Ferrari had endured the previous season, the SF70H—named for the company's seventieth anniversary—proved to be something of a revelation. Sergio Marchionne's restructure of the technical department had sought to remove an impediment that had bedeviled Ferrari for many years: a blame culture that tended to stifle original thinking. Under a new system of working groups in which out-there ideas could be proposed and evaluated without fear or favor, Scuderia unveiled a car that was radically different from its predecessor.

While the front wing and suspension layout was broadly similar to the SF16-H, the new car pushed the rules to the maximum in the sidepod area, where the leading edges of the turning vanes and flow conditioners wrapped around high-mounted air intakes. The height of these slots meant air passing toward them was neither blocked nor impeded by the wishbones, and it enabled the designers to include deeply scalloped undercuts that promoted air along the floor of the car. Rivals believed that the floor had been built in such a way that it could flex downward ahead of the rear wheels at speed, facilitating greater downforce.

←

Mercedes's domination for three consecutive seasons prompted a knee-jerk change to the technical regulations with the aim of producing closer racing and more dramatic-looking cars. The change proved partially successful as Ferrari enjoyed their most competitive season in years.

SF70H SPECIFICATIONS

Engine	1,600 cc 90-degree turbocharged hybrid V-6	Suspension	Double wishbones with pushrod-actuated torsion bars/dampers (f), pullrod-actuated torsion bars/dampers (r)
Power	930 bhp @ 15,000 rpm	Brakes	Discs f/r
Gearbox	Eight-speed semiautomatic	Tires	Pirelli
Chassis	Carbon fiber monocoque	Weight	728 kg

←
The SF70H's sophisticated rear brake design was shaped to give aerodynamic benefits and conceal cleverly tuned fluidic switches.

The wheel hubs also concealed air ducts, fed by the brakes, with fluidic switches that could be tuned to generate downforce while cornering and reducing drag on the straights. Drag would certainly become an issue this season as the heavier, wider cars made for fewer overtaking opportunities. This was underscored at the first race of the year, where Mercedes's Lewis Hamilton started from pole position but then pitted for new tires earlier than his rivals and got stuck behind the Red Bull of Max Verstappen. Sebastian Vettel inherited a lead he would hold until the checkered flag, ending Ferrari's win drought.

Vettel won again in Bahrain and Monaco and remained in the lead of the championship until round twelve of the twenty. But as Mercedes overcame the shortcomings of their car, Ferrari's season imploded. Tire problems consigned Vettel to seventh in the British Grand Prix, neither Ferrari driver was on the pace on home ground at Monza, and in Singapore Vettel crashed into his own teammate at the start. An engine problem in Malaysia that forced him to start last, followed by a spark plug failure in Japan, dropped Vettel out of contention.

→
Sebastian Vettel closed out the season with third place in the Abu Dhabi Grand Prix.

←
Though the new rules mandated wider cars, designers had spent years shrink-wrapping the mechanicals for aerodynamic gain and were not about to let up now. Building out the floor and the outer element of the crash structure at the front of the sidepod to the minimum width satisfied the letter of the law, while the rest of the car remained compact.

Since the failures that had tipped the championship scales against Ferrari late in the 2017 season had largely been caused by operational blunders or reliability glitches, Maranello approached 2018 with an evolutionary car. Other teams copying their aerodynamic approach indicated that Ferrari had become Formula 1's trendsetter if not the actual title winner.

The SF71H carried over the chassis layout (pushrod front, pullrod rear) and the aerodynamic philosophy of its predecessor but adopted an even more extreme version of the "letterbox" sidepod air inlets. This configuration not only enabled Ferrari to avoid airflow disruption from the front suspension, but also to mount the mandatory side-impact protection structures in such a way that they provided no obstacle either. The SF71H's inlets were narrower than before, with a similar-size aperture on top of the sidepod, and this entire section of bodywork was narrower than specified in the regulations. Legality was provided by a horizontal wing-shaped plane and a boomerang-shaped flow conditioner—which acted as part of the impact structure—on each side.

Packaging the main part of the body as tightly as possible theoretically enabled Ferrari to maximize use of the floor and its many slotted elements to boost downforce and condition the airflow around the rear wheels. But this area was now much more difficult to simulate in the wind tunnel and in computational fluid dynamics because the wider front wheels introduced in 2017 created a more turbulent wake, especially at wider steering angles.

A key visual difference from the 2017 car was the addition of the new mandatory cockpit-protection system, known as the halo. But there were other regulation-induced changes within and without. "Shark fins" on the engine cover had been outlawed, as had the coat hanger–shaped t-wings many teams fitted ahead of the gearbox. Drivers were now limited to three power units per season, and the FIA also clamped down further on the practice of burning oil and other additives to gain a performance boost. Innuendo concerning this had surrounded both Ferrari and Mercedes from mid-2017. Cars now had to carry sensors in both their main and auxiliary oil tanks in order to verify that oil consumption had not passed the permitted limits. From the Spanish Grand Prix onward, teams were explicitly forbidden from transferring oil from the auxiliary tank to the main during qualifying, to avoid disguising excess consumption.

Ferrari's engine was now believed to be equal to or better than Mercedes's and it became the focus of

← The SF71H featured many carryover elements from its predecessor, along with a more aggressive version of its letterbox sidepod air intakes.

SF71H SPECIFICATIONS

Engine	1,600 cc 90-degree turbocharged hybrid V-6	Suspension	Double wishbones with pushrod-actuated torsion bars/dampers (f), pullrod-actuated torsion bars/dampers (r)
Power	960 bhp @ 15,000 rpm	Brakes	Discs f/r
Gearbox	Eight-speed semiautomatic	Tires	Pirelli
Chassis	Carbon fiber monocoque	Weight	728 kg

↑
Sebastian Vettel romped
to victory in Belgium, but
Ferrari's championship
challenge then disintegrated
as new aerodynamic upgrades
hindered performance.

speculation as Sebastian Vettel won the opening two rounds of 2018 (though the first of these, in Melbourne, was an opportune one resulting from a Mercedes strategy error). Clever spark plug and ignition chamber design was believed to account for part of Ferrari's advantage, but some rivals believed their twin-battery setup—revealed after a Ferrari engine designer defected to Mercedes—was circumventing the rules capping the energy contribution of the hybrid systems. The FIA checked Ferrari's systems and declared them legal, but later added extra sensors to ensure no chicanery was taking place.

This coincided with a late-season loss in form after Vettel had added three further wins to his tally, including a barnstorming one in Belgium, where he powered past Lewis Hamilton's Mercedes on the straight. The drivers' championship was in the balance, and Hamilton

←

The new cockpit-protection system known as the halo proved controversial on account of its looks, though drivers reported it did not restrict their view as some had feared.

↓

Ferrari finished first and third at the season-opening Australian Grand Prix, promising an even more competitive year.

and Vettel had scored five wins apiece, when Hamilton pressured Vettel into an elementary mistake on the opening lap of the Italian Grand Prix and motored on to win the race. He won five of the remaining seven races as Vettel's challenge foundered. Ferrari regained form after removing the majority of an aerodynamic update that had been added for Singapore, but by then the damage had been done.

The off-season between 2018 and '19 brought further upheaval for Ferrari following the death of Sergio Marchionne that summer. There were also new aerodynamic rules to contend with, owing to FIA president Jean Todt becoming discombobulated by the lack of overtaking in 2018's season-opening race and demanding rapid change.

SF90

Marchionne was believed to have been planning to eject team principal Maurizio Arrivabene, whose abrasive management style had proved divisive, and to replace him with technical director Mattia Binotto. New president John Elkann, the grandson and anointed heir of Fiat magnate Gianni Agnelli, enacted the move over the winter.

Against a background of often rancorous debate among F1's stakeholders over wider commercial and regulatory changes coming in 2021, upon the expiration of the Concorde Agreement, some of the technical aspirations for 2021 were cherry-picked and rushed through. One of the most significant factors militating against overtaking was the disruptive wake generated by the new, wider, more aero-dependent cars: once one was within a car length of another, it could lose 50 percent or more of its downforce. The FIA's technical team—led by former Ferrari chief designer Nikolas Tombazis—took the unprecedented step of inviting teams to use their in-house resources to research ways of reducing this, with the focus on the outwash effect of the front wings.

Many, including Mercedes, didn't bother, viewing it as a waste of resources, so the rules were pushed through in rather vague form and then subject to frequent clarifications until late in 2018. The result was another year of Ferrari and Mercedes domination because they enjoyed greater resources than those trailing in their slipstream. And, crucially, they had cultivated a better understanding of the changing front-wheel wake when those wheels were in yaw—which remained an issue even with the revised rules.

Ferrari and Mercedes arrived with evolutionary packages of their previous machinery, but with very different approaches at the front. The new rules mandated simpler front wings, with flatter endplates and none of the vertical fences that had been used to generate outwash. Ferrari's philosophy of fanning out the SF90's front wing planes at a steeper angle toward the center of the car—"inboard loading"—aimed to steer the air between the front wheels and the nose rather than over or around the outside of the wheels. The flattening off of the planes toward the endplates meant less downforce, but it theoretically made the

SF90 SPECIFICATIONS

Engine	1,600 cc 90-degree turbocharged hybrid V-6	Suspension	Double wishbones with pushrod-actuated torsion bars/dampers (f), pullrod-actuated torsion bars/dampers (r)
Power	1,000 bhp @ 15,000 rpm	Brakes	Discs f/r
Gearbox	Eight-speed semiautomatic	Tires	Pirelli
Chassis	Carbon fiber monocoque	Weight	728 kg

aerodynamic loadings less peaky and subject to rapid change when the car was subject to the pitch and yaw induced by cornering.

This downforce had to be recouped elsewhere, though, and the SF90 was noticeably more elaborate in the bargeboard area than its Mercedes rival because the airflow steered between the nose and the wheels had to be optimized over the rest of the car. Early testing led Ferrari to conclude that they were perhaps 0.5 seconds faster per lap than Mercedes, who were persisting with a much flatter set of wing planes.

This optimism proved baseless once the season began. The SF90 was very quick in a straight line but was well short of the downforce figures achieved by Mercedes once the silver cars took on their definitive aero spec. Ferrari Driver Academy protégé Charles Leclerc also proved increasingly unwilling to play dutiful number two to Sebastian Vettel, who struggled until a late-season upgrade made the car more to his liking. Leclerc scored more pole positions than any other driver in 2019 and won two races, but too often the SF90 lacked the race pace to capitalize on its qualifying performance. Hamilton won the title with three rounds to go, and Vettel and Leclerc summarized Ferrari's year by colliding messily in Brazil.

← The turbulent wake of the front wheels is difficult to simulate, so teams often spend time during tests and practice sessions using these "rake" devices to check the correlation between wind tunnel research and real-world performance.

← New star Charles Leclerc made his presence felt with two victories in 2019, but friction grew between him and Sebastian Vettel over the course of the season.

← Ferrari's front suspension concept changed very little from 2017 onwards as the design team appeared to favor ease of access to facilitate set-up changes. Mercedes opted for a more aggressively packaged layout in order to design a much narrower nose cone.

Named in honor of Ferrari's forthcoming 1,000th World Championship grand prix, the SF1000 was an evolution of the SF90 concept with that car's major weaknesses addressed—theoretically. But the 2020 season did not unfold according to plan—not for Ferrari, not for anybody.

Before the COVID-19 pandemic forced the last-minute cancellation of the season-opening Australian Grand Prix, Ferrari team principal Mattia Binotto circulated an internal memo warning the team not to have too high expectations for the early races. The SF1000 had certainly been underwhelming in preseason testing in Barcelona.

On the very last day of that test, the FIA released a curiously worded statement regarding a "confidential settlement" it had reached with Ferrari regarding their engine. Suspicions that Ferrari might have found a way to circumvent the regulations and gain a power advantage grew over the final races of 2019, and to this end the FIA impounded an engine for investigation. In the wake of the settlement, FIA president Jean Todt explained that his engineers hadn't found conclusive evidence to support a firm verdict, so he sought a compromise agreement rather than have Ferrari tie the matter up in appeal courts for months. Nevertheless the FIA announced various measures including additional fuel flow sensors.

The SF1000 was designed to have more downforce than its predecessor, but this came at the cost of increased drag. In concert with an engine that seemed less powerful than before—an impression born out by Ferrari customer teams also struggling for straightline speed—this spelled trouble for drivers Sebastian Vettel and Charles Leclerc when the season finally got going with a double-header in Austria in July. Leclerc salvaged second place after struggling in qualifying, but already the alarm bells were ringing in Maranello. By round three another restructure of the technical department was likely on the way.

↑
As part of a confidential agreement with the FIA after an investigation into their 2019 engine, Ferrari began working with the governing body to help police the regulations.

←
The SF100 had more downforce than its predecessor but also more drag, resulting in a net loss of lap time once the 2020 season began.

SF1000 SPECIFICATIONS

Engine	1,600cc 90-degree turbocharged hybrid V-6	Suspension	Double wishbones with pushrod-actuated torsion bars/dampers (f), pullrod-actuated torsion bars/dampers (r)
Power	1,000 bhp @ 15,000 rpm	Brakes	Discs f/r
Gearbox	Eight-speed semiautomatic	Tires	Pirelli
Chassis	Carbon fiber monocoque	Weight	728 kg

1950

GRAND PRIX	DRIVER	CAR	GRID	RESULT
Monaco	Alberto Ascari	125	7	2
	Luigi Villoresi	125	6	DNF—axle
	Raymond Sommer	125	9	4
Switzerland	Alberto Ascari	125	5	DNF—oil pump
	Luigi Villoresi	125	4	DNF—engine
	Raymond Sommer	166F2	13	DNF—suspension
Belgium	Alberto Ascari	275	7	5
	Luigi Villoresi	125	4	6
France	Alberto Ascari	275		Withdrew
	Luigi Villoresi	275		Withdrew
Italy	Alberto Ascari	375	2	2*—engine
	Giovanni Bracco	125		Withdrew
	Dorino Serafini	375	6	2*

* Ascari took over Serafini's car on lap 46. Championship positions: Ascari 5th (11 points); Serafini, Sommer 13th (3 points); Villoresi NC (0 points)

1952

GRAND PRIX	DRIVER	CAR	GRID	RESULT
Switzerland	Giuseppe Farina	500	1	DNF—electrical
	Piero Taruffi	500	2	1
	André Simon	500	4	DNF—electrical
Indianapolis	Alberto Ascari	375	19	DNF—wheel
Belgium	Alberto Ascari	500	1	1
	Giuseppe Farina	500	2	2
	Piero Taruffi	500	3	DNF—accident
France	Alberto Ascari	500	1	1
	Giuseppe Farina	500	2	2
	Piero Taruffi	500	3	3
Britain	Alberto Ascari	500	2	1
	Giuseppe Farina	500	1	6
	Piero Taruffi	500	3	2
Germany	Alberto Ascari	500	1	1
	Giuseppe Farina	500	2	2
	Piero Taruffi	500	5	4
Netherlands	Alberto Ascari	500	1	1
	Giuseppe Farina	500	2	2
	Luigi Villoresi	500	4	3
Italy	Alberto Ascari	500	1	1
	Giuseppe Farina	500	3	4
	Piero Taruffi	500	6	7
	André Simon	500	8	6
	Luigi Villoresi	500	2	3

Championship positions: Ascari 1st (36 points); Farina 2nd (24 points); Taruffi 3rd (22 points); Villoresi 8th (8 points)

1952

GRAND PRIX	DRIVER	CAR	GRID	RESULT
Switzerland	Giuseppe Farina	500	1	DNF—electrical
	Piero Taruffi	500	2	1
	André Simon	500	4	DNF—electrical
Indianapolis	Alberto Ascari	375	19	DNF—wheel
Belgium	Alberto Ascari	500	1	1
	Giuseppe Farina	500	2	2
	Piero Taruffi	500	3	DNF—accident
France	Alberto Ascari	500	1	1
	Giuseppe Farina	500	2	2
	Piero Taruffi	500	3	3
Britain	Alberto Ascari	500	2	1
	Giuseppe Farina	500	1	6
	Piero Taruffi	500	3	2
Germany	Alberto Ascari	500	1	1
	Giuseppe Farina	500	2	2
	Piero Taruffi	500	5	4
Netherlands	Alberto Ascari	500	1	1
	Giuseppe Farina	500	2	2
	Luigi Villoresi	500	4	3
Italy	Alberto Ascari	500	1	1
	Giuseppe Farina	500	3	4
	Piero Taruffi	500	6	7
	André Simon	500	8	6
	Luigi Villoresi	500	2	3

Championship positions: Ascari 1st (36 points); Farina 2nd (24 points); Taruffi 3rd (22 points); Villoresi 8th (8 points)

1953

GRAND PRIX	DRIVER	CAR	GRID	RESULT
Argentina	Alberto Ascari	500	1	1
	Giuseppe Farina	500	4	DNF—accident
	Luigi Villoresi	500	3	2
	Mike Hawthorn	500	6	4
Netherlands	Alberto Ascari	500	1	1
	Giuseppe Farina	500	3	2
	Luigi Villoresi	500	4	DNF—throttle
	Mike Hawthorn	500	6	4
Belgium	Alberto Ascari	500	2	1
	Giuseppe Farina	500	4	DNF—engine
	Luigi Villoresi	500	5	2
	Mike Hawthorn	500	7	6
France	Alberto Ascari	500	1	4
	Giuseppe Farina	500	6	5
	Luigi Villoresi	500	3	6
	Mike Hawthorn	500	7	1
Britain	Alberto Ascari	500	1	1
	Giuseppe Farina	500	5	3
	Luigi Villoresi	500	6	DNF—axle
	Mike Hawthorn	500	3	5

1953 (CONTINUED)

GRAND PRIX	DRIVER	CAR	GRID	RESULT
Germany	Alberto Ascari	500	1	8*—engine
	Giuseppe Farina	500	3	1
	Luigi Villoresi	500	6	8*
	Mike Hawthorn	500	4	3

*Ascari and Villoresi swapped cars on lap 10; Ascari stopped with engine failure on lap 15

GRAND PRIX	DRIVER	CAR	GRID	RESULT
Switzerland	Alberto Ascari	500	2	1
	Giuseppe Farina	500	3	2
	Luigi Villoresi	500	6	6
	Mike Hawthorn	500	7	3
Italy	Alberto Ascari	500	1	DNF—accident
	Giuseppe Farina	500	3	2
	Luigi Villoresi	500	5	3
	Mike Hawthorn	500	6	4
	Umberto Maglioli	553	11	8
	Piero Carini	553	20	DNF—engine

Championship positions: Ascari 1st (34.5 points); Farina 3rd (26 points); Hawthorn 4th (19 points); Villoresi 5th (17 points)

1954

GRAND PRIX	DRIVER	CAR	GRID	RESULT
Argentina	Giuseppe Farina	625	1	2
	José Froilán González	625	2	3
	Mike Hawthorn	625	4	DSQ—push start
	Umberto Maglioli	625	11	9
Belgium	Giuseppe Farina	553	3	DNF—ignition
	José Froilán González	553	2	4*—engine
	Mike Hawthorn	625	5	4*
	Maurice Trintignant	625	6	2

* González took over Hawthorn's car on lap 20

GRAND PRIX	DRIVER	CAR	GRID	RESULT
France	José Froilán González	553	4	DNF—engine
	Mike Hawthorn	553	8	DNF—engine
	Maurice Trintignant	625	9	DNF—engine
Britain	José Froilán González	625	2	1
	Mike Hawthorn	625	3	2
	Maurice Trintignant	625	8	5
Germany	José Froilán González	625	5	2*
	Mike Hawthorn	625	2	2*—axle
	Maurice Trintignant	625	7	3
	Piero Taruffi	625	11	6

*Hawthorn took over González's car on lap 16

GRAND PRIX	DRIVER	CAR	GRID	RESULT
Switzerland	José Froilán González	625	1	2
	Mike Hawthorn	625	6	DNF—oil pump
	Maurice Trintignant	625	4	DNF—engine
	Umberto Maglioli	553	11	7
	Robert Manzon	553	No time	DNS
Italy	José Froilán González	553	5	3*—gearbox
	Mike Hawthorn	625	7	2
	Maurice Trintignant	625	11	5
	Alberto Ascari	625	2	DNF—engine

1954 (CONTINUED)

GRAND PRIX	DRIVER	CAR	GRID	RESULT
	Umberto Maglioli	625	13	3*

*González took over Maglioli's car on lap 30

GRAND PRIX	DRIVER	CAR	GRID	RESULT
Spain	Mike Hawthorn	553	3	1
	Maurice Trintignant	553	8	DNF—gearbox

Championship positions: González 2nd (25.1 points); Hawthorn 3rd (24.6 points); Trintignant 4th (17 points); Farina 8th (6 points); Maglioli 18th (2 points)

1955

GRAND PRIX	DRIVER	CAR	GRID	RESULT
Argentina	Giuseppe Farina	625	5	2* 3*
	Maurice Trintignant	625	14	2* 3*—engine
	José Froilán González	625	1	3*
	Umberto Maglioli	625	NP	3*

* Only three Ferraris entered. Car 14 retired on lap 36. Car 12 shared by González (58 laps), Farina (32 laps) and Trintignant (6 laps) to second place. Car 10 shared by Farina (20 laps), Maglioli (40 laps) and Trintignant (34 laps) to third place

GRAND PRIX	DRIVER	CAR	GRID	RESULT
Monaco	Giuseppe Farina	625	14	4
	Maurice Trintignant	625	9	1
	Harry Schell	555	18	DNF—engine
	Piero Taruffi/Paul Frère	555	15	8
Belgium	Giuseppe Farina	555	4	3
	Maurice Trintignant	555	10	6
	Harry Schell	555	DNS*	
	Paul Frère	555	8	4

* Ferrari had been granted three entries; Schell present as a reserve driver

GRAND PRIX	DRIVER	CAR	GRID	RESULT
Netherlands	Mike Hawthorn	555	5	7
	Maurice Trintignant	555	8	DNF—gearbox
	Eugenio Castellotti	555	9	5
Britain	Mike Hawthorn	625	12	6*
	Maurice Trintignant	625	13	DNF—overheating
	Eugenio Castellotti	625	10	6*—transmission

* Castellotti took over Hawthorn's car on lap 46

GRAND PRIX	DRIVER	CAR	GRID	RESULT
Italy	Giuseppe Farina	D50	5	DNS
	Luigi Villoresi	D50	8	DNS
	Mike Hawthorn	555	14	DNF—gearbox
	Maurice Trintignant	555	15	8
	Eugenio Castellotti	555	4	3
	Umberto Maglioli	555	12	6

Championship positions: Castellotti 3rd (12 points, 6 scored with Lancia); Trintignant 4th (11.3 points); Farina 5th (10.3 points); Frère 15th (3 points); González 17th (2 points); Maglioli 21st (1.3 points)

1956

GRAND PRIX	DRIVER	CAR	GRID	RESULT
Argentina	Juan Manuel Fangio	D50	1	1*—fuel pump
	Eugenio Castellotti	D50	2	DNF—gearbox
	Luigi Musso	D50	3	1*
	Peter Collins	555	9	DNF—accident
	Olivier Gendebien	555	10	5

* Fangio took over Musso's car on lap 26

1956 (CONTINUED)

GRAND PRIX	DRIVER	CAR	GRID	RESULT
Monaco	Juan Manuel Fangio	D50	1	2/4*
	Eugenio Castellotti	D50	3	4*—clutch
	Luigi Musso	D50	8	DNF—accident
	Peter Collins	D50	9	2*

* Castellotti took over Fangio's car on lap 33; Fangio then took over Collins's car on lap 54

GRAND PRIX	DRIVER	CAR	GRID	RESULT
Belgium	Juan Manuel Fangio	D50	1	DNF—transmission
	Eugenio Castellotti	D50	5	DNF—transmission
	Paul Frère	D50	8	2
	Peter Collins	D50	3	1
France	Juan Manuel Fangio	D50	1*	4
	Eugenio Castellotti	D50	2	2
	Peter Collins	D50	3	1
	Alfonso de Portago	D50	9	DNF—gearbox

* It has been claimed that Collins started from pole position after being credited with Fangio's time in error, but contemporary reports do not bear this out

GRAND PRIX	DRIVER	CAR	GRID	RESULT
Britain	Juan Manuel Fangio	D50	2	1
	Eugenio Castellotti	D50	8	10*
	Peter Collins	D50	4	2*—oil pressure
	Alfonso de Portago	D50	12	2/10*

* Collins took over de Portago's car on lap 70; de Portago took over Castellotti's car on lap 80

GRAND PRIX	DRIVER	CAR	GRID	RESULT
Germany	Juan Manuel Fangio	D50	1	1
	Eugenio Castellotti	D50	3	DNF—electrical/accident*
	Peter Collins	D50	2	DNF—fuel leak/accident*
	Luigi Musso	D50	5	DNF—accident*
	Alfonso de Portago	D50	10	DNF—accident*

* Castellotti and Collins took over the cars of Musso and de Portago but then crashed out

GRAND PRIX	DRIVER	CAR	GRID	RESULT
Italy	Juan Manuel Fangio	D50	1	2/8*
	Eugenio Castellotti	D50	2	8*—tire
	Peter Collins	D50	7	2*
	Luigi Musso	D50	3	DNF—steering
	Alfonso de Portago	D50	9	DNF—tire

* Fangio suffered a broken steering arm on lap 25 and took over Collins's car on lap 35; Castellotti took over Fangio's car after it was repaired

Championship positions: Fangio 1st (30 points); Collins 3rd (25 points); Castellotti 6th (7.5 points); Frère 7th (6 points); Musso 11th (4 points); de Portago 15th (3 points); Gendebien 19th (2 points)

1957

GRAND PRIX	DRIVER	CAR	GRID	RESULT
Argentina	Peter Collins	801	5	6*—clutch
	Eugenio Castellotti	801	4	DNF—wheel
	Luigi Musso	801	6	DNF—clutch
	Mike Hawthorn	801	7	DNF—clutch
	Cesare Perdisa/ Wolfgang von Trips	D50	11	6*
	José Froilán González/ Alfonso de Portago	D50	10	5

* Collins took over Perdisa/von Trip's car on lap 63

1957 (CONTINUED)

GRAND PRIX	DRIVER	CAR	GRID	RESULT
Monaco	Peter Collins	801	2	DNF—accident
	Mike Hawthorn	801	5	DNF—accident
	Maurice Trintignant	801	6	5
	Wolfgang von Trips	801	9	DNF—engine
France	Peter Collins	801	5	3
	Mike Hawthorn	801	7	4
	Luigi Musso	801	3	2
	Maurice Trintignant	801	8	DNF—electrical
Britain	Peter Collins	801	8	4*—water leak
	Mike Hawthorn	801	5	3
	Luigi Musso	801	10	2
	Maurice Ttrintignant	801	9	4*

* Collins took over Trintignant's car on lap 85

GRAND PRIX	DRIVER	CAR	GRID	RESULT
Germany	Peter Collins	801	4	3
	Mike Hawthorn	801	2	2
	Luigi Musso	801	8	4
Pescara	Luigi Musso	801	3	DNF—oil leak
Italy	Peter Collins	801	7	DNF—engine
	Mike Hawthorn	801	10	6
	Luigi Musso	801	9	8
	Wolfgang von Trips	801	8	3

Championship positions: Musso 3rd (16 points); Hawthorn 4th (13 points); Collins 9th (8 points); Trintignant 12th (5 points); von Trips 14th (4 points); de Portago 20th (1 point); González 20th (1 point)

1958

GRAND PRIX	DRIVER	CAR	GRID	RESULT
Argentina	Peter Collins	246	3	DNF—transmission
	Mike Hawthorn	246	2	3
	Luigi Musso	246	5	2
Monaco	Peter Collins	246	9	3
	Mike Hawthorn	246	6	DNF—fuel pump
	Luigi Musso	246	10	2
	Wolfgang von Trips	246	12	DNF—engine
Netherlands	Peter Collins	246	10	DNF—gearbox
	Mike Hawthorn	246	6	5
	Luigi Musso	246	12	7
Belgium	Peter Collins	246	4	DNF—overheating
	Mike Hawthorn	246	1	2
	Luigi Musso	246	2	DNF—accident
	Olivier Gendebien	246	6	6
France	Peter Collins	246	4	5
	Mike Hawthorn	246	1	1
	Luigi Musso	246	2	DNF—fatal accident
	Wolfgang von Trips	246	No time	3
Britain	Peter Collins	246	6	1
	Mike Hawthorn	246	4	2
	Wolfgang von Trips	246	11	DNF—engine

1958 (CONTINUED)

GRAND PRIX	DRIVER	CAR	GRID	RESULT
Germany	Peter Collins	246	4	DNF—fatal accident
	Mike Hawthorn	246	1	DNF—clutch
	Wolfgang von Trips	246	5	4
	Phil Hill	156 (F2)	10	9
Portugal	Mike Hawthorn	246	2	2
	Wolfgang von Trips	246	6	5
Italy	Mike Hawthorn	246	3	2
	Wolfgang von Trips	256	6	DNF—accident
	Phil Hill	246	7	3
	Olivier Gendebien	246	5	DNF—suspension
Morocco	Mike Hawthorn	256	1	2
	Phil Hill	246	5	3
	Olivier Gendebien	246	6	DNF—accident

Championship positions: Hawthorn 1st (42 points); Collins 5th (14 points); Trintignant 7th (12 points); Musso 8th (12 points); Hill 10th (9 points); von Trips 11th (9 points)

1959

GRAND PRIX	DRIVER	CAR	GRID	RESULT
Monaco	Tony Brooks	246	4	2
	Phil Hill	246	5	4
	Jean Behra	246	2	DNF—engine
	Cliff Allison	156 (F2)	15	DNF—accident
Netherlands	Tony Brooks	246	8	DNF—oil leak
	Phil Hill	246	12	6
	Jean Behra	246	4	5
	Cliff Allison	246	No time	9
France	Tony Brooks	256	1	1
	Phil Hill	246	3	2
	Jean Behra	246	5	DNF—engine
	Dan Gurney	246	12	DNF—radiator
	Olivier Gendebien	246	11	4
Germany	Tony Brooks	256	1	1
	Phil Hill	246	6	3
	Dan Gurney	246	3	2
	Cliff Allison	246	14	DNF—clutch
Portugal	Tony Brooks	246	10	9
	Phil Hill	246	7	DNF—accident
	Dan Gurney	246	6	3
Italy	Tony Brooks	246	2	DNF—clutch
	Phil Hill	246	5	2
	Dan Gurney	246	4	4
	Cliff Allison	246	8	5
	Olivier Gendebien	246	6	6
US	Tony Brooks	246	4	3
	Phil Hill	246	8	DNF—clutch
	Wolfgang von Trips	246	6	6
	Cliff Allison	246	7	DNF—clutch

Championship positions: Brooks 2nd (27 points); Hill 4th (20 points); Gurney 7th (13 points); Gendebien 15th (3 points); Behra 17th (2 points); Allison 17th (2 points)

1960

GRAND PRIX	DRIVER	CAR	GRID	RESULT
Argentina	Phil Hill	246	6	8
	Cliff Allison	246	7	2
	Wolfgang von Trips	246	5	5
	José Froilán González	246	11	10
Monaco	Phil Hill	246	11	3
	Cliff Allison	246	—	DNQ
	Wolfgang von Trips	246	8	8
	Richie Ginther	246P	9	6
Netherlands	Phil Hill	246	13	DNF—engine
	Wolfgang von Trips	246	15	5
	Richie Ginther	246	12	6
Belgium	Phil Hill	246	3	4
	Wolfgang von Trips	246	10	DNF—transmission
	Willy Mairesse	246	12	DNF—transmission
France	Phil Hill	246	2	12
	Wolfgang von Trips	246	6	11
	Willy Mairesse	246	5	DNF—transmission
Britain	Phil Hill	246	10	7
	Wolfgang von Trips	246	7	6
Portugal	Phil Hill	246	10	DNF—accident
	Wolfgang von Trips	246	9	4
Italy	Phil Hill	246	1	1
	Richie Ginther	246	2	2
	Willy Mairesse	246	3	3
	Wolfgang von Trips	156(F2)	6	5

Championship positions: Hill 5th (16 points, 1 scored with Yeoman Credit Racing Team); von Trips 7th (10 points); Ginther 9th (8 points); Alllison 12th (6 points); Mairesse 15th (4 points)

1961

GRAND PRIX	DRIVER	CAR	GRID	RESULT
Monaco	Phil Hill	156	5	3
	Richie Ginther	156	2	2
	Wolfgang von Trips	156	6	4
Netherlands	Phil Hill	156	1	2
	Richie Ginther	156	3	5
	Wolfgang von Trips	156	2	1
Belgium	Phil Hill	156	1	1
	Richie Ginther	156	5	3
	Wolfgang von Trips	156	2	2
	Olivier Gendebien	156	3	4
France	Phil Hill	156	1	9
	Richie Ginther	156	3	15—oil pressure
	Wolfgang von Trips	156	2	DNF—engine
Britain	Phil Hill	156	1	2
	Richie Ginther	156	2	3
	Wolfgang von Trips	156	4	1
Germany	Phil Hill	156	1	3
	Richie Ginther	156	14	8
	Wolfgang von Trips	156	5	2
	Willy Mairesse	156	13	DNF—accident

1961 (CONTINUED)

GRAND PRIX	DRIVER	CAR	GRID	RESULT
Italy	Phil Hill	156	4	1
	Richie Ginther	156	3	DNF—engine
	Wolfgang von Trips	156	1	DNF—fatal accident
	Ricardo Rodriguez	156	2	DNF—fuel pump

Championship positions: Hill 1st (34 points); von Trips 2nd (33 points); Ginther 5th (16 points Gendebien 13th (3 points)

1962

GRAND PRIX	DRIVER	CAR	GRID	RESULT
Netherlands	Phil Hill	156	9	3
	Giancarlo Baghetti	156	12	4
	Ricardo Rodriguez	156	11	DNF—accident
Monaco	Phil Hill	156	9	2
	Lorenzo Bandini	156	10	3
	Willy Mairesse	156	4	7—oil pressure
Belgium	Phil Hill	156	4	3
	Giancarlo Baghetti	156	14	DNF—ignition
	Ricardo Rodriguez	156	7	4
	Willy Mairesse	156	6	DNF—accident
Britain	Phil Hill	156	12	DNF—engine
Germany	Phil Hill	156	12	DNF—suspension
	Giancarlo Baghetti	156	13	10
	Ricardo Rodriguez	156	10	6
	Lorenzo Bandini	156	18	DNF—accident
Italy	Phil Hill	156	15	11
	Giancarlo Baghetti	156	18	5
	Ricardo Rodriguez	156	11	14
	Lorenzo Bandini	156	17	8
	Willy Mairesse	156	10	4

Championship positions: Hill 6th (14 points); Baghetti 11th (4 points); Bandini 12th (4 points); Rodriguez 13th (4 points); Mairesse 14th (3 points)

1963

GRAND PRIX	DRIVER	CAR	GRID	RESULT
Monaco	John Surtees	156/63	3	4
	Willy Mairesse	156/63	7	DNF—gearbox
Belgium	John Surtees	156/63	10	DNF—injection
	Willy Mairesse	156/63	3	DNF—injection
Netherlands	John Surtees	156/63	5	3
	Ludovico Scarfiotti	156/63	11	6
France	John Surtees	156/63	4	DNF—fuel pump
	Ludovico Scarfiotti	156/63	—	DNS
Britain	John Surtees	156/63	5	2
Germany	John Surtees	156/63	2	1
	Willy Mairesse	156/63	7	DNF—accident
Italy	John Surtees	156 Aero	1	DNF—engine
	Lorenzo Bandini	156/63	6	DNF—gearbox

1963 (CONTINUED)

GRAND PRIX	DRIVER	CAR	GRID	RESULT
US	John Surtees	156/63	3	9—engine
	Lorenzo Bandini	156/63	9	5
Mexico	John Surtees	156 Aero	2	DSQ
	Lorenzo Bandini	156 Aero	7	DNF—ignition
South Africa	John Surtees	156 Aero	4	DNF—engine
	Lorenzo Bandini	156 Aero	5	5

Championship positions: Surtees 4th (22 points); Bandini 10th (6 points); Scarfiotti 15th (1 point)

1964

GRAND PRIX	DRIVER	CAR	GRID	RESULT
Monaco	John Surtees	158	4	DNF—gearbox
	Lorenzo Bandini	156 Aero	7	10—gearbox
Netherlands	John Surtees	158	4	2
	Lorenzo Bandini	158	10	DNF—steering
Belgium	John Surtees	158	5	DNF—engine
	Lorenzo Bandini	158	9	DNF—engine
France	John Surtees	158	3	DNF—engine
	Lorenzo Bandini	158	8	9
Britain	John Surtees	158	5	3
	Lorenzo Bandini	156 Aero	8	5
Germany	John Surtees	158	1	1
	Lorenzo Bandini	156 Aero	4	3
Austria	John Surtees	158	2	DNF—suspension
	Lorenzo Bandini	156 Aero	7	1
Italy	John Surtees	158	1	1
	Lorenzo Bandini	158	7	3
	Ludovico Scarfiotti	156 Aero	16	9
US*	John Surtees	158	2	2
	Lorenzo Bandini	1512	8	DNF—engine
Mexico*	John Surtees	158	4	2
	Lorenzo Bandini	1512	3	3

* Entered as North American Racing Team
Championship positions: Surtees 1st (40 points); Bandini 4th (23 points)

1965

GRAND PRIX	DRIVER	CAR	GRID	RESULT
South Africa	John Surtees	158	2	2
	Lorenzo Bandini	1512	6	15—ignition
Monaco	John Surtees	158	5	4
	Lorenzo Bandini	1512	4	2
Belgium	John Surtees	158	6	DNF—engine
	Lorenzo Bandini	1512	15	9
France	John Surtees	158	4	3
	Lorenzo Bandini	1512	3	8—accident
Britain	John Surtees	1512	5	3
	Lorenzo Bandini	158	9	DNF—engine
Netherlands	John Surtees	1512	4	7
	Lorenzo Bandini	158	12	9

1965 (CONTINUED)

GRAND PRIX	DRIVER	CAR	GRID	RESULT
Germany	John Surtees	1512	4	DNF—gearbox
	Lorenzo Bandini	158	7	6
Italy	John Surtees	1512	2	DNF—clutch
	Lorenzo Bandini	1512	5	4
	Nino Vaccarella	158	15	12
US*	Pedro Rodriguez	1512	15	5
	Lorenzo Bandini	1512	5	4
	Bob Bondurant	158	14	9
Mexico*	Pedro Rodriguez	1512	13	7
	Lorenzo Bandini	1512	7	8

* Entered as North American Racing Team

Championship positions: Surtees 5th (13 points); Bandini 6th (13 points); Rodriguez 14th (1 point)

1966

GRAND PRIX	DRIVER	CAR	GRID	RESULT
Monaco	John Surtees	312	2	DNF—transmission
	Lorenzo Bandini	246/66	5	2
Belgium	John Surtees	312	1	1
	Lorenzo Bandini	246/66	5	3
France	Lorenzo Bandini	312	3	NC
	Mike Parkes	312	1	2
Netherlands	Lorenzo Bandini	312	9	6
	Mike Parkes	312	5	DNF—accident
Germany	Lorenzo Bandini	312	6	6
	Mike Parkes	312	7	DNF—accident
	Ludovico Scarfiotti	246/66	4	DNF—electrical
Italy	Lorenzo Bandini	312	5	DNF—ignition
	Mike Parkes	312	1	2
	Ludovico Scarfiotti	312	2	1
US	Lorenzo Bandini	312	3	DNF—engine

Championship positions: Surtees 2nd (28 points, 19 with Cooper); Parkes 8th (12 points); Bandini 9th (12 points); Scarfiotti 10th (9 points)

1967

GRAND PRIX	DRIVER	CAR	GRID	RESULT
Monaco	Lorenzo Bandini	312	2	DNF—accident
	Chris Amon	312	14	3
Netherlands	Chris Amon	312	9	4
	Mike Parkes	312	10	5
	Ludovico Scarfiotti	312	15	6
Belgium	Chris Amon	312	5	3
	Mike Parkes	312	8	DNF—accident
	Ludovico Scarfiotti	312	9	NC
France	Chris Amon	312	7	DNF—throttle
Britain	Chris Amon	312	6	3
Germany	Chris Amon	312	8	3
Canada	Chris Amon	312	4	6

1967 (CONTINUED)

GRAND PRIX	DRIVER	CAR	GRID	RESULT
Italy	Chris Amon	312	4	7
US	Chris Amon	312	4	DNF—engine
Mexico	Chris Amon	312	2	9—fuel
	Jonathan Williams	312	16	8

Championship positions: Amon 4th (20 points); Parkes 16th (2 points); Scarfiotti 19th (1 point)

1968

GRAND PRIX	DRIVER	CAR	GRID	RESULT
South Africa	Chris Amon	312	8	4
	Jacky Ickx	312	11	DNF—oil leak
	Andrea de Adamich	312	7	DNF—accident
Spain	Chris Amon	312	1	DNF—fuel pump
	Jacky Ickx	312	8	DNF—ignition
Belgium	Chris Amon	312	1	DNF—radiator
	Jacky Ickx	312	3	3
Netherlands	Chris Amon	312	1	6
	Jacky Ickx	312	6	4
France	Chris Amon	312	5	10
	Jacky Ickx	312	3	1
Britain	Chris Amon	312	3	2
	Jacky Ickx	312	12	3
Germany	Chris Amon	312	2	DNF—accident
	Jacky Ickx	312	1	4
Italy	Chris Amon	312	3	DNF—accident
	Jacky Ickx	312	4	3
	Derek Bell	312	8	DNF—fuel pump
Canada	Chris Amon	312	2	DNF—transmission
US	Chris Amon	312	4	DNF—water pump
	Derek Bell	312	15	DNF—engine
Mexico	Chris Amon	312	2	DNF—transmission
	Jacky Ickx	312	15	DNF—ignition

Championship positions: Ickx 4th (27 points); Amon 10th (10 points)

1969

GRAND PRIX	DRIVER	CAR	GRID	RESULT
South Africa	Chris Amon	312	5	DNF—engine
Spain	Chris Amon	312	2	DNF—engine
Monaco	Chris Amon	312	2	DNF—differential
Netherlands	Chris Amon	312	4	3
France	Chris Amon	312	6	DNF—engine
Britain	Chris Amon	312	5	DNF—gearbox
	Pedro Rodriguez	312	8	DNF—engine
Italy	Pedro Rodriguez	312	12	6

Championship positions: Amon 12th (4 points); Amon 14th (3 points, 2 with North American Racing Team)

1970

GRAND PRIX	DRIVER	CAR	GRID	RESULT
South Africa	Jacky Ickx	312B	5	DNF—engine
Spain	Jacky Ickx	312B	7	DNF—accident
Monaco	Jacky Ickx	312B	5	DNF—transmission
Belgium	Jacky Ickx	312B	4	8
	Ignazio Giunti	312B	8	4
Netherlands	Jacky Ickx	312B	3	3
	Clay Regazzoni	312B	6	4
France	Jacky Ickx	312B	1	DNF—engine
	Ignazio Giunti	312B	11	14
Britain	Jacky Ickx	312B	3	DNF—transmission
	Clay Regazzoni	312B	6	4
Germany	Jacky Ickx	312B	1	2
	Clay Regazzoni	312B	3	DNF—engine
Austria	Jacky Ickx	312B	3	1
	Ignazio Giunti	312B	5	7
	Clay Regazzoni	312B	2	2
Italy	Jacky Ickx	312B	1	DNF—clutch
	Ignazio Giunti	312B	5	DNF—fuel system
	Clay Regazzoni	312B	3	1
Canada	Jacky Ickx	312B	2	1
	Clay Regazzoni	312B	3	2
US	Jacky Ickx	312B	1	4
	Clay Regazzoni	312B	6	13
Mexico	Jacky Ickx	312B	3	1
	Clay Regazzoni	312B	1	2

Championship positions: Ickx 2nd (40 points); Regazzoni 3rd (33 points); Giunti 17th (3 points)

1971

GRAND PRIX	DRIVER	CAR	GRID	RESULT
South Africa	Jacky Ickx	312B	8	8
	Clay Regazzoni	312B	3	3
	Mario Andretti	312B	4	1
Spain	Jacky Ickx	312B	1	2
	Clay Regazzoni	312B	2	DNF—engine
	Mario Andretti	312B	8	DNF—engine
Monaco	Jacky Ickx	312B2	2	3
	Clay Regazzoni	312B2	11	DNF—accident
	Mario Andretti	312B	—	DNQ
Netherlands	Jacky Ickx	312B2	1	1
	Clay Regazzoni	312B2	4	3
	Mario Andretti	312B	18	DNF—fuel pump
France	Jacky Ickx	312B2	3	DNF—engine
	Clay Regazzoni	312B2	2	DNF—accident
Britain	Jacky Ickx	312B2	6	DNF—engine
	Clay Regazzoni	312B2	1	DNF—oil pressure
Germany	Jacky Ickx	312B2	2	DNF—accident
	Clay Regazzoni	312B2	4	3

1971 (CONTINUED)

GRAND PRIX	DRIVER	CAR	GRID	RESULT
	Mario Andretti	312B2	11	4
Austria	Jacky Ickx	312B2	6	DNF—engine
	Clay Regazzoni	312B2	4	DNF—engine
Italy	Jacky Ickx	312B	2	DNF—engine
	Clay Regazzoni	312B2	8	DNF—engine
Canada	Jacky Ickx	312B2	12	8
	Clay Regazzoni	312B2	18	DNF—accident
	Mario Andretti	312B2	13	13
US	Jacky Ickx	312B	7	DNF—alternator
	Clay Regazzoni	312B2	4	6

Championship positions: Ickx 4th (19 points); Regazzoni 7th (13 points); Andretti 8th (12 points)

1972

GRAND PRIX	DRIVER	CAR	GRID	RESULT
Argentina	Jacky Ickx	312B2	8	3
	Clay Regazzoni	312B2	6	4
	Mario Andretti	312B2	9	DNF—engine
South Africa	Jacky Ickx	312B2	7	8
	Clay Regazzoni	312B2	2	12
	Mario Andretti	312B2	6	4
Spain	Jacky Ickx	312B2	1	2
	Clay Regazzoni	312B2	8	3
	Mario Andretti	312B2	5	DNF—oil pressure
Monaco	Jacky Ickx	312B2	2	2
	Clay Regazzoni	312B2	3	DNF—accident
Belgium	Jacky Ickx	312B2	4	DNF—fuel system
	Clay Regazzoni	312B2	2	DNF—accident
France	Jacky Ickx	312B2	4	11
	Nanni Galli	312B2	19	13
Britain	Jacky Ickx	312B2	1	DNF—oil pressure
	Arturo Merzario	312B2	9	6
Germany	Jacky Ickx	312B2	1	1
	Clay Regazzoni	312B2	7	2
	Arturo Merzario	312B2	22	12
Austria	Jacky Ickx	312B2	9	DNF—fuel system
	Clay Regazzoni	312B2	2	DNF—fuel system
Italy	Jacky Ickx	312B2	1	DNF—electrical
	Clay Regazzoni	312B2	4	DNF—accident
	Mario Andretti	312B2	7	7
Canada	Jacky Ickx	312B2	8	12
	Clay Regazzoni	312B2	7	5
US	Jacky Ickx	312B2	12	5
	Clay Regazzoni	312B2	6	8
	Mario Andretti	312B2	10	6

Championship positions: Ickx 4th (27 points); Regazzoni 7th (15 points); Andretti 12th (4 points); Merzario 20th (1 point)

1973

GRAND PRIX	DRIVER	CAR	GRID	RESULT
Argentina	Jacky Ickx	312B2	3	4
	Arturo Merzario	312B2	14	9
Brazil	Jacky Ickx	312B2	3	5
	Arturo Merzario	312B2	17	4
South Africa	Jacky Ickx	312B2	11	DNF—accident
	Arturo Merzario	312B2	15	4
Spain	Jacky Ickx	312B3	6	12
Belgium	Jacky Ickx	312B3	3	DNF—oil pressure
Monaco	Jacky Ickx	312B3	7	DNF—transmission
	Arturo Merzario	312B3	16	DNF—oil pressure
Sweden	Jacky Ickx	312B3	8	6
France	Jacky Ickx	312B3	12	5
	Arturo Merzario	312B3	10	7
Britain	Jacky Ickx	312B3	19	8
Austria	Arturo Merzario	312B3	6	7
Italy	Jacky Ickx	312B3	14	8
	Arturo Merzario	312B3	7	DNF—suspension
Canada	Arturo Merzario	312B3	20	15
US	Arturo Merzario	312B3	11	16

Championship positions: Ickx 9th (12 points, 4 with McLaren); Merzario 12th (6 points)

1974

GRAND PRIX	DRIVER	CAR	GRID	RESULT
Argentina	Niki Lauda	312B3	8	2
	Clay Regazzoni	312B3	2	3
Brazil	Niki Lauda	312B3	3	DNF—engine
	Clay Regazzoni	312B3	8	2
South Africa	Niki Lauda	312B3	1	16—electrical
	Clay Regazzoni	312B3	6	DNF—oil pressure
Spain	Niki Lauda	312B3	1	1
	Clay Regazzoni	312B3	3	2
Belgium	Niki Lauda	312B3	3	2
	Clay Regazzoni	312B3	1	4
Monaco	Niki Lauda	312B3	1	DNF—electrical
	Clay Regazzoni	312B3	2	4
Sweden	Niki Lauda	312B3	3	DNF—gearbox
	Clay Regazzoni	312B3	4	DNF—gearbox
Netherlands	Niki Lauda	312B3	1	1
	Clay Regazzoni	312B3	2	2
France	Niki Lauda	312B3	1	2
	Clay Regazzoni	312B3	4	3
Britain	Niki Lauda	312B3	1	5
	Clay Regazzoni	312B3	7	4
Germany	Niki Lauda	312B3	1	DNF—accident
	Clay Regazzoni	312B3	2	1
Austria	Niki Lauda	312B3	1	DNF—engine
	Clay Regazzoni	312B3	8	5

1974 (CONTINUED)

GRAND PRIX	DRIVER	CAR	GRID	RESULT
Italy	Niki Lauda	312B3	1	DNF—engine
	Clay Regazzoni	312B3	5	DNF—engine
Canada	Niki Lauda	312B3	2	DNF—accident
	Clay Regazzoni	312B3	6	2
US	Niki Lauda	312B3	5	DNF—suspension
	Clay Regazzoni	312B3	9	11

Championship positions: Regazzoni 2nd (52 points); Lauda 4th (38 points)

1975

GRAND PRIX	DRIVER	CAR	GRID	RESULT
Argentina	Niki Lauda	312B3	4	6
	Clay Regazzoni	312B3	7	4
Brazil	Niki Lauda	312B3	4	5
	Clay Regazzoni	312B3	5	4
South Africa	Niki Lauda	312T	4	5
	Clay Regazzoni	312T	9	16—throttle
Spain	Niki Lauda	312T	1	DNF—accident
	Clay Regazzoni	312T	2	NC
Monaco	Niki Lauda	312T	1	1
	Clay Regazzoni	312T	6	DNF—accident
Belgium	Niki Lauda	312T	1	1
	Clay Regazzoni	312T	4	5
Sweden	Niki Lauda	312T	5	1
	Clay Regazzoni	312T	12	3
Netherlands	Niki Lauda	312T	1	2
	Clay Regazzoni	312T	2	3
France	Niki Lauda	312T	1	1
	Clay Regazzoni	312T	9	DNF—engine
Britain	Niki Lauda	312T	3	8
	Clay Regazzoni	312T	4	13
Germany	Niki Lauda	312T	1	3
	Clay Regazzoni	312T	5	DNF—engine
Austria	Niki Lauda	312T	1	6
	Clay Regazzoni	312T	5	7
Italy	Niki Lauda	312T	1	3
	Clay Regazzoni	312T	2	1
US	Niki Lauda	312T	1	1
	Clay Regazzoni	312T	11	DNF—withdrawn

Championship positions: Lauda 1st (64.5 points); Regazzoni 5th (25 points)

1976

GRAND PRIX	DRIVER	CAR	GRID	RESULT
Brazil	Niki Lauda	312T	2	1
	Clay Regazzoni	312T	4	7
South Africa	Niki Lauda	312T	2	1
	Clay Regazzoni	312T	9	DNF—engine

1976 (CONTINUED)

GRAND PRIX	DRIVER	CAR	GRID	RESULT
Long Beach	Niki Lauda	312T	4	2
	Clay Regazzoni	312T	1	1
Spain	Niki Lauda	312T2	2	2
	Clay Regazzoni	312T2	5	11
Belgium	Niki Lauda	312T2	1	1
	Clay Regazzoni	312T2	2	2
Monaco	Niki Lauda	312T2	1	1
	Clay Regazzoni	312T2	2	14—accident
Sweden	Niki Lauda	312T2	5	3
	Clay Regazzoni	312T2	11	6
France	Niki Lauda	312T2	2	DNF—engine
	Clay Regazzoni	312T2	4	DNF—engine
Britain	Niki Lauda	312T2	1	1
	Clay Regazzoni	312T2	4	DSQ
Germany	Niki Lauda	312T2	2	DNF—accident
	Clay Regazzoni	312T2	5	9
Netherlands	Clay Regazzoni	312T2	5	2
Italy	Niki Lauda	312T2	5	4
	Clay Regazzoni	312T2	9	2
	Carlos Reutemann	312T2	7	9
Canada	Niki Lauda	312T2	6	8
	Clay Regazzoni	312T2	12	6
US	Niki Lauda	312T2	5	3
	Clay Regazzoni	312T2	14	7
Japan	Niki Lauda	312T2	3	DNF—withdrawn
	Clay Regazzoni	312T2	7	5

Championship positions: Lauda 2nd (68 points); Regazzoni 5th (31 points)

1977

GRAND PRIX	DRIVER	CAR	GRID	RESULT
Argentina	Niki Lauda	312T2	4	DNF—fuel
	Carlos Reutemann	312T2	7	3
Brazil	Niki Lauda	312T2	13	3
	Carlos Reutemann	312T2	2	1
South Africa	Niki Lauda	312T2	3	1
	Carlos Reutemann	312T2	8	8
Long Beach	Niki Lauda	312T2	1	2
	Carlos Reutemann	312T2	4	DNF—accident
Spain	Niki Lauda	312T2	3	DNS
	Carlos Reutemann	312T2	4	2
Monaco	Niki Lauda	312T2	6	2
	Carlos Reutemann	312T2	3	3
Belgium	Niki Lauda	312T2	11	2
	Carlos Reutemann	312T2	7	DNF—accident
Sweden	Niki Lauda	312T2	15	DNF—handling
	Carlos Reutemann	312T2	12	3
France	Niki Lauda	312T2	9	5
	Carlos Reutemann	312T2	6	6

1977 (CONTINUED)

GRAND PRIX	DRIVER	CAR	GRID	RESULT
Britain	Niki Lauda	312T2	3	2
	Carlos Reutemann	312T2	14	15
Germany	Niki Lauda	312T2	3	1
	Carlos Reutemann	312T2	8	4
Austria	Niki Lauda	312T2	1	2
	Carlos Reutemann	312T2	5	4
Netherlands	Niki Lauda	312T2	4	1
	Carlos Reutemann	312T2	6	6
Italy	Niki Lauda	312T2	5	2
	Carlos Reutemann	312T2	2	DNF—spin
US	Niki Lauda	312T2	7	4
	Carlos Reutemann	312T2	6	6
Canada	Gilles Villeneuve	312T2	17	12—transmission
	Carlos Reutemann	312T2	12	DNF—fuel
Japan	Gilles Villeneuve	312T2	20	DNF—accident
	Carlos Reutemann	312T2	7	2

Championship positions: Lauda 1st (72 points); Reutemann 4th (42 points)

1978

GRAND PRIX	DRIVER	CAR	GRID	RESULT
Argentina	Carlos Reutemann	312T2	2	7
	Gilles Villeneuve	312T2	7	8
Brazil	Carlos Reutemann	312T2	4	1
	Gilles Villeneuve	312T2	6	DNF—spin
South Africa	Carlos Reutemann	312T3	9	DNF—spin
	Gilles Villeneuve	312T3	8	DNF—oil leak
Long Beach	Carlos Reutemann	312T3	1	1
	Gilles Villeneuve	312T3	2	DNF—accident
Monaco	Carlos Reutemann	312T3	1	8
	Gilles Villeneuve	312T3	8	DNF—accident
Belgium	Carlos Reutemann	312T3	2	3
	Gilles Villeneuve	312T3	4	4
Spain	Carlos Reutemann	312T3	3	DNF—accident
	Gilles Villeneuve	312T3	5	10
Sweden	Carlos Reutemann	312T3	8	9
	Gilles Villeneuve	312T3	7	10
France	Carlos Reutemann	312T3	8	18
	Gilles Villeneuve	312T3	9	12
Britain	Carlos Reutemann	312T3	8	1
	Gilles Villeneuve	312T3	13	DNF—transmission
Germany	Carlos Reutemann	312T3	12	DNF—fuel
	Gilles Villeneuve	312T3	15	8
Austria	Carlos Reutemann	312T3	4	DSQ
	Gilles Villeneuve	312T3	11	3
Netherlands	Carlos Reutemann	312T3	4	7
	Gilles Villeneuve	312T3	5	6
Italy	Carlos Reutemann	312T3	11	3
	Gilles Villeneuve	312T3	2	7

1978 (CONTINUED)

GRAND PRIX	DRIVER	CAR	GRID	RESULT
US	Carlos Reutemann	312T3	2	1
	Gilles Villeneuve	312T3	4	DNF—engine
Canada	Carlos Reutemann	312T3	11	3
	Gilles Villeneuve	312T3	3	1

Championship positions: Reutemann 3rd (48 points); Villeneuve 9th (17 points)

1979

GRAND PRIX	DRIVER	CAR	GRID	RESULT
Argentina	Jody Scheckter	312T3	5	DNF—accident
	Gilles Villeneuve	312T3	10	DNF—engine
Brazil	Jody Scheckter	312T3	6	6
	Gilles Villeneuve	312T3	5	5
South Africa	Jody Scheckter	312T4	2	2
	Gilles Villeneuve	312T4	3	1
Long Beach	Jody Scheckter	312T4	3	2
	Gilles Villeneuve	312T4	1	1
Spain	Jody Scheckter	312T4	5	4
	Gilles Villeneuve	312T4	3	7
Belgium	Jody Scheckter	312T4	7	1
	Gilles Villeneuve	312T4	6	7
Monaco	Jody Scheckter	312T4	1	1
	Gilles Villeneuve	312T4	2	DNF—transmission
France	Jody Scheckter	312T4	5	7
	Gilles Villeneuve	312T4	3	2
Britain	Jody Scheckter	312T4	11	5
	Gilles Villeneuve	312T4	13	14—fuel system
Germany	Jody Scheckter	312T4	5	4
	Gilles Villeneuve	312T4	9	8
Austria	Jody Scheckter	312T4	9	4
	Gilles Villeneuve	312T4	5	2
Netherlands	Jody Scheckter	312T4	5	2
	Gilles Villeneuve	312T4	6	DNF—tire failure
Italy	Jody Scheckter	312T4	3	1
	Gilles Villeneuve	312T4	5	2
Canada	Jody Scheckter	312T4	9	4
	Gilles Villeneuve	312T4	2	2
US	Jody Scheckter	312T4	16	DNF—tire failure
	Gilles Villeneuve	312T4	3	1

Championship positions: Scheckter 1st (51 points); Villeneuve 2nd (47 points)

1980

GRAND PRIX	DRIVER	CAR	GRID	RESULT
Argentina	Jody Scheckter	312T5	11	DNF—engine
	Gilles Villeneuve	312T5	8	DNF—accident
Brazil	Jody Scheckter	312T5	8	DNF—engine
	Gilles Villeneuve	312T5	3	DNF—throttle

1980 (CONTINUED)

GRAND PRIX	DRIVER	CAR	GRID	RESULT
South Africa	Jody Scheckter	312T5	9	DNF—engine
	Gilles Villeneuve	312T5	10	DNF—transmission
Long Beach	Jody Scheckter	312T5	16	5
	Gilles Villeneuve	312T5	10	DNF—transmission
Belgium	Jody Scheckter	312T5	14	8
	Gilles Villeneuve	312T5	12	6
Monaco	Jody Scheckter	312T5	17	DNF—handling
	Gilles Villeneuve	312T5	6	5
France	Jody Scheckter	312T5	19	12
	Gilles Villeneuve	312T5	17	8
Britain	Jody Scheckter	312T5	23	10
	Gilles Villeneuve	312T5	19	DNF—engine
Germany	Jody Scheckter	312T5	21	13
	Gilles Villeneuve	312T5	16	6
Austria	Jody Scheckter	312T5	22	13
	Gilles Villeneuve	312T5	15	8
Netherlands	Jody Scheckter	312T5	12	9
	Gilles Villeneuve	312T5	7	7
Italy	Jody Scheckter	312T5	16	8
	Gilles Villeneuve	312T5	8	DNF—puncture
Canada	Jody Scheckter	312T5	DNQ	
	Gilles Villeneuve	312T5	22	5
US	Jody Scheckter	312T5	23	11
	Gilles Villeneuve	312T5	18	DNF—accident

Championship positions: Villeneuve 14th (6 points); Scheckter 19th (2 points)

1981

GRAND PRIX	DRIVER	CAR	GRID	RESULT
Long Beach	Didier Pironi	126CK	11	DNF—fuel system
	Gilles Villeneuve	126CK	5	DNF—transmission
Brazil	Didier Pironi	126CK	17	DNF—accident
	Gilles Villeneuve	126CK	7	DNF—turbo
Argentina	Didier Pironi	126CK	12	DNF—engine
	Gilles Villeneuve	126CK	7	DNF—transmission
San Marino	Didier Pironi	126CK	6	5
	Gilles Villeneuve	126CK	1	7
Belgium	Didier Pironi	126CK	3	8
	Gilles Villeneuve	126CK	7	4
Monaco	Didier Pironi	126CK	17	4
	Gilles Villeneuve	126CK	2	1
Spain	Didier Pironi	126CK	13	15
	Gilles Villeneuve	126CK	7	1
France	Didier Pironi	126CK	14	5
	Gilles Villeneuve	126CK	11	DNF—electrical
Britain	Didier Pironi	126CK	4	DNF—turbo
	Gilles Villeneuve	126CK	8	DNF—spin
Germany	Didier Pironi	126CK	5	DNF—electrical
	Gilles Villeneuve	126CK	8	10

1981 (CONTINUED)

GRAND PRIX	DRIVER	CAR	GRID	RESULT
Austria	Didier Pironi	126CK	8	9
	Gilles Villeneuve	126CK	3	DNF—accident
Netherlands	Didier Pironi	126CK	12	DNF—accident
	Gilles Villeneuve	126CK	16	DNF—accident
Italy	Didier Pironi	126CK	8	5
	Gilles Villeneuve	126CK	9	DNF—engine
Canada	Didier Pironi	126CK	12	DNF—ignition
	Gilles Villeneuve	126CK	11	3
Las Vegas	Didier Pironi	126CK	18	9
	Gilles Villeneuve	126CK	3	DSQ

Championship positions: Villeneuve 7th (25 points); Pironi 13th (9 points)

1982

GRAND PRIX	DRIVER	CAR	GRID	RESULT
South Africa	Didier Pironi	126C2	6	18
	Gilles Villeneuve	126C2	3	DNF—turbo
Brazil	Didier Pironi	126C2	8	6
	Gilles Villeneuve	126C2	2	DNF—spin
Long Beach	Didier Pironi	126C2	9	DNF—spin
	Gilles Villeneuve	126C2	7	DNF—DSQ
San Marino	Didier Pironi	126C2	4	1
	Gilles Villeneuve	126C2	3	2
Belgium	Didier Pironi	126C2		Withdrew
	Gilles Villeneuve	126C2		DNQ—fatal accident
Monaco	Didier Pironi	126C2	5	2
Detroit	Didier Pironi	126C2	4	3
Canada	Didier Pironi	126C2	1	9
Netherlands	Didier Pironi	126C2	4	1
	Patrick Tambay	126C2	6	8
Britain	Didier Pironi	126C2	4	2
	Patrick Tambay	126C2	13	3
France	Didier Pironi	126C2	3	3
	Patrick Tambay	126C2	5	4
German	Didier Pironi	126C2	1	DNS—accident
	Patrick Tambay	126C2	5	1
Austria	Patrick Tambay	126C2	4	4
Switzerland	Patrick Tambay	126C2	10	DNS
Italy	Mario Andretti	126C2	1	2
	Patrick Tambay	126C2	3	3
Las Vegas	Mario Andretti	126C2	7	DNF—spin
	Patrick Tambay	126C2	8	DNS

Championship positions: Pironi 2nd (39 points); Tambay 7th (25 points); Villeneuve 15th (6 points); Andretti 19th (4 points)

1983

GRAND PRIX	DRIVER	CAR	GRID	RESULT
Brazil	René Arnoux	126C2B	6	10
	Patrick Tambay	126C2B	3	5

1983 (CONTINUED)

GRAND PRIX	DRIVER	CAR	GRID	RESULT
Long Beach	René Arnoux	126C2B	2	3
	Patrick Tambay	126C2B	1	DNF—accident
France	René Arnoux	126C2B	4	7
	Patrick Tambay	126C2B	11	4
San Marino	René Arnoux	126C2B	1	3
	Patrick Tambay	126C2B	3	1
Monaco	René Arnoux	126C2B	2	DNF—suspension
	Patrick Tambay	126C2B	4	4
Belgium	René Arnoux	126C2B	5	DNF—engine
	Patrick Tambay	126C2B	2	2
Detroit	René Arnoux	126C2B	1	DNF—electrical
	Patrick Tambay	126C2B	3	DNF—engine
Canada	René Arnoux	126C2B	1	1
	Patrick Tambay	126C2B	4	3
Britain	René Arnoux	126C3	1	5
	Patrick Tambay	126C3	2	3
Germany	René Arnoux	126C3	2	1
	Patrick Tambay	126C3	1	DNF—engine
Austria	René Arnoux	126C3	2	2
	Patrick Tambay	126C3	1	DNF—ignition
Netherlands	René Arnoux	126C3	10	1
	Patrick Tambay	126C3	3	2
Italy	René Arnoux	126C3	3	2
	Patrick Tambay	126C3	2	4
Europe	René Arnoux	126C3	5	9
	Patrick Tambay	126C3	6	DNF—spin
South Africa	René Arnoux	126C3	4	DNF—engine
	Patrick Tambay	126C3	1	DNF—turbo

Championship positions: Arnoux 3rd (49 points); Tambay 4th (40 points)

1984

GRAND PRIX	DRIVER	CAR	GRID	RESULT
Brazil	René Arnoux	126C4	10	DNF—electrical
	Michele Alboreto	126C4	2	DNF—brakes
South Africa	René Arnoux	126C4	15	DNF—fuel injection
	Michele Alboreto	126C4	10	11—ignition
Belgium	René Arnoux	126C4	2	3
	Michele Alboreto	126C4	1	1
San Marino	René Arnoux	126C4	6	2
	Michele Alboreto	126C4	13	DNF—exhaust
France	René Arnoux	126C4	11	4
	Michele Alboreto	126C4	10	DNF—engine
Monaco	René Arnoux	126C4	3	3
	Michele Alboreto	126C4	4	6
Canada	René Arnoux	126C4	5	5
	Michele Alboreto	126C4	6	DNF—engine
Detroit	René Arnoux	126C4	15	DNF—accident
	Michele Alboreto	126C4	4	DNF—engine

1984 (CONTINUED)

GRAND PRIX	DRIVER	CAR	GRID	RESULT
Dallas	René Arnoux	126C4	4	2
	Michele Alboreto	126C4	9	DNF—spin
Britain	René Arnoux	126C4	13	6
	Michele Alboreto	126C4	9	5
Germany	René Arnoux	126C4	10	6
	Michele Alboreto	126C4	6	DNF—engine
Austria	René Arnoux	126C4	15	7
	Michele Alboreto	126C4	12	3
Netherlands	René Arnoux	126C4	15	11—electrical
	Michele Alboreto	126C4	9	DNF—engine
Italy	René Arnoux	126C4	14	DNF—gearbox
	Michele Alboreto	126C4	11	2
Europe	René Arnoux	126C4	6	5
	Michele Alboreto	126C4	5	2
Portugal	René Arnoux	126C4	17	9
	Michele Alboreto	126C4	8	4

Championship positions: Alboreto 4th (30.5 points); Arnoux 6th (27 points)

1985

GRAND PRIX	DRIVER	CAR	GRID	RESULT
Brazil	René Arnoux	156/85	7	4
	Michele Alboreto	156/85	1	2
Portugal	Stefan Johansson	156/85	11	8
	Michele Alboreto	156/85	5	2
San Marino	Stefan Johansson	156/85	15	6
	Michele Alboreto	156/85	4	DNF—electrical
Monaco	Stefan Johansson	156/85	15	DNF—accident
	Michele Alboreto	156/85	3	2
Canada	Stefan Johansson	156/85	4	2
	Michele Alboreto	156/85	3	1
Detroit	Stefan Johansson	156/85	9	2
	Michele Alboreto	156/85	3	3
France	Stefan Johansson	156/85	15	4
	Michele Alboreto	156/85	3	DNF—turbo
Britain	Stefan Johansson	156/85	11	DNF—accident
	Michele Alboreto	156/85	6	2
Germany	Stefan Johansson	156/85	2	9
	Michele Alboreto	156/85	8	1
Austria	Stefan Johansson	156/85	12	4
	Michele Alboreto	156/85	9	3
Netherlands	Stefan Johansson	156/85	17	DNF—engine
	Michele Alboreto	156/85	16	4
Italy	Stefan Johansson	156/85	10	5
	Michele Alboreto	156/85	7	13—engine
Belgium	Stefan Johansson	156/85	5	DNF—spin
	Michele Alboreto	156/85	4	DNF—clutch
Europe	Stefan Johansson	156/85	13	DNF—electrical
	Michele Alboreto	156/85	15	DNF—turbo

1985 (CONTINUED)

GRAND PRIX	DRIVER	CAR	GRID	RESULT
South Africa	Stefan Johansson	156/85	16	4
	Michele Alboreto	156/85	15	DNF—turbo
Australia	Stefan Johansson	156/85	15	5
	Michele Alboreto	156/85	5	DNF—transmission

Championship positions: Alboreto 2nd (53 points); Johansson 7th (26 points); Arnoux 17th (3 points)

1986

GRAND PRIX	DRIVER	CAR	GRID	RESULT
Brazil	Michele Alboreto	F1/86	6	DNF—fuel system
	Stefan Johansson	F1/86	8	DNF—brakes
Spain	Michele Alboreto	F1/86	13	DNF—wheel bearing
	Stefan Johansson	F1/86	11	DNF—brakes
San Marino	Michele Alboreto	F1/86	5	10—turbo
	Stefan Johansson	F1/86	7	4
Monaco	Michele Alboreto	F1/86	4	DNF—turbo
	Stefan Johansson	F1/86	15	10
Belgium	Michele Alboreto	F1/86	9	4
	Stefan Johansson	F1/86	11	3
Canada	Michele Alboreto	F1/86	11	8
	Stefan Johansson	F1/86	18	DNF—accident
Detroit	Michele Alboreto	F1/86	11	4
	Stefan Johansson	F1/86	5	DNF—electrical
France	Michele Alboreto	F1/86	6	8
	Stefan Johansson	F1/86	10	DNF—turbo
Britain	Michele Alboreto	F1/86	12	DNF—turbo
	Stefan Johansson	F1/86	18	DNF—engine
Germany	Michele Alboreto	F1/86	10	DNF—transmission
	Stefan Johansson	F1/86	11	11
Hungary	Michele Alboreto	F1/86	15	DNF—accident
	Stefan Johansson	F1/86	7	4
Austria	Michele Alboreto	F1/86	9	2
	Stefan Johansson	F1/86	14	3
Italy	Michele Alboreto	F1/86	9	DNF—engine
	Stefan Johansson	F1/86	12	3
Portugal	Michele Alboreto	F1/86	13	5
	Stefan Johansson	F1/86	8	6
Mexico	Michele Alboreto	F1/86	12	DNF—turbo
	Stefan Johansson	F1/86	14	12
Australia	Michele Alboreto	F1/86	9	DNF—accident
	Stefan Johansson	F1/86	12	3

Championship positions: Johansson 5th (23 points); Alboreto 9th (14 points)

1987

GRAND PRIX	DRIVER	CAR	GRID	RESULT
Brazil	Michele Alboreto	F1-87	9	8
	Gerhard Berger	F1-87	7	4

1987 (CONTINUED)

GRAND PRIX	DRIVER	CAR	GRID	RESULT
San Marino	Michele Alboreto	F1-87	6	3
	Gerhard Berger	F1-87	5	DNF—electrical
Belgium	Michele Alboreto	F1-87	5	DNF—transmission
	Gerhard Berger	F1-87	4	DNF—engine
Monaco	Michele Alboreto	F1-87	5	3
	Gerhard Berger	F1-87	8	4
Detroit	Michele Alboreto	F1-87	7	DNF—gearbox
	Gerhard Berger	F1-87	12	4
France	Michele Alboreto	F1-87	8	DNF—engine
	Gerhard Berger	F1-87	6	DNF—suspension
Britain	Michele Alboreto	F1-87	7	DNF—suspension
	Gerhard Berger	F1-87	8	DNF—accident
Germany	Michele Alboreto	F1-87	5	DNF—turbo
	Gerhard Berger	F1-87	10	DNF—turbo
Hungary	Michele Alboreto	F1-87	5	DNF—engine
	Gerhard Berger	F1-87	2	DNF—transmission
Austria	Michele Alboreto	F1-87	6	DNF—turbo
	Gerhard Berger	F1-87	3	DNF—turbo
Italy	Michele Alboreto	F1-87	8	DNF—turbo
	Gerhard Berger	F1-87	3	4
Portugal	Michele Alboreto	F1-87	6	DNF—gearbox
	Gerhard Berger	F1-87	1	2
Spain	Michele Alboreto	F1-87	4	15—engine
	Gerhard Berger	F1-87	3	DNF—engine
Mexico	Michele Alboreto	F1-87	9	DNF—engine
	Gerhard Berger	F1-87	2	DNF—turbo
Japan	Michele Alboreto	F1-87	4	4
	Gerhard Berger	F1-87	1	1
Australia	Michele Alboreto	F1-87	6	2
	Gerhard Berger	F1-87	1	1

Championship positions: Berger 5th (36 points); Alboreto 7th (17 points)

1988

GRAND PRIX	DRIVER	CAR	GRID	RESULT
Brazil	Michele Alboreto	F1/87-88C	6	5
	Gerhard Berger	F1/87-88C	4	2
San Marino	Michele Alboreto	F1/87-88C	10	18—engine
	Gerhard Berger	F1/87-88C	5	5
Monaco	Michele Alboreto	F1/87-88C	4	3
	Gerhard Berger	F1/87-88C	3	2
Mexico	Michele Alboreto	F1/87-88C	5	4
	Gerhard Berger	F1/87-88C	3	3
Canada	Michele Alboreto	F1/87-88C	4	DNF—engine
	Gerhard Berger	F1/87-88C	3	DNF—electrical
Detroit	Michele Alboreto	F1/87-88C	3	DNF—accident
	Gerhard Berger	F1/87-88C	2	DNF—puncture
France	Michele Alboreto	F1/87-88C	4	3
	Gerhard Berger	F1/87-88C	3	4

1988 (CONTINUED)

GRAND PRIX	DRIVER	CAR	GRID	RESULT
Britain	Michele Alboreto	F1/87-88C	2	17—fuel
	Gerhard Berger	F1/87-88C	1	9
Germany	Michele Alboreto	F1/87-88C	4	4
	Gerhard Berger	F1/87-88C	3	3
Hungary	Michele Alboreto	F1/87-88C	15	DNF—electrical
	Gerhard Berger	F1/87-88C	9	4
Belgium	Michele Alboreto	F1/87-88C	4	DNF—engine
	Gerhard Berger	F1/87-88C	3	DNF—injection
Italy	Michele Alboreto	F1/87-88C	4	2
	Gerhard Berger	F1/87-88C	3	1
Portugal	Michele Alboreto	F1/87-88C	7	5
	Gerhard Berger	F1/87-88C	4	DNF—spin
Spain	Michele Alboreto	F1/87-88C	10	DNF—engine
	Gerhard Berger	F1/87-88C	8	6
Japan	Michele Alboreto	F1/87-88C	9	11
	Gerhard Berger	F1/87-88C	3	4
Australia	Michele Alboreto	F1/87-88C	12	DNF—accident
	Gerhard Berger	F1/87-88C	4	DNF—accident

Championship positions: Berger 3rd (41 points); Alboreto 5th (24 points)

1989

GRAND PRIX	DRIVER	CAR	GRID	RESULT
Brazil	Nigel Mansell	640	6	1
	Gerhard Berger	640	3	DNF—accident
San Marino	Nigel Mansell	640	3	DNF—gearbox
	Gerhard Berger	640	5	DNF—accident
Monaco	Nigel Mansell	640	5	DNF—gearbox
Mexico	Nigel Mansell	640	3	DNF—gearbox
	Gerhard Berger	640	6	DNF—gearbox
US	Nigel Mansell	640	4	DNF—alternator
	Gerhard Berger	640	8	DNF—alternator
Canada	Nigel Mansell	640	5	DSQ
	Gerhard Berger	640	4	DNF—gearbox
France	Nigel Mansell	640	3	2
	Gerhard Berger	640	6	DNF—clutch
Britain	Nigel Mansell	640	3	2
	Gerhard Berger	640	4	DNF—gearbox
Germany	Nigel Mansell	640	3	3
	Gerhard Berger	640	4	DNF—spin
Hungary	Nigel Mansell	640	12	1
	Gerhard Berger	640	6	DNF—gearbox
Belgium	Nigel Mansell	640	6	3
	Gerhard Berger	640	3	DNF—spin
Italy	Nigel Mansell	640	3	DNF—gearbox
	Gerhard Berger	640	2	2
Portugal	Nigel Mansell	640	3	DSQ
	Gerhard Berger	640	2	1
Spain	Gerhard Berger	640	2	2

1989 (CONTINUED)

GRAND PRIX	DRIVER	CAR	GRID	RESULT
Japan	Nigel Mansell	640	4	DNF—engine
	Gerhard Berger	640	3	DNF—gearbox
Australia	Nigel Mansell	640	7	DNF—spin
	Gerhard Berger	640	14	DNF—accident

Championship positions: Mansell 4th (38 points); Berger 7th (21 points)

1990

GRAND PRIX	DRIVER	CAR	GRID	RESULT
US	Alain Prost	641	7	DNF—oil leak
	Nigel Mansell	641	17	DNF—engine
Brazil	Alain Prost	641	6	1
	Nigel Mansell	641	5	4
San Marino	Alain Prost	641	6	4
	Nigel Mansell	641	5	DNF—engine
Monaco	Alain Prost	641	2	DNF—battery
	Nigel Mansell	641	7	DNF—battery
Canada	Alain Prost	641	3	5
	Nigel Mansell	641	7	3
Mexico	Alain Prost	641	13	1
	Nigel Mansell	641	4	2
France	Alain Prost	641	4	1
	Nigel Mansell	641	1	18—engine
Britain	Alain Prost	641	5	1
	Nigel Mansell	641	1	DNF—gearbox
Germany	Alain Prost	641	3	4
	Nigel Mansell	641	4	DNF—broken wing
Hungary	Alain Prost	641	8	DNF—gearbox
	Nigel Mansell	641	5	17—accident
Belgium	Alain Prost	641	3	2
	Nigel Mansell	641	5	DNF—handling
Italy	Alain Prost	641	2	2
	Nigel Mansell	641	4	4
Portugal	Alain Prost	641	2	1
	Nigel Mansell	641	1	3
Spain	Alain Prost	641	2	1
	Nigel Mansell	641	3	2
Japan	Alain Prost	641	2	DNF—accident
	Nigel Mansell	641	3	DNF—transmission
Australia	Alain Prost	641	4	3
	Nigel Mansell	641	3	2

Championship positions: Prost 2nd (71 points); Mansell 5th (37 points)

1991

GRAND PRIX	DRIVER	CAR	GRID	RESULT
US	Alain Prost	642	2	2
	Jean Alesi	642	6	12—gearbox
Brazil	Alain Prost	642	6	4
	Jean Alesi	642	5	6

1991 (CONTINUED)

GRAND PRIX	DRIVER	CAR	GRID	RESULT
San Marino	Alain Prost	642	3	DNS
	Jean Alesi	642	7	DNF—spin
Monaco	Alain Prost	642	7	5
	Jean Alesi	642	9	3
Canada	Alain Prost	642	4	DNF—gearbox
	Jean Alesi	642	7	DNF—engine
Mexico	Alain Prost	642	7	DNF—alternator
	Jean Alesi	642	4	DNF—clutch
France	Alain Prost	643	2	2
	Jean Alesi	643	6	4
Britain	Alain Prost	643	5	3
	Jean Alesi	643	6	DNF—accident
Germany	Alain Prost	643	5	DNF—spin
	Jean Alesi	643	6	3
Hungary	Alain Prost	643	4	DNF—engine
	Jean Alesi	643	6	5
Belgium	Alain Prost	643	2	DNF—fuel leak
	Jean Alesi	643	5	DNF—engine
Italy	Alain Prost	643	5	3
	Jean Alesi	643	6	DNF—engine
Portugal	Alain Prost	643	5	DNF—engine
	Jean Alesi	643	6	3
Spain	Alain Prost	643	6	2
	Jean Alesi	643	7	4
Japan	Alain Prost	643	4	4
	Jean Alesi	643	6	DNF—engine
Australia	Gianni Morbidelli	643	8	6
	Jean Alesi	643	7	DNF—accident

Championship positions: Prost 5th (34 points); Alesi 7th (21 points); Morbidelli 24th (0.5 points)

1992

GRAND PRIX	DRIVER	CAR	GRID	RESULT
South Africa	Jean Alesi	F92A	5	DNF—engine
	Ivan Capelli	F92A	9	DNF—engine
Mexico	Jean Alesi	F92A	10	DNF—engine
	Ivan Capelli	F92A	20	DNF—accident
Brazil	Jean Alesi	F92A	6	4
	Ivan Capelli	F92A	11	5
Spain	Jean Alesi	F92A	8	10—spin
	Ivan Capelli	F92A	5	3
San Marino	Jean Alesi	F92A	7	DNF—accident
	Ivan Capelli	F92A	8	DNF—spin
Monaco	Jean Alesi	F92A	4	DNF—gearbox
	Ivan Capelli	F92A	8	DNF—spin
Canada	Jean Alesi	F92A	8	3
	Ivan Capelli	F92A	9	DNF—spin
France	Jean Alesi	F92A	6	DNF—engine
	Ivan Capelli	F92A	8	DNF—engine

1992 (CONTINUED)

GRAND PRIX	DRIVER	CAR	GRID	RESULT
Britain	Jean Alesi	F92A	8	DNF—fire extinguisher
	Ivan Capelli	F92A	14	9
Germany	Jean Alesi	F92A	5	5
	Ivan Capelli	F92A	12	DNF—engine
Hungary	Jean Alesi	F92A	9	DNF—transmission
	Ivan Capelli	F92A	10	6
Belgium	Jean Alesi	F92AT	5	DNF—puncture
	Ivan Capelli	F92A	12	DNF—engine
Italy	Jean Alesi	F92AT	3	DNF—fuel
	Ivan Capelli	F92AT	7	DNF—spin
Portugal	Jean Alesi	F92AT	10	DNF—spin
	Ivan Capelli	F92AT	16	DNF—engine
Japan	Jean Alesi	F92AT	15	5
	Nicola Larini	F92AT	11	12
Australia	Jean Alesi	F92AT	6	4
	Nicola Larini	F92AT	19	11

Championship positions: Alesi 7th (18 points); Capelli 13th (3 points)

1993

GRAND PRIX	DRIVER	CAR	GRID	RESULT
South Africa	Jean Alesi	F93A	5	DNF—suspension
	Gerhard Berger	F93A	15	6
Brazil	Jean Alesi	F93A	9	8
	Gerhard Berger	F93A	13	DNF—accident
Europe	Jean Alesi	F93A	9	DNF—gearbox
	Gerhard Berger	F93A	8	DNF—suspension
San Marino	Jean Alesi	F93A	9	DNF—clutch
	Gerhard Berger	F93A	8	DNF—gearbox
Spain	Jean Alesi	F93A	8	DNF—engine
	Gerhard Berger	F93A	11	6
Monaco	Jean Alesi	F93A	5	3
	Gerhard Berger	F93A	7	14—accident
Canada	Jean Alesi	F93A	6	DNF—engine
	Gerhard Berger	F93A	5	4
France	Jean Alesi	F93A	6	DNF—engine
	Gerhard Berger	F93A	14	14
Britain	Jean Alesi	F93A	12	9
	Gerhard Berger	F93A	13	DNF—suspension
Germany	Jean Alesi	F93A	10	7
	Gerhard Berger	F93A	9	6
Hungary	Jean Alesi	F93A	8	DNF—spin
	Gerhard Berger	F93A	6	3
Belgium	Jean Alesi	F93A	4	DNF—suspension
	Gerhard Berger	F93A	16	10
Italy	Jean Alesi	F93A	3	2
	Gerhard Berger	F93A	6	DNF—suspension

1993 (CONTINUED)

GRAND PRIX	DRIVER	CAR	GRID	RESULT
Portugal	Jean Alesi	F93A	5	4
	Gerhard Berger	F93A	8	DNF—spin
Japan	Jean Alesi	F93A	14	DNF—engine
	Gerhard Berger	F93A	5	DNF—engine
Australia	Jean Alesi	F93A	7	4
	Gerhard Berger	F93A	6	5

Championship positions: Alesi 6th (16 points); Berger 12th (12 points)

1994

GRAND PRIX	DRIVER	CAR	GRID	RESULT
Brazil	Jean Alesi	412T1	3	3
	Gerhard Berger	412T1	17	DNF—engine
Pacific	Nicola Larini	412T1	7	DNF—accident
	Gerhard Berger	412T1	5	2
San Marino	Nicola Larini	412T1	6	2
	Gerhard Berger	412T1	3	DNF—suspension
Monaco	Jean Alesi	412T1	5	5
	Gerhard Berger	412T1	3	3
Spain	Jean Alesi	412T1	6	4
	Gerhard Berger	412T1	7	DNF—gearbox
Canada	Jean Alesi	412T1	2	3
	Gerhard Berger	412T1	3	4
France	Jean Alesi	412T1B	3	DNF—accident
	Gerhard Berger	412T1B	4	3
Britain	Jean Alesi	412T1B	4	2
	Gerhard Berger	412T1B	3	DNF—engine
Germany	Jean Alesi	412T1B	2	DNF—engine
	Gerhard Berger	412T1B	1	1
Hungary	Jean Alesi	412T1B	13	DNF—gearbox
	Gerhard Berger	412T1B	4	12
Belgium	Jean Alesi	412T1B	5	DNF—engine
	Gerhard Berger	412T1B	11	DNF—engine
Italy	Jean Alesi	412T1B	1	DNF—gearbox
	Gerhard Berger	412T1B	2	2
Portugal	Jean Alesi	412T1B	5	DNF—accident
	Gerhard Berger	412T1B	1	DNF—gearbox
Europe	Jean Alesi	412T1B	16	10
	Gerhard Berger	412T1B	6	5
Japan	Jean Alesi	412T1B	7	3
	Gerhard Berger	412T1B	11	DNF—ignition
Australia	Jean Alesi	412T1B	8	6
	Gerhard Berger	412T1B	11	2

Championship positions: Berger 3rd (41 points); Alesi 5th (24 points); Larini 14th (6 points)

1995

GRAND PRIX	DRIVER	CAR	GRID	RESULT
Brazil	Jean Alesi	412T2	6	5
	Gerhard Berger	412T2	5	3
Argentina	Jean Alesi	412T2	6	2
	Gerhard Berger	412T2	8	6
San Marino	Jean Alesi	412T2	5	2
	Gerhard Berger	412T2	2	3
Spain	Jean Alesi	412T2	2	DNF—engine
	Gerhard Berger	412T2	3	3
Monaco	Jean Alesi	412T2	5	DNF—spin
	Gerhard Berger	412T2	4	3
Canada	Jean Alesi	412T2	4	1
	Gerhard Berger	412T2	5	11—accident
France	Jean Alesi	412T2	4	5
	Gerhard Berger	412T2	7	12
Britain	Jean Alesi	412T2	6	2
	Gerhard Berger	412T2	4	DNF—wheel
Germany	Jean Alesi	412T2	10	DNF—engine
	Gerhard Berger	412T2	4	3
Hungary	Jean Alesi	412T2	6	DNF—engine
	Gerhard Berger	412T2	4	3
Belgium	Jean Alesi	412T2	2	DNF—suspension
	Gerhard Berger	412T2	1	DNF—electrical
Italy	Jean Alesi	412T2	5	DNF—wheel bearing
	Gerhard Berger	412T2	3	DNF—suspension
Portugal	Jean Alesi	412T2	7	5
	Gerhard Berger	412T2	4	4
Europe	Jean Alesi	412T2	6	2
	Gerhard Berger	412T2	4	DNF—electrical
Japan	Jean Alesi	412T2	4	5
	Gerhard Berger	412T2	5	4
Australia	Jean Alesi	412T2	2	DNF—transmission
	Gerhard Berger	412T2	5	DNF—electrical

Championship positions: Alesi 5th (42 points); Berger 6th (31 points)

1996

GRAND PRIX	DRIVER	CAR	GRID	RESULT
Australia	Michael Schumacher	F310	4	DNF—brakes
	Eddie Irvine	F310	3	3
Brazil	Michael Schumacher	F310	4	3
	Eddie Irvine	F310	10	7
Argentina	Michael Schumacher	F310	2	DNF—broken wing
	Eddie Irvine	F310	10	5
Europe	Michael Schumacher	F310	3	2
	Eddie Irvine	F310	7	DNF—electrical
San Marino	Michael Schumacher	F310	1	2
	Eddie Irvine	F310	6	4
Monaco	Michael Schumacher	F310	1	DNF—spin
	Eddie Irvine	F310	7	6

1996 (CONTINUED)

GRAND PRIX	DRIVER	CAR	GRID	RESULT
Spain	Michael Schumacher	F310	3	1
	Eddie Irvine	F310	6	DNF—spin
Canada	Michael Schumacher	F310	3	DNF—transmission
	Eddie Irvine	F310	5	DNF—suspension
France	Michael Schumacher	F310	1	DNS
	Eddie Irvine	F310	22	DNF—gearbox
Britain	Michael Schumacher	F310	3	DNF—hydraulics
	Eddie Irvine	F310	10	DNF—transmission
Germany	Michael Schumacher	F310	3	4
	Eddie Irvine	F310	8	DNF—engine
Hungary	Michael Schumacher	F310	1	9—throttle
	Eddie Irvine	F310	4	DNF—gearbox
Belgium	Michael Schumacher	F310	3	1
	Eddie Irvine	F310	9	DNF—gearbox
Italy	Michael Schumacher	F310	3	1
	Eddie Irvine	F310	7	DNF—spin
Portugal	Michael Schumacher	F310	4	3
	Eddie Irvine	F310	6	5
Japan	Michael Schumacher	F310	3	2
	Eddie Irvine	F310	6	DNF—accident

Championship positions: Schumacher 3rd (59 points); Irvine 10th (11 points)

1997

GRAND PRIX	DRIVER	CAR	GRID	RESULT
Australia	Michael Schumacher	F310B	3	2
	Eddie Irvine	F310B	5	DNF—accident
Brazil	Michael Schumacher	F310B	2	5
	Eddie Irvine	F310B	14	16
Argentina	Michael Schumacher	F310B	4	DNF—accident
	Eddie Irvine	F310B	7	2
San Marino	Michael Schumacher	F310B	3	2
	Eddie Irvine	F310B	9	3
Monaco	Michael Schumacher	F310B	2	1
	Eddie Irvine	F310B	15	3
Spain	Michael Schumacher	F310B	7	4
	Eddie Irvine	F310B	11	12
Canada	Michael Schumacher	F310B	1	1
	Eddie Irvine	F310B	12	DNF—accident
France	Michael Schumacher	F310B	1	1
	Eddie Irvine	F310B	5	3
Britain	Michael Schumacher	F310B	4	DNF—wheel bearing
	Eddie Irvine	F310B	7	DNF—transmission
Germany	Michael Schumacher	F310B	4	2
	Eddie Irvine	F310B	10	DNF—accident
Hungary	Michael Schumacher	F310B	1	4
	Eddie Irvine	F310B	5	9
Belgium	Michael Schumacher	F310B	3	1
	Eddie Irvine	F310B	17	10—accident

1997 (CONTINUED)

GRAND PRIX	DRIVER	CAR	GRID	RESULT I
Italy	Michael Schumacher	F310B	9	6
	Eddie Irvine	F310B	10	8
Austria	Michael Schumacher	F310B	8	6
	Eddie Irvine	F310B	9	DNF—accident
Luxembourg	Michael Schumacher	F310B	5	DNF—accident
	Eddie Irvine	F310B	14	DNF—engine
Japan	Michael Schumacher	F310B	2	1
	Eddie Irvine	F310B	3	3
Europe	Michael Schumacher	F310B	2	DNF—accident
	Eddie Irvine	F310B	7	5

Championship positions: Schumacher DSQ (was 2nd on 78 points, but stripped of these for causing accident in final round); Irvine 7th (24 points)

1998

GRAND PRIX	DRIVER	CAR	GRID	RESULT
Australia	Michael Schumacher	F300	3	DNF—engine
	Eddie Irvine	F300	8	4
Brazil	Michael Schumacher	F300	4	3
	Eddie Irvine	F300	6	8
Argentina	Michael Schumacher	F300	2	1
	Eddie Irvine	F300	4	3
San Marino	Michael Schumacher	F300	3	2
	Eddie Irvine	F300	4	3
Spain	Michael Schumacher	F300	3	3
	Eddie Irvine	F300	6	DNF—accident
Monaco	Michael Schumacher	F300	4	10
	Eddie Irvine	F300	7	3
Canada	Michael Schumacher	F300	3	1
	Eddie Irvine	F300	8	3
France	Michael Schumacher	F300	2	1
	Eddie Irvine	F300	4	2
Britain	Michael Schumacher	F300	2	1
	Eddie Irvine	F300	5	3
Austria	Michael Schumacher	F300	4	3
	Eddie Irvine	F300	8	4
Germany	Michael Schumacher	F300	9	5
	Eddie Irvine	F300	6	8
Hungary	Michael Schumacher	F300	3	1
	Eddie Irvine	F300	5	DNF—gearbox
Belgium	Michael Schumacher	F300	4	DNF—accident
	Eddie Irvine	F300	5	DNF—spin
Italy	Michael Schumacher	F300	1	1
	Eddie Irvine	F300	5	2
Luxembourg	Michael Schumacher	F300	1	2
	Eddie Irvine	F300	2	4
Japan	Michael Schumacher	F300	1	2
	Eddie Irvine	F300	4	DNF—tire

Championship positions: Schumacher 2nd (86 points); Irvine 4th (47 points)

1999

GRAND PRIX	DRIVER	CAR	GRID	RESULT
Australia	Michael Schumacher	F399	3	8
	Eddie Irvine	F399	6	1
Brazil	Michael Schumacher	F399	4	2
	Eddie Irvine	F399	6	5
San Marino	Michael Schumacher	F399	3	1
	Eddie Irvine	F399	4	DNF—engine
Monaco	Michael Schumacher	F399	2	1
	Eddie Irvine	F399	4	2
Spain	Michael Schumacher	F399	4	3
	Eddie Irvine	F399	2	4
Canada	Michael Schumacher	F399	1	DNF—spin
	Eddie Irvine	F399	3	3
France	Michael Schumacher	F399	6	5
	Eddie Irvine	F399	17	6
Britain	Michael Schumacher	F399	2	DNS
	Eddie Irvine	F399	4	2
Austria	Mika Salo	F399	7	9
	Eddie Irvine	F399	3	1
Germany	Mika Salo	F399	4	2
	Eddie Irvine	F399	5	1
Hungary	Mika Salo	F399	18	12
	Eddie Irvine	F399	2	3
Belgium	Mika Salo	F399	9	7
	Eddie Irvine	F399	6	4
Italy	Mika Salo	F399	6	3
	Eddie Irvine	F399	8	6
Europe	Mika Salo	F399	12	DNF—brakes
	Eddie Irvine	F399	9	7
Malaysia	Michael Schumacher	F399	1	2
	Eddie Irvine	F399	2	1
Japan	Michael Schumacher	F399	1	2
	Eddie Irvine	F399	5	3

Championship positions: Irvine 2nd (74 points); Schumacher 5th (44 points); Salo 10th (10 points)

2000

GRAND PRIX	DRIVER	CAR	GRID	RESULT
Australia	Michael Schumacher	F1-2000	3	1
	Rubens Barrichello	F1-2000	4	2
Brazil	Michael Schumacher	F1-2000	3	1
	Rubens Barrichello	F1-2000	4	DNF—hydraulics
San Marino	Michael Schumacher	F1-2000	2	1
	Rubens Barrichello	F1-2000	4	4
Britain	Michael Schumacher	F1-2000	5	3
	Rubens Barrichello	F1-2000	1	DNF—hydraulics
Spain	Michael Schumacher	F1-2000	1	5
	Rubens Barrichello	F1-2000	3	3
Europe	Michael Schumacher	F1-2000	2	1
	Rubens Barrichello	F1-2000	4	4

2000 (CONTINUED)

GRAND PRIX	DRIVER	CAR	GRID	RESULT
Monaco	Michael Schumacher	F1-2000	1	DNF—suspension
	Rubens Barrichello	F1-2000	6	2
Canada	Michael Schumacher	F1-2000	1	1
	Rubens Barrichello	F1-2000	3	2
France	Michael Schumacher	F1-2000	1	DNF—engine
	Rubens Barrichello	F1-2000	3	3
Austria	Michael Schumacher	F1-2000	4	DNF—accident
	Rubens Barrichello	F1-2000	3	3
Germany	Michael Schumacher	F1-2000	2	DNF—accident
	Rubens Barrichello	F1-2000	18	1
Hungary	Michael Schumacher	F1-2000	1	2
	Rubens Barrichello	F1-2000	5	4
Belgium	Michael Schumacher	F1-2000	4	2
	Rubens Barrichello	F1-2000	10	DNF—fuel system
Italy	Michael Schumacher	F1-2000	1	1
	Rubens Barrichello	F1-2000	2	DNF—accident
US	Michael Schumacher	F1-2000	1	1
	Rubens Barrichello	F1-2000	4	2
Japan	Michael Schumacher	F1-2000	1	1
	Rubens Barrichello	F1-2000	4	4
Malaysia	Michael Schumacher	F1-2000	1	1
	Rubens Barrichello	F1-2000	4	3

Championship positions: Schumacher 1st (108 points); Barrichello 4th (62 points)

2001

GRAND PRIX	DRIVER	CAR	GRID	RESULT
Australia	Michael Schumacher	F2001	1	1
	Rubens Barrichello	F2001	2	3
Malaysia	Michael Schumacher	F2001	1	1
	Rubens Barrichello	F2001	2	2
Brazil	Michael Schumacher	F2001	1	2
	Rubens Barrichello	F2001	6	DNF—accident
San Marino	Michael Schumacher	F2001	4	DNF—suspension
	Rubens Barrichello	F2001	6	3
Spain	Michael Schumacher	F2001	1	1
	Rubens Barrichello	F2001	4	DNF—suspension
Austria	Michael Schumacher	F2001	1	2
	Rubens Barrichello	F2001	4	3
Monaco	Michael Schumacher	F2001	2	1
	Rubens Barrichello	F2001	4	2
Canada	Michael Schumacher	F2001	1	2
	Rubens Barrichello	F2001	5	DNF—spin
Europe	Michael Schumacher	F2001	1	1
	Rubens Barrichello	F2001	4	5
France	Michael Schumacher	F2001	2	1
	Rubens Barrichello	F2001	8	3
Britain	Michael Schumacher	F2001	1	2
	Rubens Barrichello	F2001	6	3

2001 (CONTINUED)

GRAND PRIX	DRIVER	CAR	GRID	RESULT
Germany	Michael Schumacher	F2001	4	DNF—fuel system
	Rubens Barrichello	F2001	6	2
Hungary	Michael Schumacher	F2001	1	1
	Rubens Barrichello	F2001	3	2
Belgium	Michael Schumacher	F2001	3	1
	Rubens Barrichello	F2001	5	5
Italy	Michael Schumacher	F2001	3	4
	Rubens Barrichello	F2001	2	2
US	Michael Schumacher	F2001	1	2
	Rubens Barrichello	F2001	5	15—engine
Japan	Michael Schumacher	F2001	1	1
	Rubens Barrichello	F2001	4	5

Championship positions: Schumacher 1st (123 points); Barrichello 3rd (56 points)

2002

GRAND PRIX	DRIVER	CAR	GRID	RESULT
Australia	Michael Schumacher	F2001	2	1
	Rubens Barrichello	F2001	1	DNF—accident
Malaysia	Michael Schumacher	F2001	1	3
	Rubens Barrichello	F2001	3	DNF—engine
Brazil	Michael Schumacher	F2002	2	1
	Rubens Barrichello	F2001	8	DNF—hydraulics
San Marino	Michael Schumacher	F2002	1	1
	Rubens Barrichello	F2002	2	2
Spain	Michael Schumacher	F2002	1	1
	Rubens Barrichello	F2002	2	DNS
Austria	Michael Schumacher	F2002	2	1
	Rubens Barrichello	F2002	3	2
Monaco	Michael Schumacher	F2002	3	2
	Rubens Barrichello	F2002	5	7
Canada	Michael Schumacher	F2002	2	1
	Rubens Barrichello	F2002	3	3
Europe	Michael Schumacher	F2002	3	1
	Rubens Barrichello	F2002	4	2
Britain	Michael Schumacher	F2002	3	1
	Rubens Barrichello	F2002	2	2
France	Michael Schumacher	F2002	2	1
	Rubens Barrichello	F2002	3	DNS
Germany	Michael Schumacher	F2002	1	1
	Rubens Barrichello	F2002	3	4
Hungary	Michael Schumacher	F2002	2	2
	Rubens Barrichello	F2002	1	1
Belgium	Michael Schumacher	F2002	1	1
	Rubens Barrichello	F2002	3	2
Italy	Michael Schumacher	F2002	2	2
	Rubens Barrichello	F2002	4	1
US	Michael Schumacher	F2002	1	2
	Rubens Barrichello	F2002	2	1

GRAND PRIX	DRIVER	CAR	GRID	RESULT
Japan	Michael Schumacher	F2002	1	1
	Rubens Barrichello	F2002	2	2

Championship positions: Schumacher 1st (144 points); Barrichello 2nd (77 points)

2003

GRAND PRIX	DRIVER	CAR	GRID	RESULT
Australia	Michael Schumacher	F2002	1	4
	Rubens Barrichello	F2002	2	DNF—spin
Malaysia	Michael Schumacher	F2002	3	6
	Rubens Barrichello	F2002	5	2
Brazil	Michael Schumacher	F2002	7	DNF—spin
	Rubens Barrichello	F2002	1	DNF—fuel
San Marino	Michael Schumacher	F2002	1	1
	Rubens Barrichello	F2002	3	3
Spain	Michael Schumacher	F2003-GA	1	1
	Rubens Barrichello	F2003-GA	2	3
Austria	Michael Schumacher	F2003-GA	1	1
	Rubens Barrichello	F2003-GA	5	3
Monaco	Michael Schumacher	F2003-GA	5	3
	Rubens Barrichello	F2003-GA	7	8
Canada	Michael Schumacher	F2003-GA	3	1
	Rubens Barrichello	F2003-GA	5	5
Europe	Michael Schumacher	F2003-GA	2	5
	Rubens Barrichello	F2003-GA	5	3
France	Michael Schumacher	F2003-GA	3	3
	Rubens Barrichello	F2003-GA	8	7
Britain	Michael Schumacher	F2003-GA	5	4
	Rubens Barrichello	F2003-GA	1	1
Germany	Michael Schumacher	F2003-GA	6	7
	Rubens Barrichello	F2003-GA	3	DNF—accident
Hungary	Michael Schumacher	F2003-GA	8	8
	Rubens Barrichello	F2003-GA	5	DNF—suspension
Italy	Michael Schumacher	F2003-GA	1	1
	Rubens Barrichello	F2003-GA	3	3
US	Michael Schumacher	F2003-GA	7	1
	Rubens Barrichello	F2003-GA	2	DNF—accident
Japan	Michael Schumacher	F2003-GA	14	8
	Rubens Barrichello	F2003-GA	1	1

Championship positions: Schumacher 1st (93 points); Barrichello 4th (65 points)

2004

GRAND PRIX	DRIVER	CAR	GRID	RESULT
Australia	Michael Schumacher	F2004	1	1
	Rubens Barrichello	F2004	2	2
Malaysia	Michael Schumacher	F2004	1	1
	Rubens Barrichello	F2004	3	4
Bahrain	Michael Schumacher	F2004	1	1
	Rubens Barrichello	F2004	2	2

GRAND PRIX	DRIVER	CAR	GRID	RESULT
San Marino	Michael Schumacher	F2004	2	1
	Rubens Barrichello	F2004	4	6
Spain	Michael Schumacher	F2004	1	1
	Rubens Barrichello	F2004	5	2
Monaco	Michael Schumacher	F2004	4	DNF—accident
	Rubens Barrichello	F2004	6	3
Europe	Michael Schumacher	F2004	1	1
	Rubens Barrichello	F2004	7	2
Canada	Michael Schumacher	F2004	6	1
	Rubens Barrichello	F2004	7	2
US	Michael Schumacher	F2004	2	1
	Rubens Barrichello	F2004	1	2
France	Michael Schumacher	F2004	2	1
	Rubens Barrichello	F2004	10	3
Britain	Michael Schumacher	F2004	4	1
	Rubens Barrichello	F2004	2	3
Germany	Michael Schumacher	F2004	1	1
	Rubens Barrichello	F2004	7	12
Hungary	Michael Schumacher	F2004	1	1
	Rubens Barrichello	F2004	2	2
Belgium	Michael Schumacher	F2004	2	2
	Rubens Barrichello	F2004	6	3
Italy	Michael Schumacher	F2004	3	2
	Rubens Barrichello	F2004	1	1
China	Michael Schumacher	F2004	20	12
	Rubens Barrichello	F2004	1	1
Japan	Michael Schumacher	F2004	1	1
	Rubens Barrichello	F2004	15	DNF—accident
Brazil	Michael Schumacher	F2004	18	7
	Rubens Barrichello	F2004	1	3

Championship positions: Schumacher 1st (148 points); Barrichello 2nd (114 points)

2005

GRAND PRIX	DRIVER	CAR	GRID	RESULT
Australia	Michael Schumacher	F2004M	19*	DNF—accident
	Rubens Barrichello	F2004M	11	2
Malaysia	Michael Schumacher	F2004M	13	7
	Rubens Barrichello	F2004M	12	DNF—handling
Bahrain	Michael Schumacher	F2005	2	DNF—hydraulics
	Rubens Barrichello	F2005	20*	9
San Marino	Michael Schumacher	F2005	13	2
	Rubens Barrichello	F2005	9	DNF—electrical
Spain	Michael Schumacher	F2005	8	DNF—puncture
	Rubens Barrichello	F2005	16*	9
Monaco	Michael Schumacher	F2005	8	7
	Rubens Barrichello	F2005	10	8
Europe	Michael Schumacher	F2005	10	5
	Rubens Barrichello	F2005	7	3

GRAND PRIX	DRIVER	CAR	GRID	RESULT
Canada	Michael Schumacher	F2005	2	2
	Rubens Barrichello	F2005	20	3
US	Michael Schumacher	F2005	5	1
	Rubens Barrichello	F2005	7	2
France	Michael Schumacher	F2005	3	3
	Rubens Barrichello	F2005	5	9
Britain	Michael Schumacher	F2005	9	6
	Rubens Barrichello	F2005	5	7
Germany	Michael Schumacher	F2005	5	5
	Rubens Barrichello	F2005	15	10
Hungary	Michael Schumacher	F2005	1	2
	Rubens Barrichello	F2005	7	10
Turkey	Michael Schumacher	F2005	19*	DNF—withdrew
	Rubens Barrichello	F2005	11	10
Italy	Michael Schumacher	F2005	6	10
	Rubens Barrichello	F2005	7	12
Belgium	Michael Schumacher	F2005	6	DNF—accident
	Rubens Barrichello	F2005	12	5
Brazil	Michael Schumacher	F2005	7	4
	Rubens Barrichello	F2005	9	6
Japan	Michael Schumacher	F2005	14	7
	Rubens Barrichello	F2005	9	11
China	Michael Schumacher	F2005	6	DNF—spin
	Rubens Barrichello	F2005	8	12

* 10-place grid penalty for engine change
Championship positions: Schumacher 3rd (62 points); Barrichello 8th (38 points)

2006

GRAND PRIX	DRIVER	CAR	GRID	RESULT
Bahrain	Michael Schumacher	248 F1	1	2
	Felipe Massa	248 F1	2	9
Malaysia	Michael Schumacher	248 F1	14	6
	Felipe Massa	248 F1	21	5
Australia	Michael Schumacher	248 F1	10	DNF—spin
	Felipe Massa	248 F1	15	DNF—accident
San Marino	Michael Schumacher	248 F1	1	1
	Felipe Massa	248 F1	4	4
Europe	Michael Schumacher	248 F1	2	1
	Felipe Massa	248 F1	3	3
Spain	Michael Schumacher	248 F1	3	2
	Felipe Massa	248 F1	4	4
Monaco	Michael Schumacher	248 F1	22	5
	Felipe Massa	248 F1	21	9
Britain	Michael Schumacher	248 F1	3	2
	Felipe Massa	248 F1	4	5
Canada	Michael Schumacher	248 F1	5	2
	Felipe Massa	248 F1	10	5
US	Michael Schumacher	248 F1	1	1
	Felipe Massa	248 F1	2	2

2006 (CONTINUED)

GRAND PRIX	DRIVER	CAR	GRID	RESULT
France	Michael Schumacher	248 F1	1	1
	Felipe Massa	248 F1	2	3
Germany	Michael Schumacher	248 F1	2	1
	Felipe Massa	248 F1	3	2
Hungary	Michael Schumacher	248 F1	11	8
	Felipe Massa	248 F1	2	7
Spain	Kimi Räikkönen	F2007	3	DNF—electrical
Turkey	Michael Schumacher	248 F1	2	3
	Felipe Massa	248 F1	1	1
Italy	Michael Schumacher	248 F1	2	1
	Felipe Massa	248 F1	4	9
China	Michael Schumacher	248 F1	6	1
	Felipe Massa	248 F1	20	DNF—accident
Japan	Michael Schumacher	248 F1	2	DNF—engine
	Felipe Massa	248 F1	1	2
Brazil	Michael Schumacher	248 F1	10	4
	Felipe Massa	248 F1	1	1

Championship positions: Schumacher 2nd (121 points); Massa 3rd (80 points)

2007

GRAND PRIX	DRIVER	CAR	GRID	RESULT
Australia	Kimi Räikkönen	F2007	1	1
	Felipe Massa	F2007	22	6
Malaysia	Kimi Räikkönen	F2007	3	3
	Felipe Massa	F2007	1	5
Bahrain	Kimi Räikkönen	F2007	3	3
	Felipe Massa	F2007	1	1
	Felipe Massa	F2007	1	1
Monaco	Kimi Räikkönen	F2007	16	8
	Felipe Massa	F2007	3	3
Canada	Kimi Räikkönen	F2007	4	5
	Felipe Massa	F2007	5	DSQ
US	Kimi Räikkönen	F2007	4	4
	Felipe Massa	F2007	3	3
France	Kimi Räikkönen	F2007	3	1
	Felipe Massa	F2007	1	2
Britain	Kimi Räikkönen	F2007	3	1
	Felipe Massa	F2007	4	5
Europe	Kimi Räikkönen	F2007	1	DNF—hydraulics
	Felipe Massa	F2007	3	2
Hungary	Kimi Räikkönen	F2007	3	2
	Felipe Massa	F2007	14	13
Turkey	Kimi Räikkönen	F2007	3	2
	Felipe Massa	F2007	1	1
Italy	Kimi Räikkönen	F2007	5	3
	Felipe Massa	F2007	3	DNF—suspension
Belgium	Kimi Räikkönen	F2007	1	1
	Felipe Massa	F2007	2	2

2007 (CONTINUED)

GRAND PRIX	DRIVER	CAR	GRID	RESULT
Japan	Kimi Räikkönen	F2007	3	3
	Felipe Massa	F2007	4	6
China	Kimi Räikkönen	F2007	2	1
	Felipe Massa	F2007	3	3
Brazil	Kimi Räikkönen	F2007	3	1
	Felipe Massa	F2007	1	2

Championship positions: Räikkönen 1st (110 points); Massa 4th (94 points)

2008

GRAND PRIX	DRIVER	CAR	GRID	RESULT
Australia	Kimi Räikkönen	F2008	15	8—engine
	Felipe Massa	F2008	4	DNF—engine
Malaysia	Kimi Räikkönen	F2008	2	1
	Felipe Massa	F2008	1	DNF—spin
Bahrain	Kimi Räikkönen	F2008	4	2
	Felipe Massa	F2008	2	1
Spain	Kimi Räikkönen	F2008	1	1
	Felipe Massa	F2008	3	2
Turkey	Kimi Räikkönen	F2008	4	3
	Felipe Massa	F2008	1	1
Monaco	Kimi Räikkönen	F2008	2	9
	Felipe Massa	F2008	1	3
Canada	Kimi Räikkönen	F2008	3	DNF—accident
	Felipe Massa	F2008	6	5
France	Kimi Räikkönen	F2008	1	2
	Felipe Massa	F2008	2	1
Britain	Kimi Räikkönen	F2008	3	4
	Felipe Massa	F2008	9	13
Germany	Kimi Räikkönen	F2008	6	6
	Felipe Massa	F2008	2	3
Hungary	Kimi Räikkönen	F2008	6	3
	Felipe Massa	F2008	3	17—engine
Europe	Kimi Räikkönen	F2008	4	DNF—engine
	Felipe Massa	F2008	1	1
Belgium	Kimi Räikkönen	F2008	4	18—spin
	Felipe Massa	F2008	2	1
Italy	Kimi Räikkönen	F2008	14	9
	Felipe Massa	F2008	6	6
Singapore	Kimi Räikkönen	F2008	3	15—spin
	Felipe Massa	F2008	1	13
Japan	Kimi Räikkönen	F2008	2	3
	Felipe Massa	F2008	5	7
China	Kimi Räikkönen	F2008	2	3
	Felipe Massa	F2008	3	2
Brazil	Kimi Räikkönen	F2008	3	3
	Felipe Massa	F2008	1	1

Championship positions: Massa 2nd (97 points); Räikkönen 3rd (75 points)

2009

GRAND PRIX	DRIVER	CAR	GRID	RESULT
Australia	Kimi Räikkönen	F60	7	15—transmission
	Felipe Massa	F60	6	DNF—suspension
Malaysia	Kimi Räikkönen	F60	7	14
	Felipe Massa	F60	16	9
China	Kimi Räikkönen	F60	8	10
	Felipe Massa	F60	13	DNF—electrical
Bahrain	Kimi Räikkönen	F60	10	6
	Felipe Massa	F60	8	14
Spain	Kimi Räikkönen	F60	16	DNF—hydraulics
	Felipe Massa	F60	4	6
Monaco	Kimi Räikkönen	F60	2	3
	Felipe Massa	F60	5	4
Turkey	Kimi Räikkönen	F60	6	9
	Felipe Massa	F60	7	6
Britain	Kimi Räikkönen	F60	9	8
	Felipe Massa	F60	11	4
Germany	Kimi Räikkönen	F60	9	DNF—radiator
	Felipe Massa	F60	8	3
Hungary	Kimi Räikkönen	F60	7	2
Europe	Kimi Räikkönen	F60	6	3
	Luca Badoer	F60	20	17
Belgium	Kimi Räikkönen	F60	6	1
	Luca Badoer	F60	20	14
Italy	Kimi Räikkönen	F60	3	3
	Giancarlo Fisichella	F60	14	9
Singapore	Kimi Räikkönen	F60	12	10
	Giancarlo Fisichella	F60	17	13
Japan	Kimi Räikkönen	F60	5	4
	Giancarlo Fisichella	F60	14	12
Brazil	Kimi Räikkönen	F60	5	6
	Giancarlo Fisichella	F60	19	10
Abu Dhabi	Kimi Räikkönen	F60	11	12
	Giancarlo Fisichella	F60	20	16

Championship positions: Räikkönen 6th (48 points); Massa 11th (22 points)

2010

GRAND PRIX	DRIVER	CAR	GRID	RESULT
Bahrain	Fernando Alonso	F10	3	1
	Felipe Massa	F10	2	2
Australia	Fernando Alonso	F10	3	3
	Felipe Massa	F10	5	4
Malaysia	Fernando Alonso	F10	19	13—engine
	Felipe Massa	F10	21	7
China	Fernando Alonso	F10	3	4
	Felipe Massa	F10	7	9
Spain	Fernando Alonso	F10	4	2
	Felipe Massa	F10	9	6
Monaco	Fernando Alonso	F10	24	6
	Felipe Massa	F10	4	4

2010 (CONTINUED)

GRAND PRIX	DRIVER	CAR	GRID	RESULT
Turkey	Fernando Alonso	F10	12	8
	Felipe Massa	F10	8	7
Canada	Fernando Alonso	F10	3	3
	Felipe Massa	F10	6	15
Europe	Fernando Alonso	F10	4	8
	Felipe Massa	F10	5	11
Britain	Fernando Alonso	F10	3	14
	Felipe Massa	F10	7	15
Germany	Fernando Alonso	F10	2	1
	Felipe Massa	F10	3	2
Hungary	Fernando Alonso	F10	3	2
	Felipe Massa	F10	4	4
Belgium	Fernando Alonso	F10	10	DNF—spin
	Felipe Massa	F10	6	4
Italy	Fernando Alonso	F10	1	1
	Felipe Massa	F10	3	3
Singapore	Fernando Alonso	F10	1	1
	Felipe Massa	F10	24*	8
Japan	Fernando Alonso	F10	4	3
	Felipe Massa	F10	12	DNF—accident
Korea	Fernando Alonso	F10	3	1
	Felipe Massa	F10	6	3
Brazil	Fernando Alonso	F10	5	3
	Felipe Massa	F10	9	15
Abu Dhabi	Fernando Alonso	F10	3	7
	Felipe Massa	F10	6	10

* 15-place grid penalty for replacing engine and gearbox
  Championship positions: Alonso 2nd (252 points); Massa 6th (144 points)

2011

GRAND PRIX	DRIVER	CAR	GRID	RESULT
Australia	Fernando Alonso	150º Italia	5	4
	Felipe Massa	150º Italia	8	7
Malaysia	Fernando Alonso	150º Italia	5	5
	Felipe Massa	150º Italia	7	6
China	Fernando Alonso	150º Italia	5	6
	Felipe Massa	150º Italia	6	7
Turkey	Fernando Alonso	150º Italia	5	3
	Felipe Massa	150º Italia	10	11
Spain	Fernando Alonso	150º Italia	4	5
	Felipe Massa	150º Italia	8	DNF—gearbox
Monaco	Fernando Alonso	150º Italia	4	2
	Felipe Massa	150º Italia	6	DNF—spin
Canada	Fernando Alonso	150º Italia	2	DNF—accident
	Felipe Massa	150º Italia	3	6
Europe	Fernando Alonso	150º Italia	4	2
	Felipe Massa	150º Italia	5	5
Britain	Fernando Alonso	150º Italia	3	1
	Felipe Massa	150º Italia	4	5

2011 (CONTINUED)

GRAND PRIX	DRIVER	CAR	GRID	RESULT
Germany	Fernando Alonso	150º Italia	4	2
	Felipe Massa	150º Italia	5	5
Hungary	Fernando Alonso	150º Italia	5	3
	Felipe Massa	150º Italia	4	6
Belgium	Fernando Alonso	150º Italia	4	4
	Felipe Massa	150º Italia	8	8
Italy	Fernando Alonso	150º Italia	4	3
	Felipe Massa	150º Italia	6	6
Singapore	Fernando Alonso	150º Italia	5	4
	Felipe Massa	150º Italia	6	9
Japan	Fernando Alonso	150º Italia	5	2
	Felipe Massa	150º Italia	4	7
Korea	Fernando Alonso	150º Italia	6	5
	Felipe Massa	150º Italia	5	6
India	Fernando Alonso	150º Italia	3	3
	Felipe Massa	150º Italia	6	DNF—suspension
Abu Dhabi	Fernando Alonso	150º Italia	5	2
	Felipe Massa	150º Italia	6	5
Brazil	Fernando Alonso	150º Italia	5	4
	Felipe Massa	150º Italia	7	5

Championship positions: Alonso 4th (257 points); Massa 6th (118 points)

2012

GRAND PRIX	DRIVER	CAR	GRID	RESULT
Australia	Fernando Alonso	F2012	12	5
	Felipe Massa	F2012	16	DNF—accident
Malaysia	Fernando Alonso	F2012	8	1
	Felipe Massa	F2012	12	15
China	Fernando Alonso	F2012	9	9
	Felipe Massa	F2012	12	13
Bahrain	Fernando Alonso	F2012	9	7
	Felipe Massa	F2012	14	9
Spain	Fernando Alonso	F2012	2	2
	Felipe Massa	F2012	16	15
Monaco	Fernando Alonso	F2012	5	3
	Felipe Massa	F2012	7	6
Canada	Fernando Alonso	F2012	3	5
	Felipe Massa	F2012	6	10
Europe	Fernando Alonso	F2012	11	1
	Felipe Massa	F2012	13	16
Britain	Fernando Alonso	F2012	1	2
	Felipe Massa	F2012	5	4
Germany	Fernando Alonso	F2012	1	1
	Felipe Massa	F2012	13	12
Hungary	Fernando Alonso	F2012	6	5
	Felipe Massa	F2012	7	9
Belgium	Fernando Alonso	F2012	5	DNF—accident
	Felipe Massa	F2012	14	5

2012 (CONTINUED)

GRAND PRIX	DRIVER	CAR	GRID	RESULT
Italy	Fernando Alonso	F2012	10	3
	Felipe Massa	F2012	3	4
Singapore	Fernando Alonso	F2012	5	3
	Felipe Massa	F2012	13	8
Japan	Fernando Alonso	F2012	6	DNF—accident
	Felipe Massa	F2012	10	2
Korea	Fernando Alonso	F2012	4	3
	Felipe Massa	F2012	6	4
India	Fernando Alonso	F2012	5	2
	Felipe Massa	F2012	6	6
Abu Dhabi	Fernando Alonso	F2012	6	2
	Felipe Massa	F2012	8	7
US	Fernando Alonso	F2012	7	3
	Felipe Massa	F2012	11*	4
Brazil	Fernando Alonso	F2012	7	2
	Felipe Massa	F2012	5	3

* 5-place grid penalty for broken gearbox seal
  Championship positions: Alonso 2nd (278 points); Massa 7th (122 points)

2013

GRAND PRIX	DRIVER	CAR	GRID	RESULT
Australia	Fernando Alonso	F138	5	2
	Felipe Massa	F138	4	4
Malaysia	Fernando Alonso	F138	3	DNF—accident
	Felipe Massa	F138	2	5
China	Fernando Alonso	F138	3	1
	Felipe Massa	F138	5	6
Bahrain	Fernando Alonso	F138	3	8
	Felipe Massa	F138	4	15
Spain	Fernando Alonso	F138	5	1
	Felipe Massa	F138	9*	3
Monaco	Fernando Alonso	F138	6	7
	Felipe Massa	F138	21*	DNF—suspension
Canada	Fernando Alonso	F138	6	2
	Felipe Massa	F138	16	8
Britain	Fernando Alonso	F138	9	3
	Felipe Massa	F138	11	6
Germany	Fernando Alonso	F138	8	4
	Felipe Massa	F138	7	DNF—spin
Hungary	Fernando Alonso	F138	5	5
	Felipe Massa	F138	7	8
Belgium	Fernando Alonso	F138	9	2
	Felipe Massa	F138	10	7
Italy	Fernando Alonso	F138	5	2
	Felipe Massa	F138	4	4
Singapore	Fernando Alonso	F138	7	2
	Felipe Massa	F138	6	6
Korea	Fernando Alonso	F138	5	6
	Felipe Massa	F138	6	9

2013 (CONTINUED)

GRAND PRIX	DRIVER	CAR	GRID	RESULT
Japan	Fernando Alonso	F138	8	4
	Felipe Massa	F138	5	10
India	Fernando Alonso	F138	8	11
	Felipe Massa	F138	5	4
Abu Dhabi	Fernando Alonso	F138	10	5
	Felipe Massa	F138	7	8
US	Fernando Alonso	F138	6	5
	Felipe Massa	F138	13	12
Brazil	Fernando Alonso	F138	3	3
	Felipe Massa	F138	9	7

3-place penalty for impeding another driver
** 5-place penalty for replacing the gearbox
Championship positions: Alonso 2nd (242 points); Massa 8th (112 points)

2014

GRAND PRIX	DRIVER	CAR	GRID	RESULT
Australia	Fernando Alonso	F14 T	5	4
	Kimi Räikkönen	F14 T	11	7
Malaysia	Fernando Alonso	F14 T	4	4
	Kimi Räikkönen	F14 T	6	12
Bahrain	Fernando Alonso	F14 T	9	9
	Kimi Räikkönen	F14 T	5	10
China	Fernando Alonso	F14 T	5	3
	Kimi Räikkönen	F14 T	11	8
Spain	Fernando Alonso	F14 T	7	6
	Kimi Räikkönen	F14 T	6	7
Monaco	Fernando Alonso	F14 T	5	4
	Kimi Räikkönen	F14 T	6	12
Canada	Fernando Alonso	F14 T	7	6
	Kimi Räikkönen	F14 T	10	10
Austria	Fernando Alonso	F14 T	4	5
	Kimi Räikkönen	F14 T	8	10
Britain	Fernando Alonso	F14 T	16	6
	Kimi Räikkönen	F14 T	18	DNF—spin
Germany	Fernando Alonso	F14 T	7	5
	Kimi Räikkönen	F14 T	12	11
Hungary	Fernando Alonso	F14 T	5	2
	Kimi Räikkönen	F14 T	16	6
Belgium	Fernando Alonso	F14 T	4	7
	Kimi Räikkönen	F14 T	8	4
Italy	Fernando Alonso	F14 T	7	DNF—engine
	Kimi Räikkönen	F14 T	11	9
Singapore	Fernando Alonso	F14 T	5	4
	Kimi Räikkönen	F14 T	7	8
Japan	Fernando Alonso	F14 T	5	DNF—electrical
	Kimi Räikkönen	F14 T	10	12
Russia	Fernando Alonso	F14 T	7	6
	Kimi Räikkönen	F14 T	8	9
US	Fernando Alonso	F14 T	6	6
	Kimi Räikkönen	F14 T	8	13

2014 (CONTINUED)

GRAND PRIX	DRIVER	CAR	GRID	RESULT
Brazil	Fernando Alonso	F14 T	8	6
	Kimi Räikkönen	F14 T	10	7
Abu Dhabi	Fernando Alonso	F14 T	8	9
	Kimi Räikkönen	F14 T	7	10

Championship positions: Alonso 6th (161 points); Räikkönen 12th (55 points)

2015

GRAND PRIX	DRIVER	CAR	GRID	RESULT
Australia	Sebastian Vettel	SF15-T	4	3
	Kimi Räikkönen	SF15-T	5	DNF—wheel
Malaysia	Sebastian Vettel	SF15-T	2	1
	Kimi Räikkönen	SF15-T	11	4
China	Sebastian Vettel	SF15-T	3	3
	Kimi Räikkönen	SF15-T	6	4
Bahrain	Sebastian Vettel	SF15-T	2	5
	Kimi Räikkönen	SF15-T	4	2
Spain	Sebastian Vettel	SF15-T	3	3
	Kimi Räikkönen	SF15-T	7	5
Monaco	Sebastian Vettel	SF15-T	3	2
	Kimi Räikkönen	SF15-T	6	6
Canada	Sebastian Vettel	SF15-T	18*	5
	Kimi Räikkönen	SF15-T	3	4
Austria	Sebastian Vettel	SF15-T	3	4
	Kimi Räikkönen	SF15-T	14	DNF—accident
Britain	Sebastian Vettel	SF15-T	4	3
	Kimi Räikkönen	SF15-T	5	8
Hungary	Sebastian Vettel	SF15-T	3	1
	Kimi Räikkönen	SF15-T	5	DNF—engine
Belgium	Sebastian Vettel	SF15-T	8	12
	Kimi Räikkönen	SF15-T	16**	7
Italy	Sebastian Vettel	SF15-T	3	2
	Kimi Räikkönen	SF15-T	2	5
Singapore	Sebastian Vettel	SF15-T	1	1
	Kimi Räikkönen	SF15-T	3	3
Japan	Sebastian Vettel	SF15-T	4	3
	Kimi Räikkönen	SF15-T	6	4
Russia	Sebastian Vettel	SF15-T	4	2
	Kimi Räikkönen	SF15-T	5	8***
US	Sebastian Vettel	SF15-T	13****	3
	Kimi Räikkönen	SF15-T	18****	DNF—spin
Mexico	Sebastian Vettel	SF15-T	3	DNF—spin
	Kimi Räikkönen	SF15-T	19*****	DNF—accident
Brazil	Sebastian Vettel	SF15-T	3	3
	Kimi Räikkönen	SF15-T	4	4
Abu Dhabi	Sebastian Vettel	SF15-T	15	4
	Kimi Räikkönen	SF15-T	3	3

* 5-place penalty for overtaking under red flag
** 5-place penalty for replacing the gearbox
*** 30-second penalty for causing a collision
**** 10-place penalty for using additional engine element
***** 35-place penalty for replacing the gearbox and using additional engine elements
Championship positions: Vettel 3rd (278 points); Räikkönen 4th (150 points)

2016

GRAND PRIX	DRIVER	CAR	GRID	RESULT
Australia	Sebastian Vettel	SF16-H	3	3
	Kimi Räikkönen	SF16-H	4	DNF—fire
Bahrain	Sebastian Vettel	SF16-H	3	DNS
	Kimi Räikkönen	SF16-H	4	2
China	Sebastian Vettel	SF16-H	4	2
	Kimi Räikkönen	SF16-H	3	5
Russia	Sebastian Vettel	SF16-H	7*	DNF—accident
	Kimi Räikkönen	SF16-H	3	3
Spain	Sebastian Vettel	SF16-H	6	3
	Kimi Räikkönen	SF16-H	5	2
Monaco	Sebastian Vettel	SF16-H	4	4
	Kimi Räikkönen	SF16-H	11*	DNF—spin
Canada	Sebastian Vettel	SF16-H	3	2
	Kimi Räikkönen	SF16-H	6	6
Europe	Sebastian Vettel	SF16-H	3	2
	Kimi Räikkönen	SF16-H	4	4
Austria	Sebastian Vettel	SF16-H	9*	DNF—tire
	Kimi Räikkönen	SF16-H	4	3
Britain	Sebastian Vettel	SF16-H	11*	9
	Kimi Räikkönen	SF16-H	5	5
Hungary	Sebastian Vettel	SF16-H	5	4
	Kimi Räikkönen	SF16-H	14	6
Germany	Sebastian Vettel	SF16-H	6	5
	Kimi Räikkönen	SF16-H	5	6
Belgium	Sebastian Vettel	SF16-H	4	6
	Kimi Räikkönen	SF16-H	3	9
Italy	Sebastian Vettel	SF16-H	3	3
	Kimi Räikkönen	SF16-H	4	4
Singapore	Sebastian Vettel	SF16-H	22**	5
	Kimi Räikkönen	SF16-H	5	4
Malaysia	Sebastian Vettel	SF16-H	5	DNF—accident
	Kimi Räikkönen	SF16-H	6	4
Japan	Sebastian Vettel	SF16-H	6***	4
	Kimi Räikkönen	SF16-H	8*	5
US	Sebastian Vettel	SF16-H	6	4
	Kimi Räikkönen	SF16-H	5	DNF—wheel
Mexico	Sebastian Vettel	SF16-H	7	5****
	Kimi Räikkönen	SF16-H	6	6
Brazil	Sebastian Vettel	SF16-H	5	5
	Kimi Räikkönen	SF16-H	3	DNF—spin
Abu Dhabi	Sebastian Vettel	SF16-H	5	3
	Kimi Räikkönen	SF16-H	4	6

* 5-place penalty for replacing the gearbox
** 25-place penalty for replacing the gearbox and using additional engine elements
*** 3-place penalty for causing a collision in MalaysianGrand Prix
**** 10-second penalty for erratic/dangerous driving
Championship positions: Vettel 4th (212 points); Räikkönen 6th (186 points)

2017

GRAND PRIX	DRIVER	CAR	GRID	RESULT
Australia	Sebastian Vettel	SF70H	2	1
	Kimi Räikkönen	SF70H	4	4
China	Sebastian Vettel	SF70H	2	2
	Kimi Räikkönen	SF70H	4	5
Bahrain	Sebastian Vettel	SF70H	3	1
	Kimi Räikkönen	SF70H	5	4
Russia	Sebastian Vettel	SF70H	1	2
	Kimi Räikkönen	SF70H	2	3
Spain	Sebastian Vettel	SF70H	2	2
	Kimi Räikkönen	SF70H	4	DNF—accident
Monaco	Sebastian Vettel	SF70H	1	1
	Kimi Räikkönen	SF70H	2	2
Canada	Sebastian Vettel	SF70H	2	4
	Kimi Räikkönen	SF70H	4	7
Azerbaijan	Sebastian Vettel	SF70H	4	4
	Kimi Räikkönen	SF70H	3	14—floor
Austria	Sebastian Vettel	SF70H	2	2
	Kimi Räikkönen	SF70H	3	5
Britain	Sebastian Vettel	SF70H	3	7
	Kimi Räikkönen	SF70H	2	3
Hungary	Sebastian Vettel	SF70H	1	1
	Kimi Räikkönen	SF70H	2	2
Belgium	Sebastian Vettel	SF70H	2	2
	Kimi Räikkönen	SF70H	4	4
Italy	Sebastian Vettel	SF70H	6	3
	Kimi Räikkönen	SF70H	5	5
Singapore	Sebastian Vettel	SF70H	1	DNF—accident
	Kimi Räikkönen	SF70H	4	DNF—accident
Malaysia	Sebastian Vettel	SF70H	20**	4
	Kimi Räikkönen	SF70H	2	DNS
Japan	Sebastian Vettel	SF70H	2	DNF—spark plug
	Kimi Räikkönen	SF70H	10*	5
US	Sebastian Vettel	SF70H	2	2
	Kimi Räikkönen	SF70H	5	3
Mexico	Sebastian Vettel	SF70H	1	4
	Kimi Räikkönen	SF70H	5	3
Brazil	Sebastian Vettel	SF70H	2	1
	Kimi Räikkönen	SF70H	3	3
Abu Dhabi	Sebastian Vettel	SF70H	3	3
	Kimi Räikkönen	SF70H	5	4

* 5-place penalty for replacing the gearbox
** 20-place penalty for using additional engine elements
Championship positions: Vettel 2nd (317 points); Räikkönen 4th (205 points)

2018

GRAND PRIX	DRIVER	CAR	GRID	RESULT
Australia	Sebastian Vettel	SF71H	3	1
	Kimi Räikkönen	SF71H	2	3
Bahrain	Sebastian Vettel	SF71H	1	1
	Kimi Räikkönen	SF71H	2	DNF—wheel
China	Sebastian Vettel	SF71H	1	8
	Kimi Räikkönen	SF71H	2	3
Azerbaijan	Sebastian Vettel	SF71H	1	4
	Kimi Räikkönen	SF71H	6	2
Spain	Sebastian Vettel	SF71H	3	4
	Kimi Räikkönen	SF71H	4	DNF—engine
Monaco	Sebastian Vettel	SF71H	2	2
	Kimi Räikkönen	SF71H	4	4
Canada	Sebastian Vettel	SF71H	1	1
	Kimi Räikkönen	SF71H	5	6
France	Sebastian Vettel	SF71H	3	5
	Kimi Räikkönen	SF71H	6	3
Austria	Sebastian Vettel	SF71H	6*	3
	Kimi Räikkönen	SF71H	3	2
Britain	Sebastian Vettel	SF71H	2	1
	Kimi Räikkönen	SF71H	3	3
Germany	Sebastian Vettel	SF71H	1	DNF—spin
	Kimi Räikkönen	SF71H	3	3
Hungary	Sebastian Vettel	SF71H	4	2
	Kimi Räikkönen	SF71H	3	3
Belgium	Sebastian Vettel	SF71H	2	1
	Kimi Räikkönen	SF71H	6	DNF—accident
Italy	Sebastian Vettel	SF71H	2	4
	Kimi Räikkönen	SF71H	1	2
Singapore	Sebastian Vettel	SF71H	3	3
	Kimi Räikkönen	SF71H	5	5
Russia	Sebastian Vettel	SF71H	3	3
	Kimi Räikkönen	SF71H	4	4
Japan	Sebastian Vettel	SF71H	8	6
	Kimi Räikkönen	SF71H	4	5
US	Sebastian Vettel	SF71H	5**	4
	Kimi Räikkönen	SF71H	2	1
Mexico	Sebastian Vettel	SF71H	4	2
	Kimi Räikkönen	SF71H	6	3
Brazil	Sebastian Vettel	SF71H	2	6
	Kimi Räikkönen	SF71H	4	3
Abu Dhabi	Sebastian Vettel	SF71H	3	2
	Kimi Räikkönen	SF71H	4	DNF—electrical

* 3-place penalty for impeding another driver
** 3-place penalty for failing to slow sufficiently under red flag
Championship positions: Vettel 2nd (320 points); Räikkönen 3rd (251 points)

2019

GRAND PRIX	DRIVER	CAR	GRID	RESULT
Australia	Sebastian Vettel	SF90	3	4
	Charles Leclerc	SF90	5	5
Bahrain	Sebastian Vettel	SF90	2	5
	Charles Leclerc	SF90	1	3
China	Sebastian Vettel	SF90	3	3
	Charles Leclerc	SF90	4	5
Azerbaijan	Sebastian Vettel	SF90	3	3
	Charles Leclerc	SF90	8	5
Spain	Sebastian Vettel	SF90	3	4
	Charles Leclerc	SF90	5	5
Monaco	Sebastian Vettel	SF90	4	2
	Charles Leclerc	SF90	15	DNF—accident
Canada	Sebastian Vettel	SF90	1	2*
	Charles Leclerc	SF90	3	3
France	Sebastian Vettel	SF90	7	5
	Charles Leclerc	SF90	3	3
Austria	Sebastian Vettel	SF90	9	4
	Charles Leclerc	SF90	1	2
Britain	Sebastian Vettel	SF90	6	16
	Charles Leclerc	SF90	3	3
Germany	Sebastian Vettel	SF90	20**	2
	Charles Leclerc	SF90	10	DNF—spin
Hungary	Sebastian Vettel	SF90	5	3
	Charles Leclerc	SF90	4	4
Belgium	Sebastian Vettel	SF90	2	4
	Charles Leclerc	SF90	1	1
Italy	Sebastian Vettel	SF90	4	13
	Charles Leclerc	SF90	1	1
Singapore	Sebastian Vettel	SF90	3	1
	Charles Leclerc	SF90	1	2
Russia	Sebastian Vettel	SF90	3	DNF—engine
	Charles Leclerc	SF90	1	3
Japan	Sebastian Vettel	SF90	1	2
	Charles Leclerc	SF90	2	6
Mexico	Sebastian Vettel	SF90	2	2
	Charles Leclerc	SF90	1	4
US	Sebastian Vettel	SF90	2	DNF—suspension
	Charles Leclerc	SF90	4	4
Brazil	Sebastian Vettel	SF90	2	DNF—accident
	Charles Leclerc	SF90	14***	DNF—accident
Abu Dhabi	**Sebastian Vettel**	**SF90**	**4**	**5**
	Charles Leclerc	SF90	3	3

* 5-second penalty for rejoining the track unsafely and forcing another car off
** 20-place penalty for using additional engine elements
*** 10-place penalty for using additional engine element
Championship positions: Leclerc 4th (264 points); Vettel 5th (240 points)

2020

GRAND PRIX	DRIVER	CAR	GRID	RESULT
Austria	Sebastian Vettel	SF1000	11	10
	Charles Leclerc	SF1000	7	2
Styria	Sebastian Vettel	SF1000	10	DNF—accident
	Charles Leclerc	SF1000	14	DNF—accident
Hungary	Sebastian Vettel	SF1000	5	6
	Charles Leclerc	SF1000	6	11
Great Britain	Sebastian Vettel	SF1000	10	10
	Charles Leclerc	SF1000	4	3
70th Anniversary	Sebastian Vettel	SF1000	11	12
	Charles Leclerc	SF1000	8	4
Spain	Sebastian Vettel	SF1000	11	7
	Charles Leclerc	SF1000	9	DNF—electrics
Belgium	Sebastian Vettel	SF1000	14	13
	Charles Leclerc	SF1000	13	14
Italy	Sebastian Vettel	SF1000	17	DNF—brakes
	Charles Leclerc	SF1000	13	DNF—spin
Tuscany	Sebastian Vettel	SF1000	14	10
	Charles Leclerc	SF1000	5	8
Russia	Sebastian Vettel	SF1000	14	13
	Charles Leclerc	SF1000	10	6
Eifel	Sebastian Vettel	SF1000	11	11
	Charles Leclerc	SF1000	4	7
Portugal	Sebastian Vettel	SF1000	15	10
	Charles Leclerc	SF1000	4	4
Emilia Romagna	Sebastian Vettel	SF1000	14	12
	Charles Leclerc	SF1000	7	5
Turkey	Sebastian Vettel	SF1000	11	3
	Charles Leclerc	SF1000	12	4
Bahrain	Sebastian Vettel	SF1000	11	13
	Charles Leclerc	SF1000	12	10
Sakhir	Sebastian Vettel	SF1000		
	Charles Leclerc	SF1000		
Abu Dhabi	Sebastian Vettel	SF1000		
	Charles Leclerc	SF1000		

INDEX